Busy People's Low-Fat Cookbook

Dawn Hall

Rutledge Hill Press™

Nashville, Tennessee

A Division of Thomas Nelson, Inc.

www.ThomasNelson.com

In memory of my gentle hero, faithful best friend, cherished lover, loving father, and courageous husband, Tracy Hall.
11/27/62–5/4/01

Copyright © 1998, 2003 by Dawn Hall.

Published by Rutledge Hill Press, a Division of Thomas Nelson, Inc., P.O. Box 141000, Nashville, Tennessee, 37214.

Library of Congress Cataloging-in-Publication Data

Hall, Dawn.
    Busy people's low-fat cookbook / Dawn Hall.
      p. cm.
    Includes index.
    ISBN 1-4016-0105-7
    1. Low-fat diet—Recipes. I. Title.
    RM237.7.H3448 2003
    641.5'638—dc21   2003001766

Printed in Hong Kong
03 04 05 06 07—5 4 3 2 1

Complete Your Busy People's Library

The recipes in these two cookbooks are all easy to prepare and cook They all contain 7 ingredients or less and can be prepared in less than 30 minutes

Down-Home Cooking Without the Down-Home Fat
1-4016-0104-9
$16.99

Includes recipes for:

- Citrus Pancakes
- Caesar Oyster Crackers
- Chicken Skillet Cobbler
- Chewy, Gooey No-Bake Freezer Cookies
- Turtle Cake

Busy People's Slow Cooker Cookbook
1-4016-0107-3
$16.99

Includes recipes for:

- Cinnamon-Kissed Chicken
- Mushroom Chowder
- Apple-Yam Casserole
- Peaches and Cream Spoon Cake
- Pistachio-Nut Snack Cake

RUTLEDGE HILL PRESS

Available at better book stores everywhere!
or at
www.RutledgeHillPress.com

Contents

Acknowledgments • vii

My Story • ix

Introduction • 1

Notes to the Cook • 21

Breakfast • 23

Appetizers & Breads • 43

Soups & Salads • 65

Side Dishes • 109

Entrées • 139

Desserts • 201

Drinks • 255

Index • 263

Acknowledgments

As I take a moment to reflect and gather my thoughts, I am overwhelmed with thankfulness. I wholeheartedly believe my talents are a gift from God, so of course I thank Him first. It's not uncommon for me to wake up at 3:30 A.M. with a low-fat, fast and easy recipe idea in my head. For years I thought, "What is wrong with me?" But after friends and family members kept requesting the recipes I'd created and encouraging me to write a cookbook, I realized that it wasn't a problem; it was a gift. A gift from God. It is to Him that I give all the praise and glory for all the good He does through me.

Next I thank my daughters Whitney and Ashley who have served as my guinea pigs for so many years. When you taste the recipes in this cookbook you may think that would be a good thing, but believe me, I've had my share of flops. I never follow a recipe. I love to create. Sometimes when eating out I'll jot down on a paper napkin what I think is in the dish, then when I'm home I try to recreate the same dish using low-fat ingredients quickly and easily. For someone to ask me not to be creative with food would be like asking a flower not to blossom. My family has never done that to me. I am truly thankful for their support and encouragement.

I greatly appreciate the help of my personal assistants: Diane Bowman-Yantiss, Karen Schwanbeck, Mable Jackson, and Robin Friend. I couldn't have done it all without you. You are the glue that keeps it all together.

Last but certainly not least I thank my publisher, Larry Stone, for believing in me, Bryan Curtis and Terri Woodmore for getting the word out, and Geoff Stone, my editor. I am grateful for all the hard work, time, and patience he put into the project.

My Story

It's been said that sometimes truth is stranger than fiction. Often this has been the case in my life. If I were not the one living my life, I'd find the truth of my life unbelievable. Many have said my story would make a great movie. Who knows? Maybe someday.

I was born in Fort Wayne, Indiana. My parents divorced when I was five. When I was ten we moved to Toledo, Ohio, when my mom remarried. I'm the oldest of seven. I feel I was born watching my weight and have struggled with being a compulsive overeater for as long as I can remember. I hate it.

I flunked first grade. In early years of elementary school my teachers always told me I wasn't focusing in class, even though I was trying to with all my might. It wasn't until adulthood that I was diagnosed with attention deficit disorder, which explains my extreme difficulty (even today) to concentrate with background noise and distractions. I graduated with honors in 1981 from Springfield High School.

I married my high school sweetheart, Tracy Wayne Hall, in 1984. I never went to college. I worked as a waitress until I was pregnant with our first child in 1986. We were blessed with two wonderful daughters born in 1987 and 1988. It took one year to physically build our small ranch home ourselves (with the help of friends) while our family lived in a tiny efficiency apartment above Tracy's parents' garage. We fondly named our new home Cozy Homestead, and we moved into it in June 1992.

I enjoyed teaching aerobics and facilitating classes for compulsive overeaters. With passion I was creating new recipes every day, and our family never ate the same meal twice for family dinners. I home-schooled our children until November 28, 1994. I'll never forget that day. It was the day my life was turned inside out and upside down and also the last day of a normal life as I can remember it.

November 28, 1994, the day after my loving husband's thirty-second birthday, was the day we found out Tracy had brain cancer. Doctors were able to surgically remove one pound of malignant tumor, leaving Tracy completely paralyzed on his entire left side. He was given six to eight months to live.

I told Tracy the day we found out about his cancer that I believed God was going to use our most challenging situation to give Himself praise and glory. That is *exactly* what God is doing to this day.

To make a long story short, in order to pay for an experimental treatment, we had to raise thousands of dollars each month because our insurance would not pay for experimental treatments. All of the recipes I had been creating over the previous five years I printed into books and sold in order to earn enough money for Tracy's treatments. My thought was we could use what little we had left in our savings to pay for a couple weeks of Tracy's treatment, or we could try to invest the money into cookbooks and hopefully earn enough to pay for his treatments indefinitely. In the beginning, when I was driving home with my first vanload of a thousand cookbooks I thought to myself, "You're nuts, Dawn. How in the world are you going to sell a thousand books? You're nuts!" Well, we sold a thousand cookbooks in five days and eighteen thousand in ten weeks. That first book was *Down Home Cookin' Without the Down Home Fat*. It was selected as one of Ohio's Best of the Best Cookbooks by Quail Ridge Press and the 1996 Best Cookbook of the Year by North American Book Dealers Exchange. Not too shabby for a homemaker who didn't know how to type or use a computer, huh? I would be a fool if I thought for even one moment that I did it. Over 650,000 cookbooks sold. It was definitely a God thing, and He gets all the credit. He did it through me and for that I am forever grateful.

I guess we weren't living with enough stress of daily financial bondage and fighting cancer and its devastating effects. We had a house fire on Valentine's Day in 2000. It was a nightmare, and I did all I could to fight the fire. I remember vividly our daughters screaming in panic and fear, "Get out of the house, Mom! It's only a house!" They were scared to death. All I knew was I didn't want our daughters to lose the house their daddy built for them. After all, how many little girls can say their daddy built their house for them? The fire left all four of us living in an assisted living nursing home for four months as builders restored our home to its original state.

The good news was that Tracy lived for six and a half years after his diagnosis, twelve times longer than the doctors ever imagined. He was a wonderful father and an amazing example of a truly godly man. He inspired countless people, me included. He was able to fulfill his dream of living to see his little girls become young ladies. Tracy died on May 5, 2001. Ironically, it wasn't the cancer that took him. It was from a fall that caused a brain hemorrhage. The experimental treatment had cured him completely. Tracy's death was not in vain. The data gathered during his use of the experimental cancer treatment will be used to help others. His skin, bones, organs, and even part of his eyes were donated to help others live. Praise God!

God still gets all the praise and glory. I believe my cookbooks are a tool that God is using to open the doors for me to share the good news of His love. As an inspirational speaker, people will come listen to me, a "cookbook lady," when they might never come to listen to a preacher. I believe my primary purpose is to encourage and inspire others to live lives with no regrets and to put God first in each of their lives.

Introduction

Since we live in a culture that is always on the go, we don't always have a lot of time to prepare healthy meals. This has contributed to fast-food lifestyles that have produced overweight people. With my line of Busy People's cookbooks I make available to everybody recipes that are easy to prepare, low in fat, and great tasting. In this book you will learn about the importance of eating low-fat foods as well as get to enjoy over 200 low-fat recipes that will stimulate your taste buds. Also look for my *Busy People's Slow Cooker Cookbook*. The slow cooker is a perfect way to prepare a meal while away from home. And if you like these recipes, keep your eyes open for future Busy People's cookbooks at a bookstore near you.

Help! I've Started Eating and I Can't Stop

It seems like most of us have been there at one time or another. Thanksgiving, Christmas day, and all-you-can-eat buffets (we want to get our money's worth!) are just a few situations when a lot of us overeat. For those of you who never overindulge, God bless you! You can go ahead and move to the next chapter, as this will probably bore you. For most of us, we eat for so many of the wrong reasons: We're happy; We're sad; We're bored; It's time to eat. You know it's true!

The Truth About Your Weight

Weight, nutrition, and health are complicated issues. When it comes to fighting the bulge, the truth is it can be hard. For some of us very hard. If you're thinking, "No joke. Now tell me something I don't know." Listen up. What you are about to read may surprise you.

The number one reason people are in hospitals today is because of lifestyle. Heart disease, cancer, and diabetes can all be positively affected by a low-fat diet. Today there are so many wonderful low-fat foods that taste delicious. We don't have to eat like a rabbit to eat healthy. If you've never tried a low-fat diet, I strongly encourage you to do so. For those of you who complain about the taste of low-fat foods yet have never tried them, all I can say is, "Don't knock it until you've tried it!"

Although many dietitians, health enthusiasts, and other people with good intentions would like to make being healthy seem simple, it is not. Some people believe: If I'd only put God first; If I'd only eat low-fat foods; If I would exercise daily; or If I only ate when I was hungry, I wouldn't have a weight problem. Other people believe that there must be some hidden abuse or emotional reason behind why people are overweight or that it's a self-control thing. It's not always that simple. Yes, sometimes it is a psychological problem, and yes, sometimes it can be as simple as changing one bad behavior or attitude towards food. However, for the most part, I feel it is much, much more complicated than just one issue. For the most part, for most people maintaining ideal weight is complex and multifaceted.

Maintaining Ideal Body Weight

Many people have tried to simplify this complicated issue with comments such as, "If you don't want to be fat, just don't eat fat." Wouldn't it be nice if it were so simple? Then there are those who say, "If you don't want to be fat, just stop eating when you feel comfortable." That's a fine idea for those who are overweight because they simply keep eating even though they are full. What about those of us who already quit eating when we are comfortable, and we happen to have a larger appetite than our bodies need? Another way of looking at this is that we don't eat too much; our bodies are just shorter than they ought to be for the weight we are. It's hard to stop eating when your stomach and watering mouth cry out, "I'm still hungry!" One way to help calm hunger cries is to drink water before, during, and after your meal. Other ideas to help satisfy a hungry tummy are:

- First thing in the morning, think positive, reinforcing thoughts about eating healthy.
- Eat a cup of vegetable soup or a clear broth before your meal.
- Eat more salad with fat-free salad dressing or fat-free green vegetables at the end of the meal to help you feel satisfied.
- Sip on decaffeinated herbal flavored teas. There's something very soothing and relaxing about sipping on flavorful teas. Or, for a unique sipping beverage place 8 to 10 tic-tacs in the filter holder of a 10-cup coffee maker instead of coffee. This will create a hot, flavorful beverage that is virtually calorie free. (One calorie per cup.)
- Drink a glass of Metamucil. (The flavored ones aren't bad.) Not only does it help you feel fuller, but it provides 3 grams of natural fiber per glass.
- Sometimes we still feel hungry because our sweet tooth is not satisfied. With this in mind, try a tic-tac or chewing a piece of gum. If that doesn't work, try a small fat-free cookie, sugar-free jello, popsicle, or a piece of fruit.

Ask the advice of your family doctor or holistic medical doctor. Explain your hunger. See if there are some natural herbs, vitamins, or minerals that may be helpful in curbing your appetite. For those who say, "It's all in your head . . . that's why you think you're hungry," a part of their statement is true. Hunger signals are released from the brain. However, being overweight usually is more complicated and complex than simply just that. If you go to a holistic medical doctor, he can actually test your blood. Sometimes a deficiency in one area or another can make you feel hungry, tired, etc.

My mother, Wendy Oberhouse, has lost over eighty pounds, and my stepfather, Donald Oberhouse, has lost seventy pounds. They've kept the weight off for years. I am so proud of them. Along with the switch to a low-fat, low-calorie lifestyle, they use herbs to help curb their large appetites. The herbs help take the edge off so they can maintain their healthier lifestyle.

Out of Sight, Out of Mind Theory

Sometimes we think we're hungry because the delicious, mouth-watering foods that are left over from the meal are staring up at us from their serving bowls. We think we're hungry when we really aren't. It tasted good, and we'd like more. Keeping this possibility in mind, only serve your vegetables and salad home-style. (They can be used as filler, if you're still hungry after the meal is eaten.) Place all other foods on dinner plates before serving.

Feeling Satisfied/Feeling Full

Learn the difference between feeling satisfied and feeling full. There is a difference. Let me say up front that it is not necessarily our fault as Americans that we are fat. You may have heard that it's better to eat five or six meals a day instead of three. That's a surefire way to put on the pounds when we think of meals like June Cleaver used to serve, with meat, potatoes, gravy, vegetable, rolls, butter, and of course dessert. Instead you should eat five or six small meals (or snacks) a day. This idea of eating smaller meals throughout the day, or grazing, is absolutely wonderful at helping keep blood sugar levels good and energy levels strong. However, *what* we graze on is of the utmost importance. Cows like to graze for most of the day, and if we grazed on greens most of the day, we'd be thinner and healthier. The problem is a lot of us are grazing on high caloric fat-free foods. Beware of compacted caloric foods. Only on special occasions like dinner out or a holiday will you eat a full meal. Instead, what I encourage you to do is break up your regular three meals a day into six. Let me explain:

Old Way of Eating

Three Low-Fat Meals a Day

Breakfast
1 slice toast, orange juice, cereal with skim milk

Lunch
turkey sandwich, Baked Lays Potato Crisps, apple, herbal tea and fat-free cookie

Dinner
barbecued chicken breast, tossed salad with fat-free dressing, roll, baked potato and green beans

Total Calories and Fat:
1225 Calories & 8 fats

New Way of Grazing

Six Snacks a Day

Breakfast
cereal with skim milk and toast

Snack
orange (instead of juice because it's more filling & satisfying to chew)

Lunch
turkey sandwich, Baked Lays, apple and tea

Snack
fat-free cookie

Dinner
barbecued chicken breast, tossed salad with fat-free salad dressing, baked potato and green beans (skip the roll)

Snack
100 calorie snack such as fat-free cookies (instead of the roll which we skipped at dinner)

Total Calories and Fat:
1225 Calories & 8 fats

As you can see, I simply broke up the meals and used part of them as snacks. You never get really full nor do you ever get really hungry. Many kids I know skip breakfast and their morning snack, and by lunch they are starving. Because they are starving they wind up eating more calories in their lunch alone than they would have in their breakfast, snack, and lunch combined. Even a fat-free 50-calorie slice of toast with 10 sprays of "I Can't Believe It's Not Butter" spray for breakfast, totaling only 60 calories and 1 gram of fat, can save you oodles and oodles of calories later by helping curb your hunger so you don't feel ravenous by lunch. Many people think like this: "Well, I didn't eat breakfast, so it's okay to go ahead and eat these fries." Those 300-calorie fries just blew your total caloric and fat intake for the day out of the water. If people eat a small breakfast or snack before lunch they probably would be able to refrain from the fries altogether.

Low-Fat Lifestyle

Some people tell you to eat whatever you want but only eat a little bit. That is good to a degree. I think it is better to eat what you are craving, but choose low-fat. Remember, choosing a low-fat lifestyle helps fight countless diseases, including heart disease, cancer, and diabetes. Why eat a Snickers at 12 grams of fat if a Milky Way Lite will do the trick and satisfy the sweet craving for only 5 grams of fat and almost half the calories? Or how about a bite-size Milky Way Lite at 1 gram of fat and 30 calories? Why eat regular French fries at 20 grams of fat and 300 calories when the baked ones are equally delicious with practically no fat and one-third of the calories? With today's endless array of wonderful low-fat, low-calorie choices, why not make the healthier choice and eat what you're craving? There are a lot more healthy options today than there were twenty years ago. What used to be a special treat fifty years ago is now the norm in many families. A special candy bar from the five-and-dime store or a hamburger, fries, and milk shake at the local diner was a special treat. Nowadays, people think nothing of having an Egg McMuffin and a side of fried hash browns for breakfast; a Quarter-Pounder with cheese, fries, and a milk shake for lunch; a candy bar for a snack; pizza for dinner; and then a bowl of ice cream before going to bed. Once in a while these foods are okay as a treat, but on a daily basis they will kill you.

Don't think of low-fat eating as a diet. Think of it as a lifestyle change. What you do to get thinner and healthier is what you need to continue doing after you've reached your goal. The Bible tells us to train up our children in the way they should go. I believe it is not only about spiritual things but physical ones also. It is a lot easier to maintain a healthy, low-fat lifestyle when you are trained that way as a child. The habits that you make when you are a child are most likely going to be the habits that you continue as an adult—especially your eating habits.

I am the oldest of seven children. We took great pride in how much we could eat. We'd have contests to see who could out eat the others. "You can eat seven ears of corn; well, I can eat eight." It may sound funny now, but to this day I struggle within. I am a recovering food addict. I tell people there's nothing a hot fudge brownie can't to help make feel better. I've used food like an alcoholic uses alcohol to numb the pain, help me feel better, keep me from being bored or lonely, to celebrate . . . the list goes on and on and on. I know how hard it is. I want to encourage any of you who struggle: There is hope. There is help. All you have to do is ask. Oftentimes when we think our stomachs are hungry, it's really our hearts that need feeding. Having faith in God and accountability from others is the key to overcoming addictions. For those needing accountability some good groups include Overeaters Anonymous, First Place, and T.O.P.S. You are not alone. There are a lot of people who struggle with food addictions. Keep believing. You will succeed!

Muscle vs. Fat

Some people say they can consume 3,000 calories a day and remain 125 pounds simply by eating a very low-fat diet. This can be extremely frustrating for those of us born watching our weight. We eat about half that many calories and weigh more. The secret to being able to eat more calories and not gain weight is in the muscle mass. One pound of muscle burns 50 calories a day whereas one pound of body fat burns 2 calories a day. Let's take two people each weighing 100 pounds. Person A is solid muscle. Person B is solid body fat. It takes twenty-five times the amount of calories to maintain muscle than it does to maintain fat.

Person	Weight	Mass	Calories per pound per day	Total calories per day
Person A	100 lbs.	Muscle	50	5000
Person B	100 lbs.	Fat	2	200

Wow! That's a tremendous difference. Forty-eight hundred more daily calories are needed to maintain 100 pounds of muscle versus 100 pounds of fat.

Basal Metabolic Rate

The basal metabolic rate (BMR) is the amount of energy your body burns when resting. This rate is measured in calories and is based on the body's build and make-up rather than on weight. On the top of the next page is a the Harris-Benedict formula for figuring out your BMR.

Adult Male:

$$66 + [6.3 \times weight\ (lb.)] + [12.9 \times height\ (in.)] - [6.8 \times age\ (yrs.)]$$

Adult Female:

$$655 + [4.3 \times weight\ (lb.)] + [4.7 \times height\ (in.)] - [4.7 \times age\ (yrs.)]$$

It's important to remember that the number one factor in our build and body makeup is genetic. In other words, we're each born with a genetic blueprint based on our ancestors. However, in the blueprint there are some things we can somewhat control by our lifestyle. People with similar genetic makeups can have a huge weight difference depending on their lifestyles.

Although each of our body types has its own blueprint we do have some control as to where in that blueprint we want to be. No matter where we choose to be it will have a price. It's also important to remember that having too much body fat is what we need to be concerned with, not necessarily what your bathroom scale says. The scale does not let you know if you are at your ideal weight for your frame. Instead of focusing on the scale and letting your weight determine how you feel about yourself, throw away the scale and focus on the real issue—living healthily. Ask yourself these questions: "Am I treating myself healthily? Am I a healthy eater? Did I take time to exercise? Am I getting enough rest?"

Good for the Gaggle

If you've ever heard the expression "What's good for the goose is good for the gander," this heading may make sense. I say, "What's good for the goose is good for the gaggle." In other words, when you choose to have a low-fat lifestyle, don't separate your low-fat food from your family's high-fat food at home. What is good for you is good for your family and your children. As I said before, it's much easier to grow up loving to eat low-fat foods rather than learning to eat them later on in life. For those of you who are concerned your children will not get enough fats or calories, check with their doctor. I have found that most children will make enough unhealthy choices on their own and will get more than enough fat. There is usually enough fat in just one school lunch for a few days! Plus there are healthy high-fat foods, such as peanut butter and nuts, they may choose to eat that you and I will normally avoid because they are so full of calories.

Helpful Hints to Eating Low-Fat

Avoid Sugar—Sugar has half the calories gram for gram compared to fats. But sugar is fattening because it's so calorie dense, and calories that aren't burned up are stored as fat.

30% or less—Follow the American Heart Association's guidelines of 30% or less of your daily calories deriving from fat. This simple rule of thumb is: 3 fat grams or less per 100 calories.

A Fat Book—Purchase a calorie counting book that contains food products by name. Highlight items in the book you like that have less than 3 grams of fat per 100 calories.

Personal Reference—Write down the items you highlighted in the book and keep it with you. This will be a quick and handy resource for you.

Modify or Substitute—Keep eating the foods you love, but modify or substitute. Let's say you have a sweet tooth. When your sweet tooth is driving you nuts, instead of going crazy, choose your favorite low-fat sweets for a healthy choice.

Example of my list for low-fat candy:
Peppermint Patty, Sugar Babies, Sugar Daddy, licorice, Milk Duds, Milky Way Lite, Sweet Tarts, most hard candies, dark chocolate covered cherries, marshmallow eggs, and Bit-O-Honey.

Isn't it nice to know we can still eat the things we've grown to love and not eat like a rabbit in order to be healthier? Some simple substitutions such as a Milky Way Lite candy bar instead of a Snickers candy bar can save oodles of fat and calories (9 fat grams and 110 calories saved!) Yet, you don't feel deprived. You feel satisfied and you've done your body good. (Or at least better!) However, let us not forget sugar is still fattening if eaten too much. Remember, moderation is the key in not ending up a big fatty.

Prepare Well—Immediately after arriving home from the market clean, cut, and prepare all your fresh fruits and vegetables for the week. The last thing you feel like doing when you're hungry is peeling a carrot. Large, clear plastic bags are absolutely wonderful for storing visually pleasing and prepared fresh vegetables and fruits. Most vegetables last for five days. (Cutting vegetables thicker helps them stay fresher longer.) If you don't have a good hour to prepare your fruits and vegetables, then spend the extra money on already prepared vegetable and fruit snacks.

Out of Sight, Out of Mind—Don't store them in drawers of the refrigerator where they are out of sight. Instead keep them on shelves up front where you will immediately see them. Keep fresh, whole fruits (apples, oranges, pears, bananas, etc.) out on the counter for snacks instead of sweets. Fat-free cookies, cakes and treats are usually higher in sugars and lower in actual nutritional value than fruits. Keep a wide variety of your favorite fat-free salad dressings on hand and refrigerated in an organized, easily visible spot at all times for using not only as a salad dressing but also as a dip for vegetables and marinade.

Exercise

It's important not only for your physical well being but also for your mental and emotional well being. When you take care of yourself, you can't help but feel better about yourself.

When you exercise . . .

- Your body releases endorphins which help you feel good and better about yourself.
- The energy you burn creates energy and makes you feel more energetic.
- You build muscle, which in turn burns more calories throughout the day (see page 8).
- You relieve stress.
- You help your body fight numerous diseases.

How to Stick to Exercising

- Exercise in the morning. Studies show that people who exercise first thing in the morning are more apt to stick with it than those who exercise at other times of the day.
- Do an aerobic exercise that you enjoy. If you don't enjoy it, no matter how wonderful your intentions are, chances are you won't stick to it.
- Find something to preoccupy your mind during your exercise. Record your favorite show and watch it while exercising, visit with a friend while exercising, listen to a book on tape, or take advantage of the alone time and pray.

- Plan it into your day as a priority. Again, remember, exercising first thing in the morning increases your chances of sticking with it for the long haul.

The Cost Factor

Buying low-fat or fat-free is more expensive when you are not consumer wise. Manufactures take out the fat and charge you more. It doesn't make sense to me, but it makes dollars and cents for the manufacturers! One way I've saved without using coupons is to make a list of the products I like to use the most. One day take time to comparison shop. Make a list of the three to four stores where you shop most often. Then write out the products you buy most often and compare the prices at the different stores.

Here's a sample of my chart:

Item	Super Value	Kroger	Sam's	Aldi's
Frozen veggies	0.89	1.20	1.00	0.79
Canned veggies	0.50	0.78	N/A	0.29
Chicken breast	1.99	3.99	2.50	2.30
Eye of round	2.49	3.99	4.29	N/A
Ultra Promise margarine	1.89	1.69	N/A	N/A
Healthy Choice cheese	2.39	1.99	N/A	N/A
Eggs - 1 dozen	0.75	1.09	0.80	0.60
Skim milk	2.29	1.89	1.89	1.89
Yogurt	0.35	0.69	0.50	0.29
Baked Lays potato chips	3.29	3.39	2.49	N/A
Baked Tostitos	3.59	3.31	2.69	N/A
Fat-free frozen yogurt	1.89	4.99	3.99	N/A

N/A = Not Available.

Make your own chart.

Item	Store #1	Store #2	Store #3	Store #4

N/A = Not Available.

Once you've filled in on the left column the items you usually use, go to each store and write in the appropriate box how much that product usually costs. See which store has the lowest prices on certain items. Once you've completed your chart and are out shopping at one of the stores, you'll know which items are cheapest at that store. The key is to plan ahead and buy the items that you know are lower priced on a regular basis at each individual store. Of course, if a store happens to have something on sale, then I stock up. Shopping this way saves me an estimated 20 to 30 percent compared to shopping all at one location.

Saving Money with Coupons

As I've already said, fat-free products are more expensive than their fatty counterparts. I feel it's worth the cost for better health. When

I have time, I do the coupon thing. My coupon book was a $5.00 investment, and it has saved me a lot of grief, time, and money. I get so many compliments on my coupon organization. Here's what you'll need:

- 100-page large photo album with clear film sheets that hold photos in place
- 1 envelope with flap cut off
- tape
- coupons
- tabs (used for filing)

Clear sheet that holds photos in place, now holds coupons in place

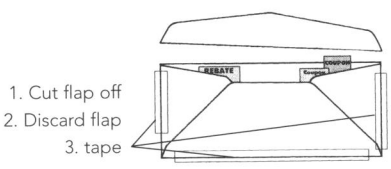

1. Cut flap off
2. Discard flap
3. tape

Label the tabs individually for easy finding. I label mine: Dairy, Breads, Meats, Fish, Chicken, Cleaning Supplies, Hair Care, etc. Each section will have its own title page. Tape the labeled tabs onto the outside edge of photo album pages so that you can easily go to any section desired. (Only one tab per page. There will be numerous pages without tabs in each section following the title page.)

Put coupons in proper sections.

Cut the flap off the envelope. Tape the envelope to the front inside cover of the photo album. Put the coupons you've pulled from the designated sections in the envelope for easy storage until check-out time. I also put rebates into the envelope.

Another way to stay within budget is to only spend cash for groceries. When you get paid take out enough cash for the grocery budget and only spend that cash on groceries. This will help you live within your means. It saves time when picking up only a few items at the grocery store because you don't have to write a check. Also, for those times when you only need a few items, do not take a cart. Carry the items in your arms or a basket. You will be a lot less tempted to impulse buy if your arms are full.

What I Like to Stock in My Kitchen

There are literally hundreds (if not thousands) of fat-free and very low-fat products on the market today. The problem (as I'm sure a lot of you know) is that many of them do *not* taste good. Eating low-fat really shouldn't be a tasteless, boring experience. My motto regarding low-fat foods is: If it doesn't taste good, don't eat it. There are too many delicious choices available for any of us to waste calories on food that doesn't taste good.

An easy rule of thumb when reading labels: if it has more than 3 grams of fat per 100 calories, don't buy it and don't use it! The only time I break that rule is for super lean beef such as:

Type of Beef	Serving Size	Fat Grams	Calories	% Fat Calories
London Broil/ Flank Steak	3 oz.	6	167	32%
Top Loin (Lean Only)	3 oz.	6	162	33%
Eye of Round	3 oz.	5	150	30%

If you enjoy eating red meat and do not want to refrain, then I encourage you to make the switch to ground eye of round. You'll be doing your heart, health, and waistline a lot of good.

The following is a sample of products I enjoy using and keep stocked in my kitchen. Look for them in your grocery store.

Butter & Margarines

Butter Buds (found in spice section)

Butter-flavored Pam Spray

Nonfat cooking sprays

I Can't Believe It's Not Butter Spray

*Ultra Fat-free Promise Margarine

Breads & Grains

Enriched flour

Fat-free flour tortillas

Graham crackers

Health Valley fat-free cookies

Health Valley fat-free granola

Fat-free breads (40 calories per slice)

Nabisco reduced-fat Ritz Crackers

Pastas from whole durum wheat
(except egg noodles)

Quaker rice cakes (caramel and
strawberry flavored)

Rice (whole grain enriched)

Whole grain and white rice

Whole-wheat flour

Beverages

Country Time lemonade (sugar free)

Crystal Light (sugar free)

Dole fruit juices (100%)

Grapefruit, orange, and prune
juices (100%)

Kool-Aid (sugar free)

Tea (instant or tea bag)

Tomato juice

Condiments

A-1 sauce

Almond extract

Barbecue sauce

Cocoa

Equal

Evaporated skim milk

Hidden Valley fat-free salad dressings

Ketchup

Kraft Free mayonnaise
and Miracle Whip

Kraft fat-free tartar sauce

Kroger fat-free ice cream toppings

Liquid smoke

Lite soy sauce

Lite teriyaki marinade

Mustard

Seven Seas "Free" ranch salad dressing

Seven Seas "Free" red wine vinegar
salad dressing

Seven Seas "Free" viva Italian
salad dressing

T. Marzetti's fat-free raspberry
salad dressing

Taco seasoning mix

Tomato sauce

Vanilla

Western fat-free salad dressing

Dairy

(Note: I am not a big fan of fat-free
cheeses or margarines, but in my
recipes, they taste good.)

Borden fat-free cheese slices
(sharp cheddar)

*Eagle brand fat-free condensed
sweetened milk

Fat-free cottage cheese

Fat-free yogurts

Fleishmann's fat-free buttery spread
(comes in a bottle)

Fleishmann's fat-free cheese spread
(comes in a bottle)

Healthy Choice fat-free cheese

Kraft fat-free cheeses

Kraft Free Parmesan cheese

Non-fat buttermilk

*Pet fat-free evaporated skim milk

*Reddi Whip fat-free whipped topping

Sargenta fat-free ricotta

Snack Food

Baked Tostitos

Dole fruit & juice bars

Fat-free ice cream

Frozen fat-free yogurts

Fudge bars (most are low-fat or fat-free)

Health Valley fat-free tarts

Hostess lite twinkies, cupcakes,
brownies, and muffins

Jello fat-free pudding and pudding cups

Keebler Elfin Delights

Little Debbie's lite oatmeal pies
and brownies

Pepperidge Farm fat-free brownies
and blondies

Pop Secret popcorn bars

Popsicles

Pretzels

Smart Pop microwave popcorn

Snack Well's cookies, tarts, and
breakfast bars

Sweet Escapes candies

Welch's frozen juice bars

Meats, Fish, Poultry

Beef (eye of round, London broil,
flank steak, top loin)

ButterBall fat-free sausage, turkey
breast, and lunchmeats

Canadian bacon (usually low in fat)

Chicken breast, skinless

Crabmeat, flake or stick (imitation)

*Eckrich fat-free meats (hot dogs,
smoked sausage, kielbasa)

Fish (flounder, grouper, pike, sole, cod,
orange roughy, monk fish, perch,
scallops)

*Healthy Choice lunch meat, hot dogs,
and smoked sausage

MorningStar Ground Meatless
(only in recipes)

Shellfish (lobster, crab, shrimp)

Tuna (packed in water)

Fruits and Veggies

Canned vegetables, no salt added

Canned fruits in fruit juice only

Cranberry sauce

Fresh vegetables

Frozen vegetables, and fruits, with no sugar added

Lite fruit cocktail

Lite pie fillings (cherry, apple, and blueberry)

Sauces

Campbell's Healthy Request low-fat & fat-free sauces

Healthy Choice spaghetti sauce

Heinz Homestyle Lite gravies (in a jar)

Hunts "Light" fat-free pasta sauce

Pepperidge Farm stroganoff gravy

Prego spaghetti and pizza sauce (low-fat)

Ragu Lite "Garden Harvest" & "Tomato & Herb"

Ragu Pizza Quick Sauce

Other Items

*Bac-O's (imitation bacon bits)

Betty Crocker Super Moist cake mixes

*Campbell's Healthy Request low-fat & fat-free soups

Chef Boy-R-Dee Spaghetti O's

*Cool Whip Free

*Egg Beaters

Gold Medal fudge brownie mix

Legumes (beans and lentils)

Martha White's light mixes

Nabisco's "Royal" Lite Cheesecake mixes

Pillsbury Lovin' Lites frostings

An asterisk (*) in front of the product means the generic brands of these items are less expensive and good.

Notes to the Cook

Splenda

Splenda is a calorie-free sugar substitute that tastes like sugar and is made from sugar but without the fattening carbohydrates. I use it in a lot of my recipes.

There are two forms of Splenda: Splenda granular and Splenda packets. Splenda granular comes in a box and measures like sugar. Splenda packets come prepackaged and do not measure like sugar. Be careful in following my recipe ingredients and use the appropriate type of Splenda. The two different forms measure differently and are not interchangeable.

Butter Buds

I use Butter Buds in a lot of my recipes. Butter Buds is a brand of all-natural, fat- and cholesterol-free butter-flavored granules that can be used in place of butter, margarine, or oil. They are available in granulated Sprinkles and a Mix that can be reconstituted with hot water to form a buttery liquid. Because they are low in fat I have depended on them for a number of my recipes. The following is a substitution chart in case you cannot find Butter Buds at your local grocer.

BUTTER BUDS® SUBSTITUTION CHART

Butter or Margarine	Butter Buds Mix (Dry)	Butter Buds Mix (Liquefied)	Butter Buds Sprinkles
1 tablespoon	1 teaspoon	1 tablespoon	$3/4$ teaspoon
2 tablespoons	2 teaspoons	2 tablespoons	$1^1/2$ teaspoons
$1/4$ cup ($1/2$ stick)	4 teaspoons ($1/2$ envelope)	$1/4$ cup	1 tablespoon
$1/2$ cup (1 stick)	8 teaspoons (1 envelope)	$1/2$ cup	2 tablespoons
1 cup (2 sticks)	2 envelopes	1 cup	$1/4$ cup

Butter Buds® is a registered trademark of Cumberland Packaging Corp., Brooklyn, New York, 11205. Used by Permission.

Breakfast

Thankfulness is an attitude we choose to have.

Banana Cream Oatmeal   29

Blueberry Crumb Cake   40

Blueberry Custard Bake   36

Breakfast Burrito   35

Breakfast Fruit-Filled Pockets   41

Broccoli, Ham & Cheese Frittata   39

Cherry Oatmeal   26

Cherry Pizza   38

Cinnamon Drops   31

Cinnamon Rolls (minisize)   37

Coconut Cream Oatmeal   25

Cran-Apple Oatmeal   28

Cranberry Orange Scones   33

"Fake Bacon"   30

Manhandler Breakfast Bake   34

Mm!   32

Peaches & Cream Oatmeal   27

Coconut Cream Oatmeal

This hearty, stick-to-your-bones breakfast is a special treat, with its creamy, toasted coconut flavor. It's a great way to start a cold day.

2	tablespoons coconut, flaked	1/2	cup fat-free, sweetened condensed skim milk
1/4	teaspoon light salt, optional		
4	cups water	1	teaspoon coconut extract
2	cups quick-cooking oats		

- Broil the coconut on a cookie sheet for 15 seconds until toasty brown.
- Bring the salt and water to a boil in a medium-size pan. Add the oats and cook for 1 minute, stirring occasionally.
- Remove from the heat. Stir in the condensed milk, coconut extract, and toasted coconut. Stir until all the ingredients are well blended.
- Cover and let sit for 2 to 3 minutes. The oatmeal will thicken as it sits, yet it will have a creamy consistency to it.
- Serve warm.

Note: The fat in this recipe is primarily the fat that naturally grows in oats. It's good for the body.

Yield: 4 (1-cup) servings

Calories: 277; Fat: 2g (9% fat); Cholesterol: 2mg; Carbohydrate: 52g; Dietary Fiber: 4g; Protein: 9g; Sodium: 52mg

Total time: 7 minutes or less

Menu idea: This is good with half of a grapefruit and skim milk, tea, or coffee.

Cherry Oatmeal

The slight tartness of the cherries is a pleasant, fruity surprise. Children especially like this oatmeal.

6 cups water	1 (21-ounce) can light cherry pie filling
1/4 teaspoon salt, optional	
3 cups old-fashioned oats	3/4 cup strawberry-flavored powdered sugar*
1 teaspoon almond extract	

- Bring the water and salt to a boil on high heat in a large pan or Dutch oven.
- Add the oats.
- Reduce the heat to medium, but keep the oats boiling for 5 minutes, stirring occasionally.
- After 5 minutes remove the oatmeal from the heat.
- Add the almond extract, cherry pie filling, and powdered sugar.
- Stir until well mixed. Cover and let sit for 2 minutes longer.
- Serve immediately while hot.

*Note: If you don't have strawberry-flavored powdered sugar, regular powdered sugar is fine. Some people may like their oatmeal sweeter. I set sugar on the table so each person can sweeten his own oatmeal as desired.

Note: The fat in this recipe is primarily the fat that naturally grows in oats. It's good for the body.

Yield: 7 (1-cup) servings

Calories: 220; Fat: 2g (9% fat); Cholesterol: 0mg; Carbohydrate: 44g; Dietary Fiber: 5g; Protein: 6g; Sodium: 12mg

Total time: 10 minutes or less

Menu idea: This is good served with tea, coffee, or skim milk.

Peaches & Cream Oatmeal

The slight tartness and gentle texture of the peaches combined with the sweet creamy oatmeal gives this a tasty flavor.

4	cups water	2	cups quick-cooking oats
	Dash of light salt, optional	$1/2$	cup fat-free, sweetened condensed skim milk
$1/2$	cup finely chopped dried peaches	1	teaspoon vanilla

- In a medium-size pan on high heat bring the water and salt if using to a boil.
- Reduce the heat to low.
- Stir in the peaches and oats. Let the mixture cook for 1 minute.
- Turn off the heat and stir in the condensed milk and vanilla.
- Cover and let sit for 3 minutes.

Note: The fat in this recipe is primarily the fat that naturally grows in oats. It's good for the body.

Yield: 5 (1-cup) servings

Calories: 253; Fat: 2g (8% fat); Cholesterol: 2mg ; Carbohydrate: 51g; Dietary Fiber: 5g; Protein: 8g; Sodium: 35mg

Total time: 7 minutes or less

Menu idea: Fresh sliced peaches or oranges on the side and skim milk, tea, or coffee.

Cran-Apple Oatmeal

This will wake up your taste buds. The sweet tartness adds a zesty touch to an old-time breakfast favorite.

2^1/2 cups apple cider
1^1/2 cups quick-cooking oats

^{1}/3 cup sweetened dried cranberries

- In a medium-size pan bring the apple cider to a boil.
- Add the oats and dried cranberries. Let the mixture cook for 1 minute and then turn off the heat.
- Cover and let the oats sit for 3 minutes.

Yield: 3 (1-cup) servings

Calories: 253; Fat: 2g (8% fat); Cholesterol: 2mg; Carbohydrate: 51g; Dietary Fiber: 5g; Protein: 8g; Sodium: 35mg

Total time: 7 minutes or less

Menu idea: This recipe is good served with skim milk, tea, or coffee.

Banana Cream Oatmeal

If you like banana cream pie, you'll love this. It's my daughter Ashley's favorite of all my different flavored oatmeal recipes.

4 cups water	1/2 cup fat-free, sweetened condensed skim milk
2 cups quick-cooking oats	
2 medium bananas, thinly sliced	

- In a medium-size saucepan bring the water to a boil over high heat.
- Once the water boils, reduce the heat to medium and add the oats.
- Cook for 1 minute, stirring occasionally.
- Remove the oats from the heat and add the banana slices and condensed milk.
- Cover and let the oatmeal sit for 2 to 3 minutes. It will thicken as it sits.
- Serve warm.

Note: The fat in this recipe is primarily the fat that naturally grows in oats. It's good for the body.

Yield: 4 (1½-cup) servings

Calories: 320; Fat: 3g (8% fat); Cholesterol: 2mg ; Carbohydrate: 65g; Dietary Fiber: 6g; Protein: 10g; Sodium: 42mg

Total time: 7 minutes or less

Menu idea: This is great with skim milk, tea, or coffee.

"Fake Bacon"

Paula Kamler from Joplin, Missouri, sent me this recipe.

4 slices thin ham, not honey glazed

- Microwave the ham on a tray until crispy and reduced in size by about half. My microwave takes 2 minutes. Others may vary.

Yield: 1 serving

Calories: 99; Fat: 5g (43% fat); Cholesterol: 31mg; Carbohydrate: 1g; Dietary Fiber: 0g; Protein: 13g; Sodium: 828mg

Preparation time: 1 minute or less
Microwave time: 2 minutes
Total time: 3 minutes or less

Menu ideas: "Fake bacon" can be used for breakfast, BLT sandwich, or crumbled for a salad.

Cinnamon Drops

Move over, traditional fatty cinnamon rolls; Cinnamon Drops are here.

1/2 cup sugar	1/4 cup fat-free buttery spread
2 tablespoons cinnamon	2 tablespoons low-fat, creamy
2 (7 1/2-ounce) cans Pillsbury buttermilk biscuits	deluxe frosting, optional

- Preheat the oven to 350 degrees.
- Spray a 9 x 13-inch pan with nonfat cooking spray.
- Mix the sugar and cinnamon together in a small bowl.
- Cut each biscuit into quarters.
- Put a little dab of buttery spread on each biscuit piece and coat with the cinnamon-sugar mixture.
- Set the coated dough pieces on the prepared baking pan with the pieces touching each other. Some overlapping will occur. If there is cinnamon-sugar remaining, sprinkle it over the dough in the pan.
- Bake for 15 minutes.
- If frosting is desired, microwave it for approximately 10 to 15 seconds to melt it into a glaze. Drizzle the glaze over the Cinnamon Drops.
- Let them cool for several minutes before eating.

Yield: 16 servings

Calories: 93; Fat:1g (8% fat); Cholesterol: 0mg; Carbohydrate: 20g; Dietary Fiber: 1g; Protein: 2g; Sodium: 243mg

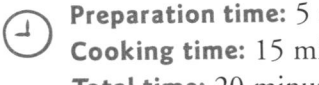

Preparation time: 5 minutes
Cooking time: 15 minutes
Total time: 20 minutes or less

Menu ideas: Terrific for brunch buffets or for a special breakfast instead of toast.

Mm!

This scrumptious crumb cake makes an excellent breakfast cake, coffee cake, snack cake, or dessert.

1 (10-ounce) package frozen strawberries, thawed	1 (18¹/4-ounce) box reduced-fat, yellow cake mix (I use Betty Crocker Super Moist.) Do not make as directed on box.
1 (8-ounce) package fat-free cream cheese, softened	

- Preheat the oven to 350 degrees.
- Set aside 1 cup of the dry cake mix.
- Line a 9 x 13-inch pan with foil for easier clean-up. Coat the foil with nonfat cooking spray.
- With a mixer on low speed, beat together the strawberries and cream cheese for 1 minute.
- Add half of the remaining cake mix to the cream mixture and continue beating until well mixed, and then add the other half. *Do not* use the 1 cup reserved. Beat for 2 minutes on medium speed.
- Spread the batter into the prepared pan. Sprinkle the 1 cup reserved cake mix on top of the batter.
- Bake for 30 minutes or until a knife inserted in the center comes out clean.

Yield: 15 servings

Calories: 159; Fat: 2g (8% fat); Cholesterol: 0mg; Carbohydrate: 20g; Dietary Fiber: 1g; Protein: 2g; Sodium: 243mg

Preparation time: 10 minutes or less
Baking time: 30 minutes
Total time: 40 minutes or less

Menu idea: This is good served with tea, coffee, or skim milk and a piece of fruit

Cranberry Orange Scones

These flavorful drop biscuits are great for breakfast by themselves or served with egg dishes. A slightly sweet treat at dinner with meals, they're delicious served hot.

2 egg whites	**Glaze:**
1 (10-ounce) jar cranberry orange crushed fruit	2 tablespoons raspberry preserves
3 cups reduced-fat baking mix (I use Bisquick.)	$1/2$ cup powdered sugar
	1 tablespoon skim milk

- Preheat the oven to 350 degrees.
- Spray two cookie sheets with nonfat cooking spray.
- Beat the egg whites with the crushed fruit until well mixed.
- Stir in the biscuit mix. The dough will be stiff and sticky.
- Drop 14 rounded tablespoons of the dough onto the prepared cookie sheets.
- Bake for 15 minutes or until the bottoms are golden brown.
- While the scones are baking, make the glaze by mixing the raspberry preserves, powdered sugar, and skim milk in a bowl.
- With a spoon, drizzle the glaze lightly over the biscuits while they are still hot and fresh from the oven.
- Let them cool for several minutes before eating. The hot fruit could burn your mouth.

Yield: 14 servings

Calories: 160; Fat: 2g (9% fat); Cholesterol: 0mg; Carbohydrate: 34g; Dietary Fiber: 0g; Protein: 3g; Sodium: 314mg

Preparation time: 5 minutes
Baking time: 15 minutes
Total time: 20 minutes or less

Menu ideas: These are perfect for breakfast, brunch, buffets, egg-based entrées, and omelets.

Manhandler Breakfast Bake

This is an excellent, simple, whip-it-up-fast entrée that is perfect for a hearty breakfast or brunch.

3 (8-ounce) packages egg substitute	1/2 pound Canadian bacon, thinly sliced and cut into bite-size pieces
1 (8-ounce) bag fat-free, shredded pizza cheese (a blend of nonfat mozzarella and nonfat cheddar cheese)	1 (7 1/2-ounce) can Pillsbury buttermilk biscuits

- Preheat the oven to 350 degrees.
- Spray a 9 x 13-inch pan with nonfat cooking spray.
- In a bowl mix the egg, cheese, and Canadian bacon.
- Arrange the biscuits on the bottom of the baking pan.
- Pour the egg mixture over the biscuits. You may need to press the biscuits down so they are covered with the mixture.
- Bake for 30 minutes or until a knife inserted in the center comes out clean.
- Serve hot.
- If desired lightly sprinkle with light salt.

Yield: 6 large servings

Calories: 239; Fat: 2g (9% fat); Cholesterol: 3mg; Carbohydrate: 32g; Dietary Fiber: 1g; Protein: 4g; Sodium: 310mg

Preparation time: 5 minutes or less
Baking time: 30 minutes
Total time: 35 minutes or less

Menu idea: Serve with a fruit cup and skim milk, coffee, or tea.

Breakfast Burrito

Move over, McDonald's. I've created our own breakfast burrito that's fast and easy to prepare. It's delicious and a lot lower in fat and calories than yours. These can be made in advance, refrigerated, and warmed in the microwave when needed.

1/2 pound low-fat kielbasa, diced into tiny pieces	1/2 cup fat-free shredded cheddar cheese
8 egg whites	10 fat-free, soft flour tortillas
1/4 cup chunky salsa	

- In a large non-stick skillet heat the diced kielbasa over medium-high heat, approximately 3 to 4 minutes.
- In a medium bowl beat the egg whites and chunky salsa together. Cook the egg/salsa mixture with the kielbasa as you would scrambled eggs, stirring every 30 seconds. When the eggs are completely cooked, yet still slightly damp, stir in the cheddar cheese.
- Cook for about 30 seconds more, or until the cheese is melted.
- Microwave the tortillas until soft and warm, about 10 to 30 seconds.
- Fill the middle of each tortilla with the prepared breakfast mixture. Fold as you would a burrito.
- Presto! You're done.

Yield: 10 burritos

Calories: 137; Fat: 1g (4% fat); Cholesterol: 9mg; Carbohydrate: 22g; Dietary Fiber: 1g; Protein: 10g; Sodium: 570mg

Preparation time: 1 minute
Cooking time: 6 minutes
Total time: 7 minutes

Menu idea: All you need is some orange juice, coffee, or tea.

Blueberry Custard Bake

Serve as an elegant entrée for a special breakfast or brunch.

1	(3.4-ounce) instant vanilla pudding mix	5	ounces sugar-free blueberry spreadable fruit
16	egg whites or 16 ounces egg substitute	1	cup blueberries

- Preheat the oven to 350 degrees.
- Spray a 9 x 13-inch casserole dish with nonfat cooking spray.
- With a mixer beat the pudding mix with the egg substitute for 5 minutes on high. Pour the mixture into the prepared casserole dish.
- Bake for 30 minutes.
- In the meantime heat the blueberry preserves and blueberries in a saucepan over low heat.
- Let it cool for 2 minutes before cutting.
- Cut into eight squares and serve hot with a few tablespoonfuls of hot blueberry sauce served on top, letting the blueberry sauce flow over the top and down the sides of each individual serving.

Yield: 8 servings

Calories: 127; Fat: 0g (0% fat); Cholesterol: 0mg; Carbohydrate: 24g; Dietary Fiber: 1g; Protein: 7g; Sodium: 289mg

Preparation time: 8 minutes or less
Baking time: 30 minutes
Total time: 38 minutes or less

Menu idea: Serve this with the Cinnamon Rolls (page 37), a fruit cup, and some skim milk, coffee, or tea.

Cinnamon Rolls (minisize)

These cinnamon rolls aren't too sweet; they're just *right.*

1 (10-ounce) can pizza crust dough	1/3 cup sugar
2 tablespoons low-fat margarine	1 tablespoon low-fat vanilla frosting
2 teaspoons ground cinnamon	

- Preheat the oven to 375 degrees.
- Spray a jelly roll pan (17 x 11-inch cookie sheet with 1-inch sides) with nonfat cooking spray.
- Roll the dough out in the jelly roll pan, spreading it flat with your hands until the dough touches the edges of the pan.
- Microwave the margarine until melted.
- Drizzle the melted margarine over the dough. With your fingertips evenly spread the melted margarine over the dough.
- Mix the cinnamon and sugar together and sprinkle two-thirds of the cinnamon/sugar mixture over the melted margarine.
- Roll up the dough (jelly-roll style), beginning from the longest side.
- With your fingers pinch the seam of the dough to seal.
- Cut into twelve pieces. (This is easy to do with scissors.)
- Spray twelve mini-muffin tins with nonfat cooking spray. (Regular size muffin tins work fine also.)
- Place one mini-roll into each muffin tin.
- Sprinkle the remaining cinnamon/sugar mixture evenly on the tops.
- Bake for 15 minutes.
- Microwave the frosting for 5 seconds and immediately lightly drizzle on top of the cinnamon rolls.
- Let the rolls cool 1 to 2 minutes before eating.

Yield: 12 servings

Calories: 95; Fat: 2g (15% fat); Cholesterol: 0mg; Carbohydrate: 18g; Dietary Fiber: 1g; Protein: 2g; Sodium: 170mg

Preparation time: 10 minutes or less
Baking time: 15 minutes or less
Total time: 25 minutes or less

Menu idea: This versatile dish is great for brunch, breakfast buffets, showers, or special holidays.

Cherry Pizza

Delicious fresh out of the oven or served at room temperature, this dish is perfect for those who like to eat pizza for breakfast. It's great for dessert, too.

1   (10-ounce) can pizza dough
1   (21-ounce) can cherry pie filling
1/4   cup fat-free margarine

1   (20-ounce) package cherry oatmeal crunch mix (I use Calhoun Bend Mill brand.)
1/4   cup low-fat, creamy deluxe vanilla frosting

- Preheat the oven to 425 degrees.
- Spray a jelly roll pan (17 x 11-inch cookie sheet with 1 inch sides) with nonfat cooking spray.
- With your hands press the pizza dough evenly to cover the entire pan.
- Spread the cherry pie filling evenly over the pizza dough.
- With a knife cut the nonfat spread into the cherry oatmeal crunch mix until the mixture has a crumbly consistency with no pieces larger than pea size.
- Sprinkle the crumb mixture evenly over the pie filling.
- Bake for 12 minutes or until the crust is golden brown and the top is slightly crunchy.
- Microwave the frosting for 3 to 5 seconds, just enough to melt frosting.
- Drizzle the frosting over the cherry pizza. Let the pizza cool for a few minutes before serving.

★ **For Blueberry Pizza:** Follow the directions exactly, but substitute blueberry pie filling instead of cherry pie filling.

Yield: 15 servings

Calories: 249; Fat: 2g (15% fat); Cholesterol: 0mg; Carbohydrate: 52g; Dietary Fiber: 3g; Protein: 5g; Sodium: 281mg

Preparation time: 10 minutes or less
Baking time: 12 minutes or less
Total time: 22 minutes or less

Menu idea: Serve with skim milk, tea, or coffee. It's good for breakfast buffets, brunches, or luncheons.

Broccoli, Ham & Cheese Frittata

This is an impressive name for an easy-to-prepare meal.

$1/4$ cup finely chopped red onion or $1/4$ cup frozen chopped onion
$1/2$ pound turkey ham, chopped
$3/4$ (16-ounce) bag frozen broccoli
9 egg whites

2 drops yellow food coloring
$1/2$ cup shredded fat-free cheddar cheese
Dash of seasoned salt, optional (I use Lawry's.)

- Preheat the oven to 350 degrees.
- Spray a large skillet with nonfat cooking spray. (A Teflon-coated skillet works best but any non-stick skillet will do.)
- Cook the onion and ham for 2 to 3 minutes over medium heat.
- Microwave the broccoli for 3 minutes.
- Beat the egg whites with the yellow food coloring about 100 strokes.
- Put the broccoli in the pan with the ham and onion.
- Pour the eggs over the mixture in the pan.
- Cook on low heat for 3 minutes.
- Sprinkle the cheese on top of the mixture. Spray nonfat cooking spray over the cheese. (This helps to keep the cheese from getting tough or chewy and makes it melt better.)
- Bake for about 5 to 8 minutes, or until the eggs are fully cooked.
- Sprinkle with the seasoned salt, if desired.
- Cut the frittata into thirds and serve hot.

Yield: 3 servings

Calories: 193; Fat: 3g (16% fat); Cholesterol: 58mg; Carbohydrate: 8g; Dietary Fiber: 3g; Protein: 33g; Sodium: 1166mg

Preparation time: 6 minutes
Cooking time: 14 minutes or less
Total time: 20 minutes or less

Menu ideas: Great for breakfast, brunch, or lunch. Serve with fat-free toast, jam, and fresh melon; Cucumber Dill Salad (page 90); or Blueberry Crumb Cake (page 40).

Blueberry Crumb Cake

This cake looks like it took forever to make. But don't worry; it's one of those quickie recipes you can whip up in no time at all.

1	(18.25-ounce) yellow cake mix, dry (I use Betty Crocker Super Moist.)	4	egg whites
		1	(21-ounce) can blueberry pie filling

- Preheat the oven to 350 degrees.
- Spray two 8-inch round cake pans with nonfat cooking spray.
- Set aside ½ cup of the dry cake mix to use later.
- With a mixer beat the egg whites on low speed for 30 seconds.
- Add the blueberry pie filling and the cake mix, except for the reserved ½ cup, to the egg whites and beat on medium speed for 2 minutes.
- Spread the batter into the prepared pans.
- Sprinkle the remaining dry cake mix evenly on top of batter in both cake pans.
- Bake for 28 minutes or until a knife inserted in the center of the cake comes out clean.

Note: To serve as a dessert, put a dab of blueberry pie filling on top of each serving of crumb cake.

Yield: 16 servings

Calories: 174; Fat: 2g (10% fat); Cholesterol: 0mg; Carbohydrate: 37g; Dietary Fiber: 1g; Protein: 3g; Sodium: 219mg

Preparation time: 7 minutes
Baking time: 28 minutes
Total time: 35 minutes

Menu ideas: This festive crumb cake is terrific for breakfast in the morning and light enough for a dessert after a heavy meal.

Breakfast Fruit-Filled Pockets

While preparing for a TV show, I came up with this creative and tasty recipe.

1	(7½-ounce) can Pillsbury buttermilk biscuits	1	teaspoon ground cinnamon
1	(21-ounce) can cherry pie filling or blueberry or strawberry	2	tablespoons sugar
1	egg white, beaten	3	tablespoons low-fat vanilla frosting

- Preheat the oven to 425 degrees.
- Spray a cookie sheet with nonfat cooking spray.
- Spray your hands with nonfat cooking spray. With your hands flatten each biscuit (dough) into a 3-inch circle.
- Put 1 rounded teaspoonful pie filling into the center of each circle.
- Brush a little beaten egg white on the outer ¼-inch rim of dough. This will act as the glue to hold the dough together.
- Fold the dough in half to shape like a half moon. With a fork press the dough edges together to seal.
- Mix the ground cinnamon and sugar together. Sprinkle on top of each pocket.
- Bake for 10 minutes or until golden brown.
- Once the pockets are done, microwave the frosting for 10 to 20 seconds, just enough to melt the frosting.
- Drizzle the frosting over the tops of the pockets.
- Let the pockets cool a few minutes before eating. Otherwise the piping hot filling will burn your mouth.

Yield: 10 servings

Calories: 150 ; Fat: 1g (7% fat); Cholesterol: 0mg; Carbohydrate: 33g; Dietary Fiber: 1g; Protein: 2g; Sodium: 205mg

Preparation time: 15 minutes or less
Cooking time: 10 minutes
Total time: 25 minutes or less

Menu ideas: These are great for breakfast, brunch buffets, or snacks. Also serve these pockets for a warm and delicious on-the-run breakfast.

Appetizers & Breads

Wisdom is knowing when not to say what's on your mind.

Buttermilk Ranch Dressing   53

Cheese Biscuits   63

Chicken & Onion Cheese Spread   46

Chicken Onion Dip   50

Cucumber Sandwiches   57

Deviled Eggs   47

Dijon Mayo Spread for Sandwiches   56

Garlic Toast   61

Ham & Cheese Spread   45

Italian Dunkers   58

Mexican Cheese Moons   55

Mild Mustard/Dill Dipping Sauce   54

Party Poppers   51

Pinwheel Dinner Rolls   64

Ruby Raspberry Fruit Dip   52

Southwestern Corn Muffins   62

Sweet Corn Bread   60

Sweet & Sour Teenie Weenies   49

Tomato Biscuits   59

Vegetable Dip   48

Ham & Cheese Spread

For years I've had to stay away from the deli's ham and cheese spread. It was one of my favorite high-fat foods that I did miss. But no more. My spread is absolutely, positively delicious. On a scale of one to ten, I think mine's a twelve.

$1/4$	cup fat-free whipped salad dressing	1	tablespoon mustard
3	tablespoons fat-free Thousand Island dressing	$3/4$	pound extra lean ham
		1	cup fat-free shredded cheddar cheese

- In a small bowl with a fork, mix the whipped dressing, Thousand Island, and mustard together until creamy and well mixed.
- Cut the ham into $1/4$-inch, or smaller, pieces and put them into a blender or food processor. Grind, using the pulse button for a few seconds to turn appliance on and off quickly. You may need to use a spatula to rearrange pieces that are not getting ground. Continue pulsing for 3- to 5-second intervals until all the ham pieces are ground.
- Add the ground ham to the cream mixture, along with the shredded cheddar cheese. Stir until well mixed.
- Serve as is, or cover and keep chilled until ready to use. Refrigerated, the spread will keep up to 5 days.

Yield: 6 ($1/4$-cup) servings

Calories: 115; Fat: 3g (24% fat); Cholesterol: 25mg; Carbohydrate: 5g; Dietary Fiber: 1g; Protein: 16g; Sodium: 1040mg

Total preparation time: 10 minutes or less

Menu ideas: As an appetizer, use as a filling to stuff cherry tomatoes or serve with fat-free crackers. It's also great on fat-free bread as a sandwich with lettuce.

Chicken & Onion Cheese Spread

This multiple-use spread is scrumptious no matter how it's used.

1	(10-ounce) can premium chunk white chicken in water, not drained	1/2	cup fat-free sour cream
2	(8-ounce) fat-free cream cheese packages, softened	1	(1-ounce) envelope dry onion soup mix
		1/4	cup chopped green or red pepper, optional

- Mix the chicken with its water, cream cheese, sour cream, soup mix, and pepper together with a hand mixer on low speed for about 1 to 2 minutes until well mixed.
- Serve with crackers. Or see menu ideas listed below.

Yield: 30 (2-tablespoon) servings

Calories: 30; Fat: 0g (0% fat); Cholesterol: 5mg; Carbohydrate: 2g; Dietary Fiber: 0g; Protein: 4g; Sodium: 198mg

 Preparation time: 6 minutes or less

 Menu ideas: Use as a vegetable dip or stuff in celery sticks. Spread on soft flour tortillas, top with lettuce and tomatoes, and roll up. Or spread the mix on a piece of toast for an open-face sandwich, and if desired top with a fresh green pepper ring.

Deviled Eggs

Sharon Swick from Delta, Ohio, sent me this one.

5 hard-cooked eggs, chilled	1/2 teaspoon mustard
1 cup egg substitute	1/2 teaspoon vinegar
3 tablespoons fat-free whipped salad dressing	1/2 teaspoon salt, optional
1/4 teaspoon horseradish	Black pepper and paprika, optional

- Cut the hard-cooked eggs in half and discard the yolks.
- Spray a skillet with nonfat cooking spray.
- Over medium heat scramble the egg substitute in the skillet until done.
- Place the scrambled eggs, salad dressing, horseradish, mustard, vinegar, and salt in a food processor and mix until smooth.
- Fill the egg whites with the mixture and sprinkle with the paprika.

Note: If you prefer a sweeter taste, use less mustard and add 1 to 2 tablespoons sweet relish.

Yield: 10 servings (1 half per serving)

Calories: 25; Fat: 0g (0% fat); Cholesterol: 0mg; Carbohydrate: 1g; Dietary Fiber: 0g; Protein: 4g; Sodium: 121mg

Preparation time: 10 minutes

Menu ideas: Serve as an appetizer; they're also great for picnics.

Vegetable Dip

This was given to me by Vickie Barber of Swanton, Ohio.

1 quart low-fat mayonnaise	1 teaspoon garlic powder
1 (16-ounce) container fat-free sour cream	2 teaspoons dill weed
1 teaspoon onion powder	2 to 3 teaspoons parsley flakes

- In a bowl with a tight fitting lid mix together the mayonnaise, sour cream, onion powder, garlic powder, dill weed, and parsley.
- Chill and serve.

Yield: 48 (2-tablespoon) servings

Calories: 44; Fat: 1g (28% fat); Cholesterol: 2mg; Carbohydrate: 7g; Dietary Fiber: 0g; Protein: 1g; Sodium: 194mg

Preparation time: 6 minutes or less

Menu ideas: Serve with your favorite vegetables, low-fat crackers, or baked potato chips.

Sweet & Sour Teenie Weenies

This appetizer is especially popular with children.

I	(14-ounce) package fat-free hot dogs	2	tablespoons mustard
1/4	cup grape jelly		

- Slice each wiener diagonally into five pieces.
- In a medium-size serving bowl mix the jelly and mustard together until well mixed.
- Heat the mixture on high in the microwave for 15 seconds.
- In a bowl coat the wieners with the sauce.
- In the microwave cook on high for a total of 3 to 5 minutes, depending on your microwave.
- Coat the wieners with the sauce after each 1 minute of cooking. Keep heating until they are completely warmed.
- Serve with toothpicks.

Note: This recipe can be tripled and kept warm on low in a slow cooker for long periods of time, up to 4 hours.

Yield: 16 servings (2½ pieces per serving)

Calories: 31; Fat: 0g (0% fat); Cholesterol: 7mg; Carbohydrate: 4g; Dietary Fiber: 0g; Protein: 3g; Sodium: 264mg

Preparation time: 4 minutes or less
Microwave time: 6 minutes or less
Total time: 10 minutes or less

Menu idea: This is a simple hors d'oeuvre that is good to take to potluck parties.

Chicken Onion Dip

A friend of mine introduced me to a high-fat version of this recipe. I modified it to low-fat. It's now a family favorite.

2 (8-ounce) packages fat-free cream cheese, softened	2/3 cup chopped sweet onion (I use Vidalia onions.)
1 (10-ounce) can premium chunk chicken in water, not drained	1 teaspoon mustard

- Mix the cream cheese, chicken with water, onion, and mustard in a medium bowl. Mix with a fork until well blended.
- Keep chilled until ready to serve.

Yield: 15 (1½-ounce) servings

Calories: 55; Fat: 0g (0% fat); Cholesterol: 13mg; Carbohydrate: 6g; Dietary Fiber: 0g; Protein: 6g; Sodium: 101mg

Total preparation time: 5 to 6 minutes

Menu ideas: This recipe is quite versatile. As a salad, serve on a bed of leafy greens topped with croutons. This can also serve as an appetizer by stuffing inside cherry tomatoes and sprinkling with paprika. You can spread it on toast to make a sandwich or warm it in the microwave until bubbly for a nice dip.

Party Poppers

These spicy sausage slices are a perfect warm appetizer to serve for any occasion. Please note: They are spicy.

1/4 cup white zinfandel	1 (14-ounce) low-fat smoked sausage
1/2 cup barbecue sauce	

- In a small bowl mix the wine and barbecue sauce together.
- Cut the sausage into 1/3-inch-thick slices.
- Dip the sausage slices into the sauce.
- Grill on a non-stick griddle or pan at 250 degrees for 1 to 2 minutes. Turn over. With a teaspoon give each sausage slice a dab more sauce. Heat for 1 to 2 minutes more.
- Insert a toothpick into each slice.
- Reduce the heat to low, just enough to keep these tasty, spicy, delectables warm until ready to serve.

Yield: 14 (1-ounce) servings

Calories: 47; Fat: 1g (18% fat); Cholesterol: 10mg; Carbohydrate: 5g; Dietary Fiber: 0g; Protein: 4g; Sodium: 395mg

Preparation time: 5 minutes or less
Cooking time: 5 minutes
Total time: 10 minutes or less

Menu ideas: This recipe is great for parties or as an appetizer for a nice dinner.

Ruby Raspberry Fruit Dip

My daughter Whitney and I created this sweet, smooth, creamy dip to use with fresh fruit. We both loved it. It also tastes good as a dip for pretzels. If you like a sweet and salty combination, you'll like it with pretzels.

I cup marshmallow creme	1/4 cup fat-free raspberry salad dressing (I use T. Marzetti.)

- In a bowl mix the marshmallow and salad dressing together and serve. This is excellent served at room temperature.

Yield: 10 (2-tablespoon) servings

Calories: 58; Fat: 0g (0% fat); Cholesterol: 0mg; Carbohydrate: 15g; Dietary Fiber: 0g; Protein: 0g; Sodium: 52mg

 Preparation time: 2 to 5 minutes
Total time: 5 minutes

Menu ideas: Serve with brunch or serve as a delectable treat.

Buttermilk Ranch Dressing

I created this for all those who can't stand fat-free dressing. This will really fool them. Don't tell them and they won't know.

1 1/2 cups low-fat buttermilk	1 cup skim milk
1 tablespoon light whipped salad dressing	1 (2-ounce) packet low-fat Hidden Valley Original Ranch salad dressing
3/4 cup fat-free sour cream	

- With a whisk beat the buttermilk, salad dressing, sour cream, milk, and ranch dressing together for about 2 minutes.
- Refrigerate until chilled. Then serve.

Yield: 26 (2-tablespoon) servings

Calories: 24 ; Fat: 0g (0% fat); Cholesterol: 2mg; Carbohydrate: 4g; Dietary Fiber: 0g; Protein: 1g; Sodium: 183mg

Preparation time: 5 minutes or less

Menu ideas: Serve over your favorite salad or as a dip with your favorite vegetables.

Mild Mustard/Dill Dipping Sauce

Just the right zip *for your dip.*

1 tablespoon mustard	¹/₈ teaspoon dried dill weed
¹/₃ cup fat-free sour cream	

- In a bowl mix the mustard, sour cream, and dill weed together until well blended.

Yield: 6 servings

Calories: 17; Fat: 0g (0% fat); Cholesterol: 2mg; Carbohydrate: 3g; Dietary Fiber: 0g; Protein: 1g; Sodium: 39mg

Preparation time: 3 minutes

Menu ideas: This can either be served with Breaded Pork Tenderloins (page 184), or it is good as a vegetable dip.

Mexican Cheese Moons

These tasty delights make wonderful appetizers or hors d'oeuvres. Their half- moon shape and golden brown crust with colorful seasonings on top make them appealing to everyone. Children like the special surprise of the creamy filling inside.

2 teaspoons plus 1 teaspoon taco seasoning mix	1/2 cup fat-free shredded cheddar cheese
1/2 cup fat-free cream cheese	2 (10-count) cans Pillsbury buttermilk biscuits
1/2 cup salsa	

- Preheat the oven to 400 degrees.
- For easier cleanup, line two cookie sheets with foil. Spray the foil with nonfat cooking spray.
- In a blender mix the 1 teaspoon taco seasoning mix, cream cheese, salsa, and cheddar cheese and blend until well mixed.
- Press one biscuit at a time between the palms of your hands to flatten the dough into a small oval (about 3½ to 4 inches). You may want to spray your hands with nonfat cooking spray so the biscuits won't stick to you.
- With a measuring spoon, put one level tablespoon of the prepared filling inside the flattened dough. Fold the dough in half and pinch the edges together firmly to seal.
- Place the folded biscuit onto the prepared cookie sheet. Continue flattening and stuffing the biscuits one at a time. (There will be five biscuits left over.)
- Lightly sprinkle the tops of the folded biscuits with the remaining 2 teaspoons taco seasoning mix.
- Bake for 8 minutes or until the tops and bottoms are golden brown.
- Let them cool for several minutes before serving. These are best served warm.

Yield: 15 moons

Calories: 86; Fat: 1g (10% fat); Cholesterol: 2mg; Carbohydrate: 14g; Dietary Fiber: 0g; Protein: 4g; Sodium: 403mg

Preparation time: 5 to 10 minutes
Baking time: 8 minutes
Total time: 18 minutes or less

Menu idea: Serve with taco sauce for dipping.

Dijon Mayo Spread for Sandwiches

This is from Sharon Swick of Delta, Ohio, and she really enjoys this one.

1	cup fat-free mayonnaise	Dash of garlic salt
1	tablespoon Dijon mustard	Dash of pepper

- In a bowl mix the mayonnaise, mustard, salt, and pepper by hand.
- Chill and use as needed.

Yield: 8 (2-tablespoon) servings

Calories: 22; Fat: 0g (0% fat); Cholesterol: 0mg; Carbohydrate: 6g; Dietary Fiber: 0g; Protein: 0g; Sodium: 255mg

Preparation time: 5 minutes or less

Menu idea: Enjoy this tasty spread on your favorite sandwich.

Cucumber Sandwiches

This was given to me by Vickie Barber from Swanton, Ohio.

2 (8-ounce) packages fat-free cream cheese, softened	I (14-ounce) package pita bread (4 pieces), cut into quarters
I (0.7-ounce) package Italian salad dressing mix, dry	I to 2 cucumbers, peeled and thinly sliced

- In a bowl thoroughly mix the cream cheese and salad dressing mix.
- Spread the mixture into the pita bread quarters and fill with slices of cucumber.

Yield: 16 servings

Calories: 113; Fat: 0g (0% fat); Cholesterol: 5mg; Carbohydrate: 19g; Dietary Fiber: 1g; Protein: 7g; Sodium: 452mg

Preparation time: 5 minutes or less

Menu idea: Great as a finger-food-type sandwich for lunch along with a fresh vegetable tray and Vegetable Dip (page 48).

Italian Dunkers

This appetizer was created by my daughters, Whitney and Ashley. If you like pizza, you'll like this.

4	hot dog buns	4	slices fat-free cheddar cheese, cut in half
	Italian seasonings	1	(14-ounce) jar pizza sauce

- Cut the hot dog buns in half lengthwise.
- Sprinkle the split buns with Italian seasoning.
- Lay a cheese slice on the top of each half bun.
- Microwave until the cheese softens.
- Microwave the sauce.
- Dip the cheese-covered buns into the sauce.
- Presto! You're done.

Yield: 8 Dunkers

Calories: 88; Fat: 2g (16% fat); Cholesterol: 0mg; Carbohydrate: 15g; Dietary Fiber: 2g; Protein: 4g; Sodium: 328mg

Preparation time: 4 to 5 minutes
Microwave time: 5 to 10 seconds
Total time: 5 minutes or less

Menu ideas: This is great as a snack or lunch.

Tomato Biscuits

You'll have no ho-hum biscuits when you pop these in your mouth.

I	(7¹/2-ounce) can Pillsbury buttermilk biscuits	I	medium ripe tomato, cut into I0 slices
¹/3	cup fat-free grated topping (I use Kraft.)	¹/4	cup grated Parmesan cheese
			Garlic salt, optional

- Preheat the oven to 425 degrees.
- Line a cookie sheet with aluminum foil.
- Spray the foil with nonfat cooking spray.
- Press each biscuit individually into the grated topping and place onto the prepared cookie sheet.
- Arrange 1 tomato slice on each biscuit.
- Sprinkle the Parmesan cheese evenly over all the biscuits.
- Sprinkle each biscuit lightly with the garlic salt if desired.
- Bake for 10 to 13 minutes or until golden brown.
- Serve immediately.

Yield: 10 biscuits

Calories: 68; Fat: 1g (17% fat); Cholesterol: 4mg; Carbohydrate: 11g; Dietary Fiber: 0g; Protein: 3g ; Sodium: 241mg

Preparation time: 10 minutes
Baking time: 10 minutes
Total time: 20 minutes or less

Menu ideas: These would taste great with Spicy Thick Vegetarian Chili (page 75), or any Italian entrée.

Sweet Corn Bread

This is from Sharon Swick of Delta, Ohio, and a favorite of her husband, Bob.

1/3 cup Egg Beaters	1 teaspoon salt, optional
1 cup evaporated skim milk	1 1/4 cups reduced-fat biscuit mix
1/2 cup brown sugar	(I use Bisquick.)
2 teaspoons Molly McButter, dry	3/4 cup cornmeal

- Preheat the oven to 400 degrees.
- Spray a 9-inch-square baking dish with nonfat cooking spray.
- In a large bowl combine the Egg Beaters, evaporated milk, and brown sugar.
- Add the Molly McButter and salt. Mix thoroughly.
- Add the biscuit mix and cornmeal and stir until well mixed.
- Pour into the baking dish and bake for 20 to 25 minutes or until golden brown.

Yield: 9 servings

Calories: 179; Fat: 1g (7% fat); Cholesterol: 1mg; Carbohydrate: 36g; Dietary Fiber: 1g; Protein: 5g; Sodium: 254mg

Preparation time: 10 minutes or less
Baking time: 25 minutes or less
Total time: 35 minutes or less

Menu ideas: Serve on the side with one of your favorite soups, or with your main entrée, instead of regular bread. Also good with Mexican-style and pork-based entrées.

Garlic Toast

This is perfect for fast and easy meals that aren't fancy.

1	slice fat-free bread	Garlic salt
5	sprays I Can't Believe It's Not Butter spray	Dried parsley , optional

- Toast the slice of bread.
- Spray one side of the toast with I Can't Believe It's Not Butter.
- Sprinkle lightly with garlic salt first, and then sprinkle lightly with dried parsley if desired.

Yield: 1 serving

Calories: 71; Fat: 0g (0% fat); Cholesterol: 0mg; Carbohydrate: 15g; Dietary Fiber: 1g; Protein: 2g; Sodium: 161mg

Preparation time: 3 minutes or less

Menu idea: Garlic Toast is great with any Italian entrée.

Southwestern Corn Muffins

The slight zest of these corn muffins goes perfectly with chili. I especially like them with my Spicy Thick Vegetarian Chili (page 75). Now we're talkin' some good old-fashioned eatin'!

$1/3$ cup plus I tablespoon chunky salsa	2 egg whites
2 tablespoons cinnamon-flavored applesauce	I ($6^{1}/2$-ounce) corn bread and muffin mix

- Preheat the oven to 400 degrees.
- Spray six medium muffin cups with nonfat cooking spray, or line a muffin tin with cupcake liners.
- In a bowl combine the salsa, applesauce, and egg whites until well mixed.
- Add the corn bread mix and stir until well mixed. The batter will be lumpy.
- Spoon the batter evenly into the cups.
- Bake for 15 minutes or until the tops are lightly browned.
- Remove the muffins immediately.

Note: These muffins can be made ahead of time and quickly reheated in the microwave for toasty, warm muffins anytime.

Yield: 6 servings

Calories: 137; Fat: 3g (21% fat); Cholesterol: 7mg; Carbohydrate: 23g; Dietary Fiber: 0g; Protein: 3g ; Sodium: 346mg

Preparation time: 4 to 5 minutes
Baking time: 15 minutes
Total time: 20 minutes or less

Menu ideas: Serve with chili or with your favorite soup or Mexican entrée.

Cheese Biscuits

I got this recipe idea from a favorite seafood restaurant. Betcha don't have the slightest idea what restaurant that could be, do ya? These are not half as fattening, but don't let that fool you. These babies are delicious.

2	cups skim milk	2	teaspoons garlic salt
1	(8-ounce) package fat-free, fancy shredded cheddar cheese	5	cups reduced-fat biscuit mix
2	tablespoons Butter Buds Sprinkles	48	sprays I Can't Believe It's Not Butter spray

- Preheat the oven to 350 degrees.
- Spray two cookie sheets with nonfat cooking spray.
- In a large mixing bowl pour the milk over the cheese and let it sit for 3 minutes.
- Add the Sprinkles and garlic salt to the milk, stirring until they are dissolved.
- Stir in the biscuit mix. The dough will become very stiff. You may find it easier to finish mixing with your hands. Keep mixing until there is no biscuit mix on the bottom or sides of the bowl.
- Drop the dough by rounded tablespoons onto the prepared cookie sheets. This is easy to do with two spoons.
- Bake for 15 to 17 minutes or until the tops are golden brown.
- Spray each biscuit with 2 sprays of the I Can't Believe It's Not Butter before serving.

Yield: 24 servings (1 biscuit per serving)

Calories: 117; Fat: 2g (13% fat); Cholesterol: 1mg; Carbohydrate: 19g; Dietary Fiber: 0g; Protein: 5g; Sodium: 530mg

Preparation time: 5 minutes
Baking time: 15 to 17 minutes
Total time: 22 minutes or less

Menu ideas: Here's another recipe that would be wonderful with chili or soup.

Pinwheel Dinner Rolls

These are as pretty as they are delicious.

1	(10-ounce) tube Pillsbury pizza dough	1	teaspoon garlic salt
52	sprays I Can't Believe It's Not Butter spray	1	tablespoon crushed dried parsley

- Preheat the oven to 425 degrees.
- Spray a cookie sheet with nonfat cooking spray.
- Unroll the pizza dough and press it out to ¼-inch thickness onto the cookie sheet.
- Spray 40 sprays of I Can't Believe It's Not Butter evenly over the dough.
- Sprinkle the garlic salt and parsley evenly on top.
- Roll the dough (jelly-roll style) starting from the long side of the dough.
- Once completely rolled, pinch the seam to seal.
- Cut into twelve pieces to form pinwheels and place on the prepared cookie sheet so the top of each pinwheel is facing up.
- Bake for 8 to 10 minutes or until golden brown.
- Spray the tops of each roll with one spray of I Can't Believe It's Not Butter before serving.

Yield: 12 rolls

Calories: 63; Fat: 1g (12% fat); Cholesterol: 1mg; Carbohydrate: 19g; Dietary Fiber: 0g; Protein: 5g; Sodium: 530mg

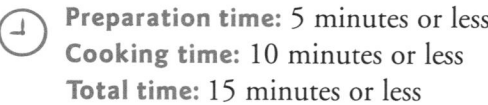 **Preparation time:** 5 minutes or less
Cooking time: 10 minutes or less
Total time: 15 minutes or less

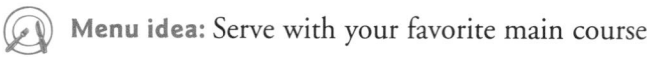 **Menu idea:** Serve with your favorite main course.

Soups & Salads

If you want to be blessed then be a blessing to others.

Apple Cottage Salad 99

Bacon, Lettuce, and Tomato Salad 96

Broccoli & Cauliflower Salad 102

Broccoli & Ham Salad 85

California Medley Soup 70

Caribbean Chicken Salad
   Sandwiches 107

Chicken Corn Chowder 74

Corn Chowder 73

Cranberry Apple Salad 92

Crunchy Cucumbers with Cream 82

Cucumber Dill Salad 90

Ham & Cheese Potato Salad 93

Mexican Chicken Salad 80

Mother-Daughter Salad 97

Mother's Day Salad 98

Oriental Chicken Soup 76

Peaches & Cream Gelatin Salad 77

Peppered Potato Salad 105

Polynesian Fruit Salad 78

Popeye's Favorite Salad 100

Sassy Slaw 91

Seafood Pasta Salad 87

Seafood Salad 86

Seaside Salad 84

Smokey Bean Soup 69

Southwestern Chicken Soup 68

Southwestern Three Bean Salad 81

Southwestern Vegetarian Soup 72

Spicy Thick Vegetarian Chili 75

Spring Salad 103

Spring Salad with Chicken 104

Steak & Potato Cattlemen's Soup 67

Sweet & Sour Fresh Vegetable
   Garden Salad 83

Taco Vegetable Soup 71

Tangy Tossed Salad 95

Tropical Passion Fruit Salad 89

Very Berry Fruit Salad 79

Warm Cran-Apple Salad 94

Zesty Summer Cottage Salad 88

Zesty Chilled Fruit Salad 101

Zesty Potato Salad 106

Zesty Egg Salad Sandwiches 108

Steak & Potato Cattlemen's Soup

This recipe is a terrific way to use leftover steak and potatoes or an eye of round roast and potatoes.

2½ cups (1 pound) eye of round steak, cooked and cut into bite-size pieces

2½ cups (2 large potatoes) potatoes with skins on, cooked and cut into bite-size pieces

4 ounces fresh mushrooms, sliced

½ cup barbecue sauce

½ cup chopped onions (Frozen onions work well.)

1 (1¼-ounce) envelope dry onion soup mix

4 cups water

Slow cooker method:
- Spray a slow cooker with nonfat cooking spray.
- Mix the ingredients together in the slow cooker.
- Cover and cook on low for 4 hours.

Stovetop method:
- Spray a Dutch oven or large saucepan with nonfat cooking spray.
- Mix the ingredients together in the Dutch oven.
- Over medium-low heat cook for 5 to 10 minutes or until fully heated.

Microwave method:
- Spray a microwavable covered dish with nonfat cooking spray.
- Mix the ingredients together in the microwavable dish.
- Cover and cook on high power in a carousel microwave for 8 minutes.
- Stir and, if needed, cook an additional 2 to 3 minutes.

Yield: 6 (1-cup) servings

Calories: 216; Fat: 4g (19% fat); Cholesterol: 52mg; Carbohydrate: 19g; Dietary Fiber: 2g; Protein: 25g; Sodium: 749mg

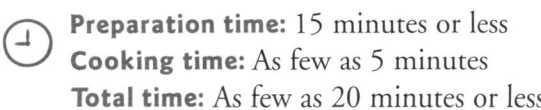

Preparation time: 15 minutes or less
Cooking time: As few as 5 minutes
Total time: As few as 20 minutes or less

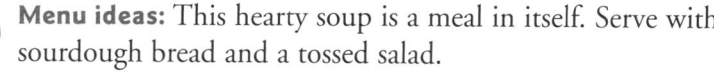

Menu ideas: This hearty soup is a meal in itself. Serve with sourdough bread and a tossed salad.

Southwestern Chicken Soup

This soup has a slight bite, which gives it a unique flavor. It's a good alternative to traditional chicken noodle soup when someone is feeling under the weather.

2	pounds boneless, skinless chicken breasts, cut into bite-size pieces	12	chicken bouillon cubes
		2	cups salsa
3	quarts water	1	box Spanish rice (I use Rice-a-Roni.)

- In a large pot mix the chicken, water, bouillon, salsa, and Spanish rice.
- Bring to a boil.
- Boil 3 to 4 minutes.
- Reduce the heat and simmer for 10 minutes.
- Serve hot.

Yield: 18 (1-cup) servings

Calories: 110; Fat: 4g (9% fat); Cholesterol: 30mg; Carbohydrate: 10g; Dietary Fiber: 0g; Protein: 13g; Sodium: 1088mg

Preparation time: 10 minutes or less
Cooking time: 20 minutes
Total time: 30 minutes or less

Menu idea: This is very tasty with a grilled cheese sandwich (on the side) or corn bread.

Smokey Bean Soup

There's nothing like comin' home to the wonderful aroma of this mouth-watering soup awaiting you. It's so hearty, you could almost call it a stew.

I (48-ounce) jar mixed beans	I (1½-ounce) envelope dried onion soup mix
3/4 pound smoked, lean ham lunchmeat or turkey ham, chopped	3/4 teaspoon dried thyme , optional
I teaspoon liquid smoke	I (16-ounce) bag frozen vegetables
	48 ounces water

Stovetop:
- In a large pan mash the beans with a slotted spoon. Add the ham, liquid smoke, soup mix, thyme, frozen vegetables, and water.
- Bring the soup to a boil, and then simmer for 12 minutes.

Slow cooker:
- In the slow cooker mash the beans with a slotted spoon. Add the ham, liquid smoke, soup mix, thyme, frozen vegetables, and water.
- Stir the ingredients until well mixed and the soup mix is completely dissolved.
- Cover and cook on low for about 5 hours*
- Before serving, if you want the broth thicker, simply mash with the potato masher and stir.
- Serve hot.

Note: The soup actually needs only 5 hours on low in the slow cooker before it's ready to eat. It's hard to overcook this soup, so don't worry if it's in the slow cooker for longer than 10 hours.

Yield: 15 (1-cup) servings

Calories: 162; Fat: 2g (11% fat); Cholesterol: 7mg; Carbohydrate: 24g; Dietary Fiber: 5g; Protein: 12g ; Sodium: 935mg

Preparation time: 10 minutes or less
Cooking time: Varies depending on your cooking method

Menu idea: This is good served with corn bread and a pot of greens on the side.

California Medley Soup

This is a "make me feel good" soup. It smells good, it tastes good, and it makes you feel warm and cozy inside. It's a great soup for anyone trying to lose weight.

1	gallon water	4	large boneless, skinless chicken breasts, cut into bite-size pieces (approximately 1 pound)
12	chicken-flavored bouillon cubes		
1	(1-ounce) envelope dry onion soup mix	2	pounds frozen California-blend vegetables (broccoli, cauliflower, and carrots)

- In a large soup pot bring the water to a boil and add the bouillon cubes and soup mix.
- Add the chicken and vegetables.
- Bring to a boil again.
- Reduce the heat, cover, and simmer for 6 minutes.
- Remove to a plate about 2 cups of the vegetables with a slotted spoon.
- Mash the vegetables with a potato masher and then return them to the saucepan.
- Simmer for another minute, just enough time for the mashed vegetables to reheat.
- Serve hot.

Yield: 18 (1-cup) servings

Calories: 50; Fat: 1g (10% fat); Cholesterol: 15mg; Carbohydrate: 4g; Dietary Fiber: 1g; Protein: 7g; Sodium: 822mg

Preparation time: 10 minutes or less
Cooking time: 20 minutes
Total time: 30 minutes or less

Menu ideas: Fat-free crackers and tossed salad or fat-free cottage cheese with canned tropical fruit complement this soup wonderfully.

Taco Vegetable Soup

My family thinks this flavorful, zesty soup is delicious served with crushed baked tortilla chips sprinkled on top of each serving.

I pound ground turkey breast	I (49¹/2-ounce) can chicken broth with floating fat removed
2 (16-ounce) packages frozen vegetables	I (16-ounce) jar salsa
I (1¹/2-ounce package) taco seasoning mix	Baked tortilla chips , optional

- In a large soup pot mix the turkey breast, vegetables, taco seasoning, chicken broth, and salsa.
- Bring to a boil.
- Reduce the heat to low.
- Cover and simmer for 13 minutes.
- If desired served with crushed baked tortilla chips sprinkled on top of each serving.

Note: If you like a spicier soup, add a few drops of Tabasco sauce.

Yield: 12 (1-cup) servings

Calories: 126; Fat: 1g (11% fat); Cholesterol: 26mg; Carbohydrate: 14g; Dietary Fiber: 0g; Protein: 11g; Sodium: 1077mg

Preparation time: 5 minutes or less
Cooking time: 13 minutes or less
Total time: 18 minutes or less

Menu idea: Serve this with Mexican Chicken Salad (page 80), and Southwestern Corn Muffins (page 62).

Southwestern Vegetarian Soup

This soup is great on a cold winter day.

6	cups chicken broth (or 6 bouillon cubes with 6 cups water)	I	(16-ounce) package frozen vegetables
2	cups salsa, your favorite	I	(31-ounce) can fat-free refried beans
I	(I 1/2-ounce) package taco seasoning mix		Baked tortilla chips , optional

Stovetop:

- In a large soup pot stir the chicken broth, salsa, taco seasoning, vegetables, and refried beans until the beans are dissolved.
- Bring the soup to a boil and then reduce the heat to low.
- Cover and simmer for 12 minutes.
- If desired sprinkle crushed baked tortilla chips on individual servings of soup before eating.

Slow cooker:

- In a slow cooker stir the chicken broth, salsa, taco seasoning, vegetables, and refried beans until the beans are dissolved.
- Cover and cook on low for 8 hours or on high for 4 hours.
- If desired sprinkle crushed baked tortilla chips on individual servings of soup before eating.

Note: For a spicier soup add a few drops Tabasco sauce.

Yield: 12 (1-cup) servings

Calories: 111; Fat: 0g (0% fat); Cholesterol: 0mg; Carbohydrate: 20g; Dietary Fiber: 4g; Protein: 4g; Sodium: 1393mg

Preparation time: 5 minutes or less
Cooking time: As few as 15 minutes or less
Total time: 20 minutes or less

Menu idea: Serve this with Mexican Chicken Salad (page 80) and Southwestern Corn Muffins (page 62).

Corn Chowder

This soup makes a great accompaniment to any sandwich. Actually, a half sandwich with a cup of corn chowder is very filling for me.

2/3	cup fat-free shredded cheddar cheese	2	(15-ounce) cans cream-style corn
I	teaspoon onion salt	I	(14 1/2-ounce) can fat-free chicken broth
I	(II-ounce) can sweet corn and diced peppers	1/4	teaspoon ground pepper, optional

- In a Dutch oven or large saucepan combine the cheese, onion salt, corn and peppers, cream-style corn, chicken broth, and pepper, if using.
- Bring to a boil over medium-high heat, stirring constantly.
- Remove the soup from the heat and let it sit for 3 to 4 minutes to cool a little before serving.

Yield: 6 (1-cup) servings

Calories: 170; Fat: 1g (7% fat); Cholesterol: 1mg; Carbohydrate: 36g; Dietary Fiber: 3g; Protein: 8g; Sodium: 1295mg

Preparation time: 6 minutes or less
Cooking time: 5 minutes
Total time: 11 minutes or less

Menu ideas: This chowder is great with half of a sandwich or a tossed salad.

Chicken Corn Chowder

This soup makes a great accompaniment to any sandwich. Actually, a half sandwich with a cup of corn chowder is very filling for me.

2/3 cup fat-free shredded cheddar cheese	1 (14¹/2-ounce) can fat-free chicken broth
1 teaspoon onion salt	1 cup cooked, diced chicken breast
1 (11-ounce) can sweet corn and diced peppers	ground pepper
2 (15-ounce) cans cream-style corn	

- In a Dutch oven or large saucepan combine the cheese, onion salt, corn and peppers, cream-style corn, chicken broth, chicken, and pepper to taste.
- Bring to a boil over medium-high heat, stirring constantly.
- Remove the soup from the heat and let it sit for 3 to 4 minutes to cool a little before serving.

Yield: 7 (1-cup) servings

Calories: 180; Fat: 2g (10% fat); Cholesterol: 18mg; Carbohydrate: 31g; Dietary Fiber: 2g; Protein: 13g; Sodium: 1126mg

Preparation time: 6 minutes or less
Cooking time: 5 minutes
Total time: 11 minutes or less

Menu ideas: Either chowder is good with a tossed salad, crackers, or Mint Mousse (page 212).

Spicy Thick Vegetarian Chili

This thick, hearty, stick-to-your-bones-but-not-your-thighs chili is power packed with protein and fiber.

2	(15-ounce) cans Mexican-style hot chili beans	2	cups chunky salsa
1	(16-ounce) can vegetarian refried beans	1	(6-ounce) can tomato paste
1	(15-ounce) can black beans	1	(12-ounce) bag shredded, fat-free cheddar cheese

- In a 3-quart or larger non-stick soup pot combine the chili beans, refried beans, black beans, salsa, and tomato paste.
- Cook over medium heat until thoroughly heated and well mixed.
- Sprinkle a little cheddar cheese on top of each bowl of chili.

Note: To thin the chili, add water or tomato juice 1 cup at a time until desired consistency is reached.

Note: For spicier chili add Tabasco sauce.

Yield: 9 (1-cup) servings

Calories: 197; Fat: 2g (7% fat); Cholesterol: 0mg; Carbohydrate: 33g; Dietary Fiber: 9g; Protein: 10g; Sodium: 1014mg

Preparation time: 4 minutes or less
Cooking time: 6 minutes
Total time: 10 minutes or less

Menu idea: Serve this with Southwestern Corn Muffins (page 62).

Oriental Chicken Soup

This flavorful oriental soup is delicious on cold days. It's loaded with colorful vegetables and is as eye appealing as it is delicious.

6	chicken breasts (I use Tyson mesquite flavor.)	1	(12-ounce) bottle teriyaki baste and glaze
4	pounds frozen stir-fry vegetables	2	tablespoons garlic salt
		18	cups chicken broth with visible fat removed

- In a large soup pot combine the chicken, vegetables, teriyaki, garlic salt, and chicken broth.
- Bring to a boil and then reduce the heat to low.
- Remove the chicken breast and cut into pieces.
- Add the chicken pieces back to the soup.
- Let the soup simmer for several minutes to reheat the chicken pieces.

Yield: 29 (1-cup) servings

Calories: 89; Fat: 1g (13% fat); Cholesterol: 21mg; Carbohydrate: 9g; Dietary Fiber: 1g; Protein: 11g; Sodium: 1742mg

 Preparation time: 10 minutes or less
Cooking time: 10 minutes
Total time: 20 minutes or less

 Menu idea: Since this has your meat already in it, it would be great as an entrée with bread on the side.

Peaches & Cream Gelatin Salad

Sharon Swick from Delta, Ohio, sent me this peachy treat.

> 1 (29-ounce) can peaches in their own juice, drained, reserving 1 cup juice
> 1/2 cup fat-free cream cheese
> 1/3 cup fat-free sour cream
> 1/4 cup sugar or 1/4 cup calorie-free sugar (I use Splenda.)
> 1 (3-ounce) package peach-flavored gelatin, dry

- In a food processor combine half the drained peaches, cream cheese, sour cream, and sugar.
- Blend until smooth.
- Add the remaining peaches, saving 4 or 5 slices to garnish the top of the salad. Blend until smooth.
- Heat over medium heat the 1 cup of reserved juice until almost boiling.
- Remove the juice from the heat and add the peach gelatin, stirring until dissolved.
- Let the gelatin cool slightly and combine it with the cream cheese mixture.
- Cover and refrigerate until chilled, about 3 hours.

Yield: 6 (1/2-cup) servings

(with sugar) Calories: 176; Fat: 0g (0% fat); Cholesterol: 6mg; Carbohydrate: 40g; Dietary Fiber: 2g; Protein: 6g; Sodium: 182mg
(with Splenda) Calories: 147; Fat: 0g (0% fat); Cholesterol: 6mg; Carbohydrate: 32g; Dietary Fiber: 2g; Protein: 6g; Sodium: 182mg

Preparation time: 12 minutes or less
Cooking time: 5 minutes
Total time: 17 minutes or less

Menu idea: This would be wonderful after dining on Herbed Beef Tenderloin with Seasoned Potatoes and Buttered Mushrooms (page 196).

Polynesian Fruit Salad

This is a nutritious and delicious way to get calcium.

1	(20-ounce) can crushed pineapple in its own juice	2	cups fat-free cottage cheese
7	ice cubes	1	cup fat-free whipped topping
1	(1.7-ounce) box sugar-free, fat-free instant vanilla pudding, dry	2	medium bananas, sliced

- Into a measuring cup squeeze out as much pineapple juice as possible. Add up to 7 ice cubes to make 2 cups of liquid.
- Pour the juice and ice cubes into a medium-size mixing bowl.
- Add the pudding mix and stir briskly for 2 minutes.
- Remove any ice cubes that have not dissolved.
- Add the drained pineapple to the pudding mixture. Stir until well mixed.
- Stir the cottage cheese and whipped topping into the pudding mixture until well mixed.
- Gently stir in the bananas.
- Serve as is or keep chilled until ready to serve.

Yield: 13 (½-cup) servings

Calories: 84; Fat: 0g (0% fat); Cholesterol: 2mg; Carbohydrate: 16g; Dietary Fiber: 1g; Protein: 4g; Sodium: 229mg

 Total preparation time: 7 minutes or less

 Menu ideas: This is great served for lunch as a main course stuffed in half a cantaloupe or honeydew. It's delicious as a nutritious combination side dish and dessert with any dinner.

Very Berry Fruit Salad

Not only is this delicious, it's also nutritious.

1	(1.7-ounce) box sugar-free, fat-free instant vanilla pudding, dry	1	quart fresh blackberries or fresh blueberries
2	cups skim milk	2	medium bananas, cut into 1/4-inch slices

- With a whisk beat the pudding with the skim milk in a bowl for 2 minutes.
- Gently stir in the berries until well mixed.
- Keep chilled until ready to serve.
- Stir in the bananas when ready to serve.

Yield: 8 ($\frac{1}{2}$-cup) servings

(with blackberries) Calories: 105; Fat: 1g (4% fat); Cholesterol: 1mg; Carbohydrate: 24g; Dietary Fiber: 5g; Protein: 3g; Sodium: 281mg
(with blueberries) Calories: 108; Fat: 1g (4% fat); Cholesterol: 1mg; Carbohydrate: 25g; Dietary Fiber: 3g; Protein: 3g; Sodium: 285mg

Preparation time: 5 minutes or less

Menu ideas: This is a perfect ending to any heavy meal. It's also great for brunches or buffets.

Mexican Chicken Salad

This salad is the perfect flavor combination for a delicious lunch.

$1/2$ cup chunky salsa	(or chicken-breast lunchmeat), cut into bite-size pieces
$1/3$ cup fat-free ranch salad dressing	1 large head iceberg lettuce, shredded, about 2 pounds
$1/3$ cup fat-free French dressing	1 fat-free tortilla, cut into $1/4$-inch strips and the strips cut into 1-inch lengths
$1/3$ cup shredded fat-free cheddar cheese	
$1/2$ pound cooked chicken breasts	

- In a bowl mix the salsa, ranch dressing, French dressing, cheese, and chicken. Keep refrigerated until ready to serve.
- When you are ready to serve, toss the shredded lettuce with the mixture and tortilla strips.

Note: Do not mix the lettuce with the chicken and tortilla chips beforehand or the salad will become soggy.

Yield: 8 (1-cup) servings

Calories: 110; Fat: 1g (12% fat); Cholesterol: 25mg; Carbohydrate: 12g; Dietary Fiber: 2g; Protein: 11g; Sodium: 381mg

Yield: 4 (2-cup) servings

Calories: 220; Fat: 3g (12% fat); Cholesterol: 49mg; Carbohydrate: 23g; Dietary Fiber: 3g; Protein: 22g; Sodium: 761mg

Preparation time: 10 minutes or less

Menu ideas: This makes a great meal for lunch or a light dinner and is a wonderful side salad for any fish, chicken, or Mexican entrée.

Southwestern Three Bean Salad

The zip in this salad will add zest to any meal.

1 (19-ounce) can black bean soup, drained	1 (15½-ounce) can light red kidney beans, drained
½ cup reduced-fat red wine vinegar salad dressing	1 (16-ounce) jar chunky salsa
	1 (15½-ounce) can navy beans, drained

- In a large bowl mix together the soup, vinegar, kidney beans, salsa, and navy beans.
- Voila!

Note: If you like spicy food, add a few drops of Tabasco sauce.

Yield: 12 (½-cup) servings

Calories: 91 ; Fat: 0g (0% fat); Cholesterol: 0mg; Carbohydrate: 15g; Dietary Fiber: 4g; Protein: 4g; Sodium: 578mg

Preparation time: 5 minutes or less

Menu ideas: This makes a great side salad for a Mexican meal. It's also a terrific dip with fat-free tortilla chips.

Crunchy Cucumbers with Cream

These cucumbers are crisp, crunchy, and seasoned just right.

1	(1-ounce) packet low-fat Hidden Valley Original Ranch, dry	5	medium-size cucumbers, peeled and sliced
1	(16-ounce) container fat-free sour cream	1	medium onion, sliced in $1/2$-inch rings

- In a large bowl stir together the dry salad mix with the sour cream until well mixed.
- Add the cucumbers and onions.
- Stir until all the vegetables are coated with the cream and the onions are separated.
- Keep chilled until ready to eat.

Note: After a few days the cucumbers become less crunchy. I prefer them crunchy.

Yield: 20 ($1/2$-cup) servings

Calories: 40; Fat: 0g (0% fat); Cholesterol: 4mg; Carbohydrate: 8g; Dietary Fiber: 1g; Protein: 2g; Sodium: 119mg

Total preparation time: 15 minutes or less

Menu ideas: These are scrumptious for any barbecue or cookout. They complement all types of grilled meats such as chicken, pork, or beef.

Sweet & Sour Fresh Vegetable Garden Salad

This crunchy, sweet-and-sour salad puts zing into any meal.

4	ears of fresh sweet white corn	1	(4-ounce) jar pimientos, not drained
2	small cucumbers, cut into 1/4-inch pieces (about 3 1/2 cups)	3/4	cup brown sugar
2	small green peppers, cut into 1/4-inch pieces (about 1 1/2 cups)	2/3	cup apple cider vinegar
		4	ice cubes

- Cut the kernels from the corn.
- In a medium-size serving bowl combine the cucumbers, peppers, corn, and pimientos.
- In a microwavable container stir together the brown sugar and apple cider vinegar.
- Microwave on high for 2 minutes.
- Stir the ice cubes into the hot vinegar. Keep stirring until ice cubes are completely dissolved.
- Pour the vinegar mixture over the vegetables. Stir until all the vegetables are coated.
- Serve immediately or keep chilled until ready to eat.

Yield: 17 (1/2-cup) servings

Calories: 72; Fat: 0g (0% fat); Cholesterol: 0mg; Carbohydrate: 18g; Dietary Fiber: 1g; Protein: 1g; Sodium: 10mg

Preparation time: 25 minutes
Cooking time: 2 minutes plus 2 minutes cooling time
Total time: 30 minutes or less

Menu ideas: This salad is good for cookouts, picnics, potlucks, and fish- or chicken-based entrées.

Seaside Salad

This is a sensational salad that is great for special occasions.

1 large head iceberg lettuce shredded	1 large cucumber, cut into ¼-inch pieces
1 (8-ounce) package imitation crabmeat pieces	¼ cup fat-free coleslaw dressing (I use T. Marzetti.)
2 large tomatoes, sliced	

- In a bowl gently toss the lettuce, crabmeat, tomatoes, cucumber, and dressing together.

Note: Put the dressing on right before serving; otherwise it gets soggy.

Yield: 6 side salads

Calories: 84; Fat: 1g (10% fat); Cholesterol: 13mg; Carbohydrate: 14g; Dietary Fiber: 2g; Protein: 6g; Sodium: 462mg

Yield: 2 dinner salads

Calories: 251; Fat: 3g (10% fat); Cholesterol: 38mg; Carbohydrate: 41g; Dietary Fiber: 7g; Protein: 19g; Sodium: 1387mg

Preparation time: 10 minutes or less

Menu ideas: As a main entrée serve with fat-free crackers. As a side salad it goes great with fish-based entrées or soups.

Broccoli & Ham Salad

This salad is good, but for a fresher, crispier salad use fresh pieces of broccoli.

1/2 cup fat-free coleslaw dressing (I use T. Marzetti.)	1/2 pound pre-cooked lean ham, chopped
1/2 cup low-fat mayonnaise	2 pounds frozen broccoli cuts, thawed
4 ounces shredded fat-free mild cheddar cheese	1/4 cup chopped raisins
	1/2 cup chopped red onion

- Mix the dressing, mayonnaise, and cheese together.
- Let the mixture sit for several minutes before stirring in the ham, broccoli, raisins, and onion.

Yield: 10 (1/2-cup) servings

Calories: 124; Fat: 2g (16% fat); Cholesterol: 18mg; Carbohydrate: 17g; Dietary Fiber: 3g; Protein: 11g; Sodium: 711mg

Yield: 5 (1-cup) servings

Calories: 248 ; Fat: 4g (16% fat); Cholesterol: 36mg; Carbohydrate: 33g; Dietary Fiber: 6g; Protein: 21g; Sodium: 1422mg

Preparation time: 15 minutes or less

Menu ideas: This is delicious as an entrée by itself or as a side salad for a cookout. As an entrée, serve with fresh melon slices, and tomato slices on the side.

Seafood Salad

This is an extra special recipe for those extra special occasions such as showers and luncheons.

1	(8-ounce) package imitation lobster meat	1	pound cooked shrimp, peeled and deveined
1	(8-ounce) package imitation scallop meat	2	cups cucumbers, chopped, with seeds removed
1	(8-ounce) package imitation king crabmeat pieces	8	ounces fat-free Thousand Island dressing

- Mix together the imitation lobster, scallops, crabmeat, shrimp, cucumbers, and dressing. Keep chilled until ready to serve.
- Serve on toasted fat-free bread with lettuce or roll the seafood salad in a soft flour tortilla or serve a dab on crackers.

Note: To remove the seeds of the cucumber, cut it in half lengthwise. With a spoon, scrape down the center to remove the seeds.

Yield: 7 (1-cup) servings

Calories: 206 ; Fat: 2g (9% fat); Cholesterol: 146mg; Carbohydrate: 20g; Dietary Fiber: 1g; Protein: 25g; Sodium: 1238mg

Total preparation time: 8 minutes or less

Menu ideas: This is good in a pita half served as a sandwich or on a bed of fresh greens for individual salads.

Seafood Pasta Salad

This is an added bonus to the Seafood Salad.

1 pound bowtie pasta	1 pound cooked shrimp, peeled and deveined
1 (8-ounce) package imitation lobster meat	2 cups cucumbers, chopped, with seeds removed
1 (8-ounce) package imitation scallop meat	16 ounces fat-free Thousand Island dressing
1 (8-ounce) package imitation king crabmeat	

- In a large soup pot boil the pasta for 11 minutes, and then rinse with cold water.
- Mix together the lobster, scallops, crabmeat, shrimp, cucumbers, and dressing.
- Toss the seafood mixture with the pasta. Keep chilled until ready to serve.
- Serve on a bed of lettuce or by itself.

Note: To remove the seeds of the cucumber, cut it in half lengthwise. With a spoon, scrape down the center to remove the seeds.

Yield: 15 (1-cup) servings

Calories: 227; Fat: 1g (6% fat); Cholesterol: 68mg; Carbohydrate: 36g; Dietary Fiber: 2g; Protein: 16g; Sodium: 708mg

Preparation time: 9 minutes or less
Cooking time: 11 minutes
Total time: 20 minutes or less

Menu ideas: Serve with fresh cut tomatoes or cucumber salad. Add Perfect Pineapple Cookies (page 226) or sherbet for dessert.

Zesty Summer Cottage Salad

There's nothing to whipping up this dish in a hurry. It's easy to prepare, versatile, and tasty.

24 ounces low-fat cottage cheese	1 packet Butter Buds or 1 tablespoon Butter Buds Sprinkles
1/3 cup chopped fresh chives or green onion tops	
1/2 cup fat-free sour cream	1/8 teaspoon ground pepper

- Mix together the cottage cheese, chives, sour cream, Butter Buds, and pepper.
- Serve chilled.

Yield: 8 (1/2-cup) servings

Calories: 82; Fat: 1g (10% fat); Cholesterol: 6mg; Carbohydrate: 6g; Dietary Fiber: 0g; Protein: 12g; Sodium: 365mg

Preparation time: 5 minutes or less

Menu ideas: This creamy salad is delicious served with barbecue entrées. It's also good as a dip on baked tortillas or spread on a toasted bagel and topped with a slice of tomato.

Tropical Passion Fruit Salad

This light, creamy fruit salad is a hit with everyone. I like to eat it as a complete lunch in itself.

3/4 cup fat-free sour cream
1 tablespoon sugar substitute (I use Splenda.)
1 teaspoon coconut extract (imitation coconut extract is fine)

1 (15 1/4-ounce) can fruit in light syrup, drained
1 (8-ounce) package fat-free cottage cheese
1 small banana, sliced into 1/4-inch slices

- Mix the sour cream, sugar substitute, and coconut extract together in a serving bowl with a spoon.
- Once well mixed, add the fruit, cottage cheese, and banana slices. Gently stir until well mixed.
- Serve chilled.

Note: Keep the canned fruit refrigerated before using so it's already chilled when you're ready to eat.

Yield: 6 (1/2-cup) servings

Calories: 102; Fat: 0g (0% fat); Cholesterol: 7mg; Carbohydrate: 18g; Dietary Fiber: 1g; Protein: 6g; Sodium: 166mg

Preparation time: 6 minutes or less

Menu ideas: This recipe is good for picnics, potlucks, or with fish, chicken, or ham entrées.

Cucumber Dill Salad

This colorful, crispy salad is a great substitute for a tossed salad with any home-style entrée.

3 large cucumbers or enough for 6 cups cucumber slices	1 (12-ounce) bottle fat-free creamy dill dressing (I use Medford Farms.)
1/4 cup shredded carrots, optional	

- Peel the cucumbers and cut them into 1/4-inch-thick slices.
- Toss the cucumbers, carrots, if using, and dressing together in a mixing bowl.

Yield: 12 (1/2-cup) servings

Calories: 55; Fat: 0g (0% fat); Cholesterol: 0mg; Carbohydrate: 12g; Dietary Fiber: 1g; Protein: 1g; Sodium: 355mg

Preparation time: 7 minutes or less

Menu ideas: This crispy, crunchy dish is great to nibble on as a snack or as a side salad. It's just right for cookouts, picnics, potlucks, and showers.

Sassy Slaw

My secret ingredients turn regular coleslaw into an extra special dish that always gets rave reviews.

1	(20-ounce) can crushed pineapple in juice	3/4	cup fat-free coleslaw dressing (I use T. Marzetti.)
1	(16-ounce) package coleslaw	1/2	teaspoon ground cinnamon

- Discard 1 cup of juice from the can of pineapple.
- Thoroughly mix the pineapple (with remaining juice), coleslaw, dressing, and cinnamon in a medium-size bowl.
- Keep chilled until ready to use.

Yield: 10 ($\frac{1}{2}$-cup) servings

Calories: 58; Fat: 0g (0% fat); Cholesterol: 9mg; Carbohydrate: 14g; Dietary Fiber: 1g; Protein: 1g; Sodium: 242mg

Total preparation time: 5 minutes or less

Menu ideas: This is a delicious side vegetable for any cookout or barbecue. It's great with chicken, pork, fish, or beef entrées.

Cranberry Apple Salad

Putting together a unique and delicious original recipe to serve at the holidays couldn't be any easier than this.

I	(21-ounce) can apple pie filling	I	teaspoon ground cinnamon
I	(16-ounce) can whole-berry cranberry sauce		

- Before emptying the can, insert a sharp knife into the can of apple pie filling and cut the apples into small pieces.
- In a bowl mix together the apple pie filling, cranberry sauce, and cinnamon.
- Refrigerate for at least 20 minutes to chill.
- Serve chilled.

Note: To save preparation time store the cans of apple pie filling and cranberry sauce in the refrigerator before preparing the recipe.

Yield: 8 ($\frac{1}{2}$-cup) servings

Calories: 162; Fat: 0g (0% fat); Cholesterol: 0mg; Carbohydrate: 42g; Dietary Fiber: 1g; Protein: 0g; Sodium: 49mg

Total preparation time: 5 minutes (if filling already chilled)

Menu ideas: This is tasty on its own or as a topping for angel food cake or frozen yogurt. Good with any holiday dinner.

★ **For Cranberry Apple Pancakes:** Make pancakes as directed on a box of pancake mix. Heat the Cranberry Apple Salad in a microwave until warm. Spoon the warmed Cranberry Apple Salad over the pancakes and top with fat-free whipped topping.

Ham & Cheese Potato Salad

This hearty, meat and potatoes dish is the answer to a hungry man's hot summer day.

2 teaspoons mustard	1 (8-ounce) package fat-free shredded cheddar cheese
1 (9-ounce) jar fat-free tartar sauce	
2 teaspoons dried parsley	2 pounds potatoes (about 6 medium), cooked and cubed
2 pounds extra lean pre-cooked ham, cut into $1/4$-inch pieces	$3/4$ cup chopped red onion

- In a large bowl mix together the mustard, tartar sauce, and parsley.
- Add the ham, cheese, potatoes, and onion.
- Gently stir until all the ingredients are well coated with the dressing.
- Serve immediately or cover and keep chilled until ready to serve.

Yield: 20 side salads

Calories: 119; Fat: 2g (17% fat); Cholesterol: 23mg; Carbohydrate: 11g; Dietary Fiber: 1g; Protein: 13g; Sodium: 822mg

Yield: 10 dinner salads

Calories: 237; Fat: 5g (17% fat); Cholesterol: 45mg; Carbohydrate: 23g; Dietary Fiber: 2g; Protein: 27g; Sodium: 1644mg

Total time: 20 minutes or less

Menu ideas: This is great as an entrée served with a fresh vegetable tray with fat-free salad dressing as a dip.

Warm Cran-Apple Salad

This salad is a tasty change to an old favorite.

I (16-ounce) can whole-berry cranberry sauce	I teaspoon ground cinnamon
	I cup miniature marshmallows
I large apple, peeled and chopped (I use a Granny Smith.)	I tablespoon finely chopped walnuts

- Preheat the oven to 400 degrees.
- Spray a 1-quart casserole dish with nonfat cooking spray.
- Mix the cranberry sauce, chopped apple, and cinnamon together.
- Pour the mixture into the prepared casserole dish.
- Arrange marshmallows evenly on top.
- Bake for 7 to 10 minutes or until the tops of the marshmallows are a toasty golden brown.
- Sprinkle the chopped walnuts on top.
- Serve warm.

Yield: 6 servings

Calories: 171; Fat: 1g (5% fat); Cholesterol: 0mg; Carbohydrate: 42g; Dietary Fiber: 2g; Protein: 1g; Sodium: 26mg

Preparation time: 10 minutes or less
Baking time: 7 to10 minutes
Total time: 20 minutes or less

Menu ideas: I like serving this side salad with pork, ham, chicken, or turkey entrées. Great for the holidays instead of the traditional cranberry salad or jellied cranberry sauce.

Tangy Tossed Salad

I like the tangy zest of this salad. The dressing definitely adds zip to a normally boring salad.

2 cups chopped turkey-ham (approximately 1/2 pound)	1 cup fat-free shredded cheddar cheese
1 (12-ounce) bottle fat-free coleslaw dressing (I use T. Marzetti.)	1/4 cup chopped red onion, about 1/4 medium red onion
	2 heads leaf lettuce, chopped

- In a bowl mix the turkey-ham, dressing, cheese, and onion together until well coated.
- Stir in the lettuce just before serving.
- Serve chilled.

Yield: 8 side salads

Calories: 126; Fat: 1g (10% fat); Cholesterol: 41mg; Carbohydrate: 17g; Dietary Fiber: 1g; Protein: 11g; Sodium: 908mg

Yield: 4 dinner salads

Calories: 251; Fat: 3g (10% fat); Cholesterol: 81mg; Carbohydrate: 34g; Dietary Fiber: 2g; Protein: 22g; Sodium: 1816mg

Preparation time: 20 minutes or less

Menu idea: This salad is terrific as a meal for lunch or a side salad. As a main meal serve it with fat-free crackers and Apple Berry Bake (page 208) for dessert.

Bacon, Lettuce, and Tomato Salad

If you like BLT sandwiches, you'll love this salad.

Dressing:
- 3/4 cup fat-free sour cream
- 3/4 cup fat-free mayonnaise
- 1/3 cup Splenda or 1/3 cup sugar
- 1 teaspoon liquid smoke
- 1 (3 1/4-ounce) container imitation bacon bits

Salad:
- 1 quart cherry tomatoes, cut in half
- 2 medium heads Romaine lettuce, cut into bite-size pieces

- To make the dressing, mix together the sour cream, mayonnaise, Splenda, liquid smoke, and bacon bits until well blended.
- Gently toss the dressing with the tomatoes and lettuce.
- Keep chilled until ready to serve.

Note: If you want a thinner dressing, add 1/4 cup skim milk.

Note: Do not put the dressing on the salad until almost ready to serve, or the lettuce will get soggy.

Yield: 10 servings

Calories: 110; Fat: 3g (23% fat); Cholesterol: 5mg; Carbohydrate: 15g; Dietary Fiber: 3g; Protein: 7g; Sodium: 332mg

Total preparation time: 15 minutes or less

Menu ideas: This is good as a side salad with fish, chicken, beef, or pork.

Mother-Daughter Salad

My seven-year-old daughter was bored one day. I needed to take a pasta salad to a shower, so I invited my bored daughter to help. Together we created this unique, delicious, and visually beautiful salad. This creative blend of flavors is a raving hit every time.

12 ounces cooked chicken breast, cut into small pieces	1 (3-ounce) can real bacon bits
1/2 cup dried peaches or dried apricots, cut into tiny pieces	1 1/3 cups light apricot syrup
1/3 cup dried, sweetened cranberries, chopped	2 tablespoons chopped fresh chives, optional
	4 cups cooked small pasta shells

- Mix together the chicken, peaches or apricots, cranberries, bacon bits, apricot syrup, and chives.
- Gently toss the pasta with the chicken mixture. Make sure all the ingredients are coated well with the apricot syrup, which acts as the dressing in this recipe.
- Serve chilled.

Yield: 6 (1-cup) entrée servings

Calories: 391; Fat: 5g (12% fat); Cholesterol: 58mg; Carbohydrate: 57g; Dietary Fiber: 2g; Protein: 27g; Sodium: 515mg

Yield: 12 (1/2-cup) side-dish servings

Calories: 180; Fat: 2g (12% fat); Cholesterol: 27mg; Carbohydrate: 26g; Dietary Fiber: 1g; Protein: 13g; Sodium: 238mg

Preparation time: 14 minutes or less
Cooking time: (for pasta shells and chicken) 11 minutes
Total time: 25 minutes or less

Menu ideas: This is great to serve at showers or potlucks. As the main dish, a thick Fruity Frothy (page 261) complements this meal nicely. I like to serve this salad on a fresh Romaine or leafy lettuce leaf to accent the pretty hues of the burgundy-colored cranberries and green chives.

Mother's Day Salad

I got the idea for this salad from an exquisite, beautiful restaurant in Michigan called the Hathaway House. I enjoyed the flavor combination so much that I was determined to create my own version at a fraction of the fats and calories of their salad. I am thrilled at my results. Knowing my version is not fattening makes mine taste even better.

1	(10-ounce) can mandarin oranges in light syrup	1	large head fresh Romaine lettuce, torn into bite-size pieces
1/2	cup fat-free raspberry salad dressing or more to taste if desired	1 1/2	ounces bacon bits
		1/2	ounce crumbled feta cheese

- Drain the juice from the mandarin oranges into a large bowl.
- Stir together the salad dressing and the juice until well blended.
- Toss the lettuce, oranges, bacon bits, and dressing mixture until the lettuce is well coated.
- Sprinkle with very tiny pieces of crumbled feta cheese before serving.
- Serve chilled.

Yield: 4 servings

Calories: 155; Fat: 3g (17% fat); Cholesterol: 11mg; Carbohydrate: 28g; Dietary Fiber: 2g; Protein: 7g; Sodium: 613mg

Preparation time: 5 minutes or less

Menu ideas: This is nice served for a special Mother's Day luncheon or served as a side salad with an entrée.

Apple Cottage Salad

This is a satisfying salad that is filling enough to eat for lunch. It's also sweet enough to curb a sweet tooth at dinner if you're not serving dessert.

1 large red delicious apple, peeled and finely chopped	12 ounces fat-free cottage cheese
1/2 teaspoon light salt	3/4 cup apple butter
1 teaspoon ground cinnamon	2 tablespoons finely chopped walnuts or pecans, optional
1 tablespoon sugar or Splenda that measures like sugar	

- Sprinkle the chopped apples with the salt, cinnamon, and sugar. Toss until well coated.
- Stir the cottage cheese and apple butter into the apple mixture.
- Sprinkle the chopped nuts on top.
- Keep refrigerated until ready to serve.

Yield: 6 servings

(with Splenda) Calories: 121; Fat: 0g (0% fat); Cholesterol: 2mg; Carbohydrate: 24g; Dietary Fiber: 2g; Protein: 6g; Sodium: 294mg
(with sugar) Calories: 129; Fat: 0g (0% fat); Cholesterol: 2mg; Carbohydrate: 26g; Dietary Fiber: 2g; Protein: 6g; Sodium: 294mg

Preparation time: 10 minutes or less

Menu idea: Serve this on a bed of crisp lettuce along with a glass of Spiced Tea (page 262).

Popeye's Favorite Salad

Even Olive Oyl couldn't create a more delicious spinach salad than this one. The grilled onions on this salad are what make it so special.

1	large sweet white onion, cut into ¹/2-inch slices	1	(10-ounce) package baby spinach, washed and ready to eat
	Salt, optional	6	whites of hard-cooked eggs, chopped
1	pound eye of round steaks		Fat-free raspberry salad dressing (I use T. Marzetti's.)
	Garlic salt, optional		

- Spray both sides of the onion slices with nonfat cooking spray. If desired, lightly sprinkle one side of each onion slice with salt.
- Over medium heat grill the steaks and onion slices. Cook to desired doneness.
- Cut the steaks into long, thin strips. If desired sprinkle lightly with garlic salt.
- Cut the grilled onion slices into quarters.
- Pour the spinach into a large salad bowl.
- Top with the chopped egg whites, grilled onions, and steak strips.
- Serve immediately or keep chilled for later use. This is good with the meat and onions either hot off the grill or chilled.

Yield: 4 dinner salads

Calories: 199; Fat: 4g (19% fat); Cholesterol: 59mg; Carbohydrate: 7g; Dietary Fiber: 3g; Protein: 33g; Sodium: 192mg

Yield: 8 side salads

Calories: 100; Fat: 2g (19% fat); Cholesterol: 29mg; Carbohydrate: 4g; Dietary Fiber: 1g; Protein: 16g; Sodium: 96mg

Preparation time: 5 minutes or less
Grilling time: 10 minutes or less
Boiling time: 10 or less (boil eggs while steak is cooking)
Total time: 15 minutes or less

Menu idea: This is a meal in itself when served with rolls or garlic bread.

Zesty Chilled Fruit Salad

What an exquisite blend of flavors!

10	ice cubes
2	(11-ounce) cans of mandarin oranges in light syrup
1	(20-ounce) can chunk pineapple in its own juice
1	(0.8-ounce) package no-sugar-added, lemon flavored pudding mix, dry
1	(21-ounce) can blueberry pie filling
5	medium bananas, cut into bite-size slices
1/2	(10 1/2-ounce) bag miniature marshmallows

- Place the ice cubes in a bowl. Set a large empty bowl inside the bowl with the ice.
- Drain the juices from the oranges and pineapple into the empty bowl.
- Briskly stir the lemon pudding into the juice and stir for 2 minutes.
- Gently stir in the oranges, pineapple chunks, blueberry pie filling, banana slices, and marshmallows.
- Keep chilled until ready to serve. This tastes best chilled.
- If desired, keep the canned fruit refrigerated, prepare, and serve immediately.

Yield: 10 (1-cup) servings

Calories: 235; Fat: 0g (0% fat); Cholesterol: 0mg; Carbohydrate: 59g; Dietary Fiber: 3g; Protein: 1g; Sodium: 110mg

Preparation time: 10 minutes or less

Menu ideas: Good as a topping over angel food cake, fat-free pound cake, or frozen yogurt.

Broccoli & Cauliflower Salad

The sweet banana peppers give this extra zing.

1/2 (2.8-ounce) container real bacon pieces	1/4 cup chopped sweet banana pepper rings
1 (16-ounce) package fresh broccoli and cauliflower	1/4 cup chopped red onion
1/2 cup fat-free coleslaw dressing (I use T. Marzetti's.)	1 large fresh carrot, chopped

- Microwave the bacon pieces for 10 seconds in a medium-size serving bowl to soften.
- Stir the vegetables, dressing, pepper rings, onion, and carrot in with the bacon bits until well mixed.
- Keep chilled until ready to eat.

Yield: 6 (2/3-cup) servings

Calories: 81; Fat: 2g (19% fat); Cholesterol: 15mg; Carbohydrate: 13g; Dietary Fiber: 2g; Protein: 5g; Sodium: 590mg

Preparation time: 10 minutes

Menu ideas: This is great as a side dish with lean ham, chicken, or lean pork on the grill. It's also good with baked potatoes, cake, or pudding-type desserts. It's great for picnics and potlucks.

Spring Salad

Don't let this title fool you. This salad is delicious in all seasons—spring, summer, fall, or winter.

8 ounces fat-free coleslaw dressing (I use T. Marzetti.)	6 hard-cooked egg whites, chopped, discarding the yolks
1 (8-ounce) container fat-free sour cream	1 (4-ounce) package fat-free shredded mozzarella cheese
1 cup chopped red onion (any sweet onion will do)	2 large heads fresh Romaine lettuce, approximately 10 cups

- Mix together the coleslaw dressing and fat-free sour cream until well blended. Continue stirring and add the onion, egg whites, and cheese until well coated with the dressing.
- Gently toss the lettuce with the dressing.
- Serve immediately.

Note: Do not put the dressing on the salad until ready to serve. It is okay to prepare the dressing with the cheese, egg, and onions ahead of time; however, keep it separate from the lettuce until ready to serve. If lettuce is stirred with dressing too far in advance, the salad will become soggy.

Yield: 8 servings

Calories: 129; Fat: 0g (0% fat); Cholesterol: 22mg; Carbohydrate: 21g; Dietary Fiber: 2g; Protein: 10g; Sodium: 632mg

Preparation time: 10 minutes or less
Cooking time: 10 minutes or less (derived from cooking eggs)
Total time: 20 minutes or less

Menu idea: This salad is excellent with picnics and potlucks or just about anything your heart desires.

Spring Salad with Chicken

This is a hearty variation to the Spring Salad.

8	ounces fat-free coleslaw dressing (I use T. Marzetti.)	6	hard-cooked egg whites, chopped, discarding the yolks
1	(8-ounce) container fat-free sour cream	1	(4-ounce) package fat-free shredded mozzarella cheese
1	(10-ounce) can premium chunk white chicken in water, drained	2	large heads fresh Romaine lettuce, approximately 10 cups
1	cup chopped red onion (any sweet onion will do)		

- Mix together the coleslaw dressing and fat-free sour cream until well blended. Continue stirring and add the chicken, onion, egg whites, and cheese until well coated with the dressing.
- Gently toss the lettuce with the dressing.
- Serve immediately.

Note: Do not put the dressing on the salad until ready to serve. It is okay to prepare the dressing with the cheese, egg, and onions ahead of time; however, keep it separate from the lettuce until ready to serve. If lettuce is stirred with dressing too far in advance, the salad will become soggy.

Yield: 4 dinner salads

Calories: 288; Fat: 2g (7% fat); Cholesterol: 58mg; Carbohydrate: 36g; Dietary Fiber: 0g; Protein: 30g; Sodium: 1332mg

Yield: 8 side salads

Calories: 144; Fat: 1g (7% fat); Cholesterol: 29mg; Carbohydrate: 18g; Dietary Fiber: 2g; Protein: 15g; Sodium: 667mg

Preparation time: 10 minutes or less
Cooking time: 10 minutes or less
Total time: 20 minutes or less

Menu idea: This salad is excellent as an entrée for lunch served with reduced-fat Ritz crackers.

Peppered Potato Salad

This hearty dish is the answer to all of those who don't like sweet-tasting potato salad. Don't let the pepper in the recipe title scare you; there's only enough to give the salad flavor.

6 cups cubed potatoes with skin on	⅛ teaspoon ground pepper
1 (8-ounce) container fat-free sour cream	½ cup chopped onion
	¼ cup imitation bacon bits
3 tablespoons light whipped salad dressing	½ plus ½ teaspoon dried parsley flakes, optional

- In a large Dutch oven cook the cubed potatoes in boiling salt water for 5 to 10 minutes or until tender.
- Drain well.
- Rinse with cold water until the potatoes are cool.
- In a medium-size serving bowl stir together the sour cream, salad dressing, pepper, onion, bacon bits, and ½ teaspoon dried parsley until well mixed.
- Add the cooked, cubed potatoes to the cream mixture.
- Stir together until well mixed.
- Sprinkle with the remaining ½ teaspoon dried parsley.
- Keep chilled until ready to eat.

Yield: 12 (½-cup) servings

Calories: 100; Fat: 1g (10% fat); Cholesterol: 4mg; Carbohydrate: 19g; Dietary Fiber: 1g; Protein: 4g; Sodium: 87mg

Total preparation time: 35 minutes or less

Menu ideas: This is great for any cookout or picnic. Serve instead of a baked potato with beef, pork, fish, or chicken.

Zesty Potato Salad

There's no boring potato salad here, folks. This side salad adds zest to any blah meal.

1	(9-ounce) jar fat-free tartar sauce	1	teaspoon celery salt
3/4	cup finely chopped red onion	2	teaspoons mustard
1	teaspoon sugar	1	teaspoon dried parsley, optional
1	cup chopped celery or 1/2	2	pounds potatoes (about 6) with skins on, cooked and cubed

- Mix together the tartar sauce, onion, sugar, celery, mustard, and parsley until the dressing is well blended.
- Add the potatoes to the dressing and gently stir until the potatoes are coated with the dressing.
- Cover and keep chilled until ready to serve.

Note: The cooking and cooling of the potatoes require the most amount of time. Hopefully, you have some leftover cooked potatoes in the refrigerator. The quickest way to cook potatoes is in the microwave, approximately $3\frac{1}{2}$ minutes per potato. To cool, quickly place the hot potatoes in a sink of ice water.

Yield: 10 ($\frac{1}{2}$-cup) servings

Calories: 90; Fat: 0g (0% fat); Cholesterol: 0mg; Carbohydrate: 22g; Dietary Fiber: 2g; Protein: 3g; Sodium: 181mg

Total preparation time: 20 minutes

Menu ideas: This is great for picnics and cookouts. It adds zest to any grilled or baked plain meat entrée. It's also great with sandwiches or barbecued foods.

Caribbean Chicken Salad Sandwiches

This is the perfect size sandwich for baby or bridal showers. Men will probably want to eat two sandwiches; most women will be satisfied with one.

3 pounds boneless, skinless chicken breasts, all fat removed	1 (12-ounce) bottle teriyaki baste & glaze (I use Kikkoman's.)
1 (20-ounce) can crushed pineapple in juice	1/2 cup chopped fresh chives
	2 (12-roll packages) King's Hawaiian Rolls

- In a large, covered nonstick skillet cook the chicken breasts on medium heat for 5 minutes on each side.
- Cut the chicken into 1/4-inch pieces.
- Wash the skillet the chicken was cooked in.
- Discard 3/4 cup pineapple juice.
- Return the chicken to the skillet, along with the pineapple with juice, teriyaki, and chopped chives.
- Stir all the ingredients together over medium heat until well mixed.
- Continue cooking until fully heated, about 4 to 5 minutes.
- In the meantime, while the chicken is heating in the skillet, cut the rolls in half, making each roll into a bun.
- Fill each bun with chicken salad and serve immediately.

Yield: 24 mini-sandwiches

Calories: 183; Fat: 3g (14% fat); Cholesterol: 43mg; Carbohydrate: 22g; Dietary Fiber: 1g; Protein: 17g; Sodium: 436mg

Preparation time: 10 minutes or less
Cooking time: 15 minutes
Total time: 25 minutes or less

Menu ideas: Serve with Sassy Slaw (page 91), Crunchy Cucumbers with Cream (page 82), Very Berry Cheesecake Trifle (page 235), and Spiced Tea (page 262) to drink.

Zesty Egg-Salad Sandwiches

This brings boring egg salad to life.

I	whole hard-cooked egg	4	hard-cooked egg whites, yolks discarded
I	teaspoon water		
1/4	cup fat-free tartar sauce	6	slices fat-free bread

- Divide the egg yolk from the egg white.
- With a fork mix the egg yolk, water, and tartar sauce together until smooth and creamy.
- Chop the egg white into tiny pieces.
- Stir the egg white into the creamy mixture.
- Keep chilled until ready to serve.
- Spread on toasted bread. Top with fresh crisp lettuce.

Yield: 3 sandwiches

Calories: 205; Fat: 2g (8% fat); Cholesterol: 71mg; Carbohydrate: 34g; Dietary Fiber: 1g; Protein: 12g; Sodium: 550mg

Preparation time: 5 minutes or less
Cooking time: 10 minutes
Total time: 15 minutes or less

Menu idea: For a change of pace, serve open-face, egg salad sandwiches on toasted rye or pumpernickel. Top with thin slices of cucumber or tomato.

Side Dishes

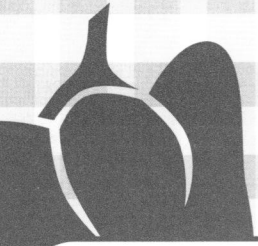

Wise people are the ones who know they don't know everything.

"B.B.B." (Best Baked Beans)   134

Broccoli Parmesan   124

Calico Corn   112

California Garlic Blend   120

Carrot with a Light, Buttery Caramel
    Glaze   121

Corn Casserole   113

Creamed Green Beans with Ham   111

Creamed Spinach   114

Garlic Red Skins   117

Green Beans Italiano   116

Hawaiian-Style Baked Beans   137

Home-Style Green Beans and
    Potatoes   135

Mashed Potatoes and Carrots   133

Mashed Potatoes Deluxe   119

Mushroom-Asparagus Casserole   129

Mushroom, Onion, and Bacon Green
    Bean Casserole   115

Oriental Vegetables   130

Sausage Pasta Salad   128

Savory Sausage and Green Bean
    Casserole   122

Sensational Sweet Potato Casserole   123

Spring Asparagus   118

Sour Cream Pasta Salad   125

Sour Cream Chicken Pasta Salad   126

Spiced Apples   132

Tuna Pasta Salad   127

Twice Baked Potatoes   131

Zesty Corn   136

Creamed Green Beans with Ham

This delightful dish is fit for a king as a side dish or entrée.

4	(15-ounce) cans green beans, drained	1	(12-ounce) can fat-free, evaporated skim milk
1/2	pound extra lean ham, chopped	1	tablespoon Butter Buds Sprinkles, dry
1	(8-ounce) can of mushroom stems and pieces, drained, optional	2	tablespoons cornstarch
		1/2	teaspoon liquid smoke

- Warm the green beans, ham, and mushrooms over medium heat in a large, non-stick skillet for 3 minutes.
- In a medium bowl mix the milk, Butter Buds, cornstarch, and liquid smoke together with a whisk until dissolved.
- Stir the milk mixture into the skillet with the green beans, ham, and mushrooms. Continue stirring over heat until thick, about 5 minutes.
- Serve hot.

Yield: 12 servings

Calories: 75; Fat: 1g (14% fat); Cholesterol: 10mg; Carbohydrate: 9g; Dietary Fiber: 1g; Protein: 7g; Sodium: 659mg

Preparation time: 7 minutes or less
Cooking time: 10 minutes or less
Total time: 17 minutes or less

Menu idea: This is great with any meat, fish, or poultry dish.

Calico Corn

This slightly sweet vegetable dish received its name because of its beautiful color combination.

2	(15¹/4-ounce) cans whole kernel corn, drained	¹/4	cup fat-free French salad dressing
I	tablespoon sugar	I	cup chunky salsa

- In a 2-quart microwavable bowl, mix together the corn, sugar, salad dressing, and salsa until well blended.
- Heat in the microwave on full power for 3 minutes or until completely warmed.

Yield: 7 (½-cup) servings

Calories: 103 ; Fat: 1g (7% fat); Cholesterol: 0mg; Carbohydrate: 23g; Dietary Fiber: 2g; Protein: 2g; Sodium: 436mg

Preparation time: 3 minutes or less
Cooking time: 3 minutes
Total time: 6 minutes or less

Menu ideas: Complements any lean meat cooked on the grill, baked, or broiled. Sprinkle chilled on top of a salad, or toss with a fresh, crisp, green lettuce salad instead of the traditional fresh tomatoes or vegetables. Serve salad dressing of your choice on the side.

Corn Casserole

I got this idea from a dear friend, Kathy Beerbower. Her recipe is absolutely delicious but loaded with too many fats and calories. This recipe is just as delicious and a lot less fattening.

1 (15¹/4-ounce) can whole kernel corn	1 (6-serving-size) box corn muffin mix—Do not make as directed on box.
1 (14³/4-ounce) can cream-style corn	¹/2 cup fat-free margarine, softened
	1 cup fat-free sour cream

- Preheat the oven to 350 degrees.
- Spray a 9 x 13-inch pan with nonfat cooking spray.
- Stir the kernel corn, cream-style corn, muffin mix, margarine, and sour cream together until well mixed and spread into the prepared pan.
- Bake for 35 to 40 minutes or until the top is golden brown.
- Serve warm.

Yield: 15 servings

Calories: 134; Fat: 2g (15% fat); Cholesterol: 3mg; Carbohydrate: 26g; Dietary Fiber: 2g; Protein: 3g; Sodium: 379mg

Preparation time: 5 minutes or less
Cooking time: 40 minutes or less
Total time: 45 minutes or less

Menu ideas: This is good with fish, chicken, turkey, omelets, quiches, or brunches.

Creamed Spinach

Popeye would have gone nuts over this smooth and creamy spinach.

2 tablespoons cornstarch	1 (5-ounce) can evaporated skim milk
1 tablespoon sugar	
1 envelope Butter Buds or 1 tablespoon Butter Buds Sprinkles	2 (10-ounce) packages frozen chopped spinach with all excess water squeezed from spinach
	1/3 cup fat-free Parmesan cheese

- In a large, non-stick skillet over no heat dissolve the cornstarch, sugar, and Butter Buds in the milk.
- Turn on the stove to medium. Add the spinach and, stirring constantly, bring to a boil.
- Sprinkle with the Parmesan cheese.
- Reduce the heat to low. Cover. Let simmer for 10 minutes.

Yield: 7 servings

Calories: 67; Fat: 0g (0% fat); Cholesterol: 5mg; Carbohydrate: 12g; Dietary Fiber: 2g; Protein: 6g; Sodium: 129mg

Preparation time: 5 minutes or less
Cooking time: 15 minutes or less
Total time: 20 minutes or less

Menu ideas: Serve this with any Italian food or main meat entrées such as chicken, turkey, fish, pork tenderloin, or lean beef.

Mushroom, Onion, and Bacon Green Bean Casserole

Don't mistake this for the classic Durkee Onion Ring Green Bean Casserole. Although this is delicious, this version has its own distinctive and delicious flavor with a fraction of the fat and calories.

4 (13-ounce) cans French-style green beans, drained	1 (16-ounce) fat-free sour cream
2 (4-ounce) cans mushroom stems and pieces	1 teaspoon liquid smoke
1 (1½-ounce) envelope dry onion soup mix	1½ plus 1½ ounces bacon bits

- With your hands squeeze as much liquid from the green beans as possible.
- Spray a 2-quart microwaveable bowl or casserole dish with nonfat cooking spray.
- Stir together the beans, mushrooms, onion soup mix, sour cream, liquid smoke, and 1½ bacon pieces. Keep stirring until well combined.
- Microwave on high for 2 to 2½ minutes. Stir. Turn bowl a half turn. Microwave again for 2 to 2½ minutes, or until completely heated. Stir again. If you have a carousel microwave, cook for 4 to 5 minutes, stirring halfway through.
- Sprinkle the remaining bacon bits on top of the casserole.
- Serve hot.

Yield: 14 (½-cup) servings

Calories: 83; Fat: 1g (15% fat); Cholesterol: 10mg; Carbohydrate: 11g; Dietary Fiber: 1g; Protein: 6g; Sodium: 839mg

Preparation time: 5 minutes or less
Cooking time: 5 minutes or less
Total time: 10 minutes or less

Menu ideas: This is good with meat entrées, such as pork tenderloin, beef tenderloin, chicken, fish, or turkey.

Green Beans Italiano

I got this idea from Kenny Rogers' restaurant. I'm not sure what he has in his recipe, but this is a pretty close match and just as good. And I can almost bet that mine is a lot less fattening. These beans are popular primarily with adults.

2 medium onions, thinly sliced (about 1¹/2 cups)	2 (16-ounce) bags frozen green beans
³/4 cup fat-free Italian dressing	¹/2 tablespoon light salt, optional
1 (14¹/2-ounce) can diced tomatoes, drained	

- In a large non-stick skillet, approximately 12 inches in diameter, sauté the onions in the salad dressing over medium heat until tender, about 2 to 3 minutes.
- Add the tomatoes and green beans. Increase the heat to medium high. Stir until well coated. Salt if desired.
- Cover and cook for 5 to 7 minutes until the beans are tender.
- Serve hot.

Yield: 12 (²/3-cup) servings

Calories: 44; Fat: 0g (0% fat); Cholesterol: 0mg; Carbohydrate: 10g; Dietary Fiber: 3g; Protein: 2g; Sodium: 256mg

Preparation time: 5 minutes or less
Cooking time: 10 minutes or less
Total time: 15 minutes or less

Menu idea: The beans go great with entrées that have a marinara sauce (red sauce) like lasagna or spaghetti.

Garlic Red Skins

Spending a little more for red potatoes instead of regular potatoes is definitely worth it for this mouth-watering, favorite side dish.

2 pounds red skin potatoes, washed	1 teaspoon light salt
2 tablespoons chopped garlic	$^1/_2$ cup fat-free butter spread
	1 teaspoon dried parsley

- Cut the potatoes into 1-inch cubes, leaving the skins on.
- Put the cubed potatoes into boiling water. Turn the heat off, let sit for 15 to 20 minutes, or until potatoes are tender when poked with a fork.
- In a large, non-stick skillet cook the garlic over medium heat with the salt and butter for just a few minutes to heat—and make the home smell yummy.
- Drain the water from the red skins.
- Stir the red skins in with the garlic butter, until potatoes are well coated.
- Pour into a serving dish. Sprinkle with the dried parsley.
- Serve immediately.

Yield: 8 servings

Calories: 95; Fat: 0g (0% fat); Cholesterol: 0mg; Carbohydrate: 24g; Dietary Fiber: 2g; Protein: 3g; Sodium: 212mg

Preparation time: 8 minutes or less
Cooking time: 15 to 20 minutes
Total time: 28 minutes or less

Menu ideas: These potatoes are good with meat entrées such as beef tenderloin, chicken, fish, or turkey.

Spring Asparagus

This is a wonderful way to eat fresh asparagus.

1 tablespoon mustard	2 pounds fresh asparagus,
$^1/_3$ cup fat-free sour cream	steamed
$^1/_8$ teaspoon dried dill weed	

- Mix the mustard, sour cream, and dill together until well blended.
- Toss gently with the freshly steamed asparagus.
- Serve immediately. If needed, this dish can be microwaved for a few minutes to warm.

Yield: 6 servings

Calories: 52; Fat: 0g (0% fat); Cholesterol: 0mg; Carbohydrate: 24g; Dietary Fiber: 2g; Protein: 3g; Sodium: 212mg

Preparation time: 5 minutes or less
Cooking time: 5 to 7 minutes
Total time: 12 minutes or less

Menu ideas: This vegetable complements pork, beef, or chicken entrées.

Mashed Potatoes Deluxe

These are the perfect substitute for those of you who like the traditional, high-fat twice baked potatoes.

2 pounds red-skin potatoes with skins on, washed and pierced with a fork	1/2 cup fat-free butter spread
1 (8-ounce) package fat-free cream cheese	1 1/4 to 1 1/2 cups skim milk
	3 teaspoons garlic salt, optional

- Microwave the potatoes in a carousel* microwave for 12 minutes or until fully cooked.
- Using a fork and sharp knife, cut the cooked potatoes into cubes, leaving skins on.
- Put the potatoes, cream cheese, butter spread, skim milk, and garlic salt, if using, into a medium-size mixing bowl. With the mixer beat on medium speed for approximately 2 minutes or until desired creamy consistency.
- Cook the entire bowl of Mashed Potatoes Deluxe in the microwave an additional 1 to 2 minutes to reheat before serving.
- Serve additional butter spread on the side if desired.

*Note: If you do not have a carousel microwave, turn potatoes a quarter turn every 3 minutes.

Yield: 8 servings

Calories: 135; Fat: 0g (0% fat); Cholesterol: 6mg; Carbohydrate: 27g; Dietary Fiber: 2g; Protein: 8g; Sodium: 235mg

Preparation time: 6 minutes
Cooking time: 14 minutes or less
Total time: 20 minutes or less

Menu ideas: Good with a pork roast, beef tenderloin, or chicken, with a good salad on the side.

California Garlic Blend

These are every bit as good as at any fine restaurant.

1	pound frozen California blend vegetables (broccoli, cauliflower, and carrots)	1	teaspoon crushed real garlic
		1/2	to 1 teaspoon light salt, optional
		1/4	cup fat-free butter spread

- Mix together in a microwavable serving bowl the vegetables, garlic, salt, if using, and butter spread.
- Cover and microwave on high for 4½ minutes. Stir well.
- Serve immediately.

Yield: 5 servings

Calories: 38; Fat: 0g (0% fat); Cholesterol: 0mg; Carbohydrate: 8g; Dietary Fiber: 2g; Protein: 2g; Sodium: 87mg

Preparation time: 3 minutes or less
Cooking time: 4½ minutes
Total time: 7½ minutes or less

Menu ideas: This is good on top of a baked potato or with a main entrée for lunch or dinner.

Carrots with a Light, Buttery Caramel Glaze

This slightly sweet glaze gives nature a helping hand by enticing children of all ages to eat more vegetables.

1 pound mini carrots, peeled	1/2 teaspoon light salt, optional
2 tablespoons fat-free butter spread	2 tablespoons fat-free caramel topping

- Place the carrots in a medium-size saucepan.
- Put just enough water in the pan to cover the carrots.
- Bring the water with the carrots to a boil.
- Turn off the heat. Cover and let sit for 10 to 13 minutes. Carrots will be tender when pierced with a fork.
- While the carrots are cooking, in a small bowl stir together the butter, salt, and caramel topping until well blended.
- Once the water is drained from the carrots, stir the buttery, caramel glaze over them.
- Serve hot.

Yield: 5 servings

Calories: 71; Fat: 0g (0% fat); Cholesterol: 0mg; Carbohydrate: 17g; Dietary Fiber: 3g; Protein: 1g; Sodium: 84mg

Preparation time: 3 minutes
Cooking time: 10 to 13 minutes
Total time: 19 minutes or less

Menu ideas: Serve with Ham Kebabs (page 164) or Manhandler Meatloaves (page 186).

Savory Sausage and Green Bean Casserole

The distinctive, savory flavor of sausage pleasingly complements these beans.

3 **(15-ounce) cans French-style green beans, drained**	1/2 **teaspoon garlic salt, optional**
1 **(10³/4-ounce) can 98% fat-free cream of mushroom soup**	1 **(4-ounce) can sliced mushrooms, drained**
1/2 **cup chopped onion (I use the frozen pre-cut onions.)**	1 **(6¹/2-ounce) package low-fat breakfast sausage, cut into tiny pieces**

- Mix the beans, soup, onion, garlic salt, if using, mushrooms, and sausage together, until well coated.
- Cook in a carousel* microwave on high for 4 to 5 minutes, or until completely heated.
- Serve immediately.

Note: If you do not have a carousel microwave, turn a half turn after 2 minutes.

Yield: 12 servings

Calories: 50; Fat: 1g (21% fat); Cholesterol: 6mg; Carbohydrate: 7g; Dietary Fiber: 1g; Protein: 3g; Sodium: 574mg

Preparation time: 10 minutes or less
Cooking time: 5 minutes or less
Total time: 15 minutes or less

Menu ideas: This is good with any meat entrée, such as chicken, turkey, fish, pork tenderloin, or beef tenderloin. It's also good with Italian food, such as lasagna or spaghetti.

Sensational Sweet Potato Casserole

This casserole is definitely a flavorful twist to an old holiday favorite.

1 (24-ounce) can sweet potatoes with syrup	Cinnamon, optional
1 (20-ounce) can apple-cranberry pie filling	

- Drain the syrup from the sweet potatoes into a measuring cup and reserve.
- Put the sweet potatoes in a medium-size bowl. With your hands or a potato masher, break the sweet potatoes into little pieces.
- Pour half of the syrup into the sweet potatoes. Discard the remaining syrup.
- With a hand-held mixer on low speed, mix the juices with the sweet potatoes until well mashed. Potatoes will be lumpy and not a very thick consistency.
- With a spoon stir the apple-cranberry pie filling into the sweet potatoes.
- Microwave on high for 2 to 3 minutes. Stir and turn the bowl a half turn. Microwave for 2 to 3 minutes more or until completely heated.
- Sprinkle with cinnamon.
- Serve hot.

Yield: 10 ($\frac{1}{2}$-cup) servings

Calories: 110; Fat: 0g (0% fat); Cholesterol: 0mg; Carbohydrate: 27g; Dietary Fiber: 2g; Protein: 1g; Sodium: 58mg

Preparation time: 5 minutes or less
Cooking time: 6 minutes or less
Total time: 11 minutes or less

Menu idea: Great as a side dish for your festive holiday dinner.

Broccoli Parmesan

Perfect for when you need a great-tasting vegetable dish fast.

1/4 cup fat-free butter spread	1/4 cup shredded Parmesan cheese, not grated
1/2 teaspoon garlic salt, optional	
1 (16-ounce) bag frozen broccoli cuts	

- Stir the butter spread, garlic salt, and broccoli in a microwaveable bowl.
- Cover and cook on high for 4 minutes. Stir. Cook for 4 more minutes on high.
- Sprinkle with Parmesan cheese and let sit for 2 minutes.
- Serve hot.

Yield: 5 servings

Calories: 52; Fat: 1g (22% fat); Cholesterol: 3mg; Carbohydrate: 7g; Dietary Fiber: 3g; Protein: 4g; Sodium: 150mg

Preparation time: 2 minutes or less
Cooking time: 10 minutes or less
Total time: 12 minutes or less

Menu ideas: Great with any meat main entrée meal, such as pork tenderloin, lean beef, chicken, fish, turkey, or Italian entrées.

Sour Cream Pasta Salad

The sour cream takes the sweet edge off of this traditional pasta salad, and it tastes terrific.

1 (16-ounce) container fat-free sour cream	2 (8-ounce) fat-free shredded cheddar cheese
3/4 cup fat-free whipped salad dressing	1 cup red sweet pepper, chopped into tiny pieces, about 1 medium pepper
2 to 3 teaspoons Durkee Salad Seasoning	1 cup chopped celery, about 3 ribs
1 (1-pound) box ziti, cooked as directed on box	2 tablespoons chopped chives, optional

- In a large bowl mix together the sour cream, whipped dressing, and salad seasoning until well blended.
- Stir in the pasta, cheese, pepper, celery, and chives, if using, until well coated with the dressing.
- Serve chilled.

Yield: 24 ($\frac{1}{2}$-cup) servings

Calories: 140; Fat: 2g (11% fat); Cholesterol: 7mg; Carbohydrate: 21g; Dietary Fiber: 1g; Protein: 9g; Sodium: 240mg

Preparation time: 12 minutes or less
Cooking time: 11 minutes or less
Total time: 23 minutes or less

Menu ideas: This is good for cookouts, barbecues, luncheons, buffets, and potlucks.

Sour Cream Chicken Pasta Salad

This is a nice variation to the sour cream pasta salad, and it tastes terrific, too.

1 (16-ounce) container fat-free sour cream	1 (1-pound) package fat-free shredded cheddar cheese
3/4 cup fat-free whipped salad dressing	1 cup red sweet pepper, chopped into tiny pieces, about 1 medium pepper
2 to 3 teaspoons Durkee Salad Seasoning	1 cup chopped celery, about 3 ribs
2 cups chopped, cooked chicken breast	2 tablespoons chopped chives, optional
1 (1-pound) box ziti-style pasta, cooked as directed on box	

- In a large bowl mix together the sour cream, whipped dressing, and salad seasoning until well blended.
- Stir in the chicken, pasta, cheese, pepper, celery, and chives, if using, until well coated with the dressing.
- Serve chilled.

Yield: 24 ($\frac{1}{2}$-cup) servings

Calories: 160; Fat: 2g (13% fat); Cholesterol: 17mg; Carbohydrate: 21g; Dietary Fiber: 1g; Protein: 13g; Sodium: 249mg

Preparation time: 12 minutes or less
Cooking time: 11 minutes or less
Total time: 23 minutes or less

Menu Idea: This is a great side dish or entrée that can be served at a picnic or potluck.

Tuna Pasta Salad

The tuna makes this pasta salad a wonderful treat.

1 (16-ounce) container fat-free sour cream	1 (1-pound) package fat-free shredded cheddar cheese
3/4 cup fat-free whipped salad dressing	1 cup red sweet pepper, chopped into tiny pieces, about 1 medium pepper
2 to 3 teaspoons Durkee Salad Seasoning	1 cup chopped celery, about 3 ribs
3 (6-ounce) cans tuna in water, drained	2 tablespoons chopped chives, optional
1 (1-pound) box ziti-style pasta, cooked as directed on box	

- In a large bowl mix together the sour cream, whipped dressing, and salad seasoning until well blended.
- Stir in the tuna, pasta, cheese, pepper, celery, and chives, if using, until well coated with the dressing.
- Serve chilled.

Yield: 24 (½-cup) servings

Calories: 185; Fat: 2g (10% fat); Cholesterol: 19mg; Carbohydrate: 21g; Dietary Fiber: 1g; Protein: 19g; Sodium: 373mg

 Menu idea: This pasta salad is filling on its own. It can also serve as a side dish for a potluck or picnic.

Sausage Pasta Salad

The sausage gives this pasta salad a nice kick.

I (16-ounce) container fat-free sour cream	I (I-pound) package fat-free shredded cheddar cheese
3/4 cup fat-free whipped salad dressing	I cup red sweet pepper, chopped into tiny pieces, about I medium pepper
2 to 3 teaspoons Durkee Salad Seasoning	I cup chopped celery, about 3 ribs
14 to 16 ounces fat-free smoked sausage, cut into bite-size pieces	2 tablespoons chopped chives, optional
I (I-pound) box ziti-style pasta, cooked as directed on box	

- In a large bowl mix together the sour cream, whipped dressing, and salad seasoning until well blended.
- Stir in the sausage, pasta, cheese, pepper, celery, and chives, if using, until well coated with the dressing.
- Serve chilled.

Yield: 24 (½-cup) servings

Calories: 157; Fat: 2g (10% fat); Cholesterol: 14mg; Carbohydrate: 22g; Dietary Fiber: 1g; Protein: 12g; Sodium: 434mg

 Menu idea: This pasta salad is filling on its own. It can also serve as a side dish for a potluck or picnic.

Mushroom-Asparagus Casserole

This definitely reminds me of old-time country cookin'.

3 (4-ounce) cans mushroom stems and pieces, drained	1/4 cup nonfat grated Parmesan cheese
5 (14 1/2-ounce) cans asparagus, drained	1/4 cup shredded nonfat mozzarella cheese
1 (12-ounce) jar home-style gravy (I use Heinz Blue Ribbon Country Flavor.)	

- Spray a two-quart casserole dish with nonfat cooking spray.
- Mix the mushrooms, asparagus, gravy, and Parmesan together in the casserole dish.
- Cover and cook in the microwave for 2 minutes. Stir and cook another 2 minutes.
- Sprinkle the top lightly with the mozzarella cheese.
- Cover and let sit several minutes before serving.
- Serve hot.

Note: The heat and moisture from the gravy and vegetables will soften the mozzarella cheese.

Yield: 18 ($\frac{1}{2}$-cup) servings

Calories: 35; Fat: 1g (21% fat); Cholesterol: 1mg; Carbohydrate: 5g; Dietary Fiber: 2g; Protein: 3g; Sodium: 438mg

Preparation time: 6 minutes or less
Cooking time: 4 minutes
Total time: 10 minutes or less

Menu ideas: This is good served with chicken Parmesan and garlic bread. It's large enough to serve for big gatherings such as potlucks and family get-togethers.

Oriental Vegetables

These vegetables give any lean cooked red meat an oriental flair, especially when you serve them with rice.

1	teaspoon garlic salt	1	(12-ounce) jar home-style gravy
2	pounds frozen oriental vegetables	1	tablespoon Splenda
		2	tablespoons soy sauce

- In a large Dutch oven or big saucepan dissolve the garlic salt in 1½ inches of water. Put the oriental vegetables in the water. The oriental vegetables will not be covered with water.
- Bring the water to a full boil.
- Turn off the heat. Cover and let sit for 10 to 12 minutes or until the vegetables are fully steamed to desired tenderness.
- Stir the gravy, Splenda, and soy sauce together in serving dish bowl. No need to heat. The heat from the cooked vegetables will heat the sauce.
- Drain the water from the vegetables. Stir the vegetables with the sauce.
- Serve hot.

Yield: 8 servings

Calories: 55; Fat: 1g (9% fat); Cholesterol: 0mg; Carbohydrate: 11g; Dietary Fiber: 2g; Protein: 4g; Sodium: 986mg

Preparation time: 7 minutes or less
Cooking time: 10 to 12 minutes
Total time: 19 minutes or less

Menu ides: Super as a side dish or add pork for a scrumptious entrée. This vegetable dish is a perfect accompaniment for the Shrimp Rice Casserole (page 170).

Twice Baked Potatoes

This recipe is also from Paula Kamler from Joplin, Missouri.

1	large baking potato	$^1/_2$ teaspoon buttermilk ranch dressing mix, dry
1	slice fat-free cheese	
2	tablespoons fat-free sour cream	1 tablespoon bacon bits
1	tablespoon Butter Buds, dry	

- Bake the potato in the microwave for approximately 3 to 4 minutes. Make sure you poke it with a fork a few times so it won't explode when cooking.
- Open and scoop the potato out of the shell.
- Mix the potato together with the cheese, sour cream, Butter Buds, and ranch dressing mix and put back into the skin.
- Microwave about 20 seconds and sprinkle with the bacon bits.

Yield: 1 serving

Calories: 321; Fat: 3g (6% fat); Cholesterol: 10mg; Carbohydrate: 89g; Dietary Fiber: 7g; Protein: 17g; Sodium: 922mg

Preparation time: 4 minutes or less
Cooking time: 3 to 4 minutes
Total time: 8 minutes or less

Menu ideas: Good for lunch with a salad. Also good with any meaty entrée such as lean sirloin steak, lean pork tenderloin, or chicken breast. Serve with a salad or cup of broth-based vegetable soup for a well-rounded meal.

Spiced Apples

This is an all-American heartland favorite.

4	Jonathan apples with skins on, sliced into $1/8$-inch slices	I	teaspoon ground cinnamon
2	tablespoons Butter Buds Sprinkles	$1/4$	cup dark brown sugar

- In a 1-quart microwavable casserole dish toss together the apple slices, Sprinkles, cinnamon, and sugar until well mixed.
- Cover with wax paper and cook on high in a carousel* microwave for 4 minutes.

*Note: If you don't have a microwave with a carousel, turn the apples a couple times during cooking.

Yield: 4 servings

Calories: 144; Fat: 1g (3% fat); Cholesterol: 0mg; Carbohydrate: 37g; Dietary Fiber: 4g; Protein: 0g; Sodium: 36mg

Preparation time: 5 minutes or less
Cooking time: 4 minutes
Total time: 9 minutes or less

Menu idea: This is delicious as a dessert served over fat-free vanilla ice cream or topped with a dab of fat-free whipped topping.

Mashed Potatoes and Carrots

This recipe is old-fashioned comfort food.

5	medium potatoes, cooked and skins removed	1/3	cup fat-free butter spread
1	(14 1/2-ounce) can sliced carrots, drained	1/3	cup fat-free chicken broth
		1/2	teaspoon celery salt

- In a medium-size mixing bowl break up the potatoes.
- Add the carrots, butter spread, broth, and celery salt to the potatoes.
- With a mixer on low, beat for 3 to 4 minutes or until creamy smooth. If needed, add more chicken broth. Note: There may be some lumps.
- Reheat in microwave for 3 to 5 minutes or until hot.

Yield: 7 servings

Calories: 95 ; Fat: 0g (0% fat); Cholesterol: 0mg; Carbohydrate: 23g; Dietary Fiber: 3g; Protein: 3g; Sodium: 292mg

Preparation time: 20 minutes or less
Cooking time: 3 to 5 minutes
Total time: 25 minutes or less

Menu ideas: This side dish tastes great with any chicken, ham, or steak entrée.

"B.B.B." (Best Baked Beans)

My daughters loved these so much that they named the recipe themselves. They are very filling, satisfying, and delicious. No one would ever believe they're fat-free. Eat as a meal or side dish. A fun way to serve these when they're the entrée is with a pie pan as the plate.

1	pound package ground meatless (I use Morningstar Farms.) or 1 pound cooked ground eye of round	2	(16-ounce) cans vegetarian baked beans fat-free
1	(15-ounce) can butter beans, drained	3/4	cup thick-and-spicy, brown-sugar-flavored barbecue sauce
		1/2	cup chopped onion, fresh or chopped frozen onions

Microwave:
- Spray a large microwavable bowl with nonfat cooking spray.
- In the bowl combine the ground meatless, butter beans, baked beans, barbecue sauce, and onions until well mixed.
- Cover and cook on high for 5 minutes.

Slow Cooker:
- Spray a slow cooker with nonfat cooking spray.
- In the cooker combine the ground meatless, butter beans, baked beans, barbecue sauce, and onions until well mixed.
- Cover and cook on low for 4 hours.

*Note: With the meat substitute this is wonderful. For those of you who don't like vegetarian meat substitute, it's good with beef, too.

Yield: 16 ($\frac{1}{2}$-cup) servings

(with ground meatless) Calories: 125; Fat: 0g (0% fat); Cholesterol: 0mg; Carbohydrate: 20g; Dietary Fiber: 5g; Protein: 12g; Sodium: 550mg
(with ground eye of round) Calories: 113; Fat: 1g (11% fat); Cholesterol: 15mg; Carbohydrate: 16g; Dietary Fiber: 3g; Protein: 10g; Sodium: 403mg

Preparation time: using ground meatless, 6 minutes or less
Cooking time: Varies depending on cooking method

Menu idea: This is a great side dish for any cookout or potluck.

Home-Style Green Beans and Potatoes

This simple side dish is a delicious way to get two for one—two vegetables in one dish.

2 (15-ounce) cans green beans, drained	2 tablespoons bacon bits
3 cooked red potatoes with skin on, cut into 1/2-inch cubes	1/8 teaspoon garlic salt, optional
2 tablespoons fat-free butter spread	Dash of pepper, optional

- Mix the green beans, potatoes, butter spread, and bacon bits in a medium-size microwavable bowl until well mixed.
- Cover and cook on high in a carousel* microwave for 3 to 4 minutes.

*Note: If you don't have a carousel, turn the bowl a couple times during cooking.

Yield: 6 servings

Calories: 70; Fat: 0g (0% fat); Cholesterol: 0mg; Carbohydrate: 15g; Dietary Fiber: 3g; Protein: 3g; Sodium: 334mg

Preparation time: 5 minutes or less
Cooking time: 4 minutes or less
Total time: 9 minutes or less

Menu ideas: This side dish tastes excellent with any chicken, ham, or steak entrée.

Zesty Corn

This dish will put a smile on your face and have your family asking for seconds.

1 (16-ounce) can cream-style yellow corn	1 cup chunky salsa
1 (16-ounce) can corn (white or yellow), drained	

- Over medium heat stir the two corns and salsa together until well mixed.
- Bring to a boil. Or cook in microwave 3 to 4 minutes until hot.
- Serve hot.

Yield: 8 servings

Calories: 82; Fat: 1g (6% fat); Cholesterol: 0mg; Carbohydrate: 19g; Dietary Fiber: 1g; Protein: 2g; Sodium: 428mg

Preparation time: 3 minutes or less
Cooking time: 5 minutes or less
Total time: 8 minutes or less

Menu ideas: Great with meat entrées, such as chicken, turkey, fish, lean beef, or pork tenderloin.

Hawaiian-Style Baked Beans

A delicious twist to an old-time favorite that is packed with protein.

2 (16-ounce) cans vegetarian baked beans	4 ounces extra lean, cooked ham, cut into bite-size pieces
1/4 cup chopped onion, fresh or frozen	1 (8-ounce) can crushed unsweetened pineapple, drained
1/4 cup teriyaki baste and glaze (I use Kikkoman.)	

Microwave:
- Spray a large microwavable bowl with nonfat cooking spray.
- Mix all the ingredients in the microwavable bowl.
- Cover and microwave on high for 3 minutes or until heated.

Stovetop:
- Spray a large saucepan with nonfat cooking spray.
- Mix all the ingredients in the saucepan.
- Bring to a boil, turn off the heat, and let it simmer for 3 to 4 minutes.

Slow cooker:
- Spray the slow cooker with nonfat cooking spray.
- In the cooker combine all the ingredients.
- Cook on low for 4 hours.

Yield: 11 (½ cup) side-dish servings

Calories: 112; Fat: 1g (7% fat); Cholesterol: 5mg; Carbohydrate: 22g; Dietary Fiber: 4g; Protein: 6g; Sodium: 622mg

Preparation time: 5 minutes or less
Cooking time: Varies depending on cooking method

Menu ideas: These are great as a meal served with Sassy Slaw (page 91) and celery sticks with fat-free dressing for dipping.

Entrées

The person who succeeds is the person who perseveres and keeps on trying.

Apricot Chicken and Rice   171

Au Gratin Casserole Dinner   177

Beanie Baby Stew   197

Beef and Broccoli Skillet Casserole   173

Beef and Potatoes with Mushroom and Onion Gravy   200

Beef Stroganoff   165

Breaded Pork Tenderloins   184

California Medley Stew   194

Caribbean Rice   195

Chicken & Green Bean Casserole   159

Chicken and Potato Stew   192

Chicken Asparagus Casserole   156

Chicken Cheesey Pizza   178

Chicken Fettuccine   152

Chicken Nuggets   141

Chicken (or Turkey) Casserole   180

Cinnamon-Kissed Chicken   144

Christmas Chicken & Rice Dinner   185

Cowboy Chow   190

Cowboy Grub (Casserole)   154

Creamed Peppery Chicken   143

Dilled Pork Steaks   162

Eight-Layer Chili Casserole   182

Farmer's Casserole   188

Ham & Cabbage Dinner   198

Ham Kebabs   164

Harvest Ham Steaks   142

Hearty Barbecue Skillet Dinner   175

Herbed Beef Tenderloin with Seasoned Potatoes & Buttered Mushrooms   196

Honey Mustard Chicken   145

Lemon Pepper Pork Tenderloin with Lemon-Kissed Potatoes   199

Manhandler Meatloaves   186

Mexicali Chicken Burritos   150

Mexican Casserole   169

Mexican Goulash   155

Mexican Pasta   149

Mexican Pizza   179

Mexican Pork Tenderloin with Rice   174

Mexican-Style Spaghetti   163

Orange Roughy   151

Pasta with Creamy Clam Sauce   153

Pizza Burritos   157

Potato Puffs   176

Presto Ham Casserole   166

Presto Poultry Casserole   168

Presto Sausage Casserole   167

Quickie Meal   183

Sausage (or Ham) Casserole   181

Shrimp Rice Casserole   170

Smothered Steak   193

Southwestern Fiesta   161

Spanish Tomatoes and Beef   146

Spicy Ricey Vegetarian Dinner   147

Steak & Potatoes Stir-Fry   158

Sweet & Sassy Entrée   160

Swiss Steak and Potatoes   189

Zesty Sausage Sandwiches   148

Zesty Sausage Skillet Dinner   172

Chicken Nuggets

My homemade version of chicken nuggets is a lot less fattening than that at fast food restaurants and just as tasty. A serving of these homemade babies have less fat than one little nugget at Mickey Ds. Wow!

1 (6-ounce) box of stuffing, any flavor (I use the corn bread flavor.)	4 egg whites 1¹/2 pounds boneless, skinless chicken breasts, all fat removed

- Preheat the oven to 425 degrees.
- Cover a cookie sheet with foil. Spray the foil with nonfat cooking spray.
- On high speed in a blender or food processor, grind the breadcrumbs and seasoning mix from stuffing for 30 seconds. Pour into a shallow bowl.
- Beat the egg whites in a blender or food processor for 15 seconds. Pour into a shallow bowl.
- Cut the chicken into nuggets.
- With a fork take the pieces of chicken, one at a time, and dip them into the ground crumbs. Dip into the egg whites. Dip again into the breadcrumbs.
- Place the prepared chicken nuggets on the cookie sheet.
- Bake for 15 minutes, and then turn the nuggets over. Bake for an additional 5 minutes.
- Serve with mustard, barbecue sauce, sweet and sour sauce, or your favorite fat-free salad dressing for dipping.

Yield: 6 (4-ounce) servings

Calories: 247; Fat: 2g (9% fat); Cholesterol: 66mg; Carbohydrate: 21g; Dietary Fiber: 1g; Protein: 32g; Sodium: 627mg

Preparation time: 15 minutes or less
Cooking time: 20 minutes
Total time: 35 minutes or less

Menu idea: These are good with Bacon, Lettuce, and Tomato Salad (page 96), Broccoli Parmesan (page 124), and light fruit cocktail.

Harvest Ham Steaks

A lip smackin' and toe tappin' creative way to use apple butter in a tasty entrée.

4	(4-ounce) ham steaks	8	teaspoons apple butter

- Spray a grill or skillet with nonfat cooking spray.
- Heat the grill to medium.
- Put the ham steaks on the grill.
- Spread 1 teaspoon of your favorite apple butter on top of each ham steak while on the grill.
- After turning the ham steak over, spread a second teaspoon of apple butter on top of each steak.
- Once bottom of ham steak is cooked, turn steak over a second time. Cook only for a couple of minutes, just enough to caramelize the apple butter.
- Serve right away.

Note: Leftover steaks taste great as cold ham sandwiches.

Note: I use extra lean ham that has 4 grams of fat per 4-ounce serving and 100 calories.

Yield: 4 (4-ounce) servings

Calories: 169; Fat: 6g (30% fat); Cholesterol: 53mg; Carbohydrate: 6g; Dietary Fiber: 0g; Protein: 22g; Sodium: 1621mg

🕐 **Cooking time:** 10 minutes or less

Menu idea: Serve these steaks with Home-Style Green Beans & Potatoes (page 135), Sassy Slaw (page 91), fat-free bread with apple butter, and Peaches & Cream Trifle (page 255) for dessert.

Creamed Peppery Chicken

This peppery chicken is as delicious as it is easy to make.

4 boneless skinless chicken breasts with fat removed, approximately 1 pound Ground black pepper	1 (8-ounce) container fat-free sour cream

- Sprinkle the chicken breasts with pepper to taste.
- In a large non-stick skillet that has been sprayed with nonfat cooking spray, cook the chicken breasts, covered, over medium heat for 4 to 5 minutes.
- Turn the pieces over and reduce the heat to low.
- Put the sour cream on top of the chicken and in the middle of the pan.
- Cover and continue cooking for 4 to 5 minutes or until completely cooked and the chicken is white all through. The sour cream will absorb the pepper flavor.

Yield: 4 servings

Calories: 187; Fat: 1g (7% fat); Cholesterol: 75mg; Carbohydrate: 11g; Dietary Fiber: 0g; Protein: 30g; Sodium: 118mg

Preparation time: 5 minutes
Cooking time: 10 minutes or less
Total time: 15 minutes or less

Menu ideas: This is excellent served on a toasted bun as a sandwich or over pasta or rice. Or serve alone as an entrée with Mashed Potatoes Deluxe (page 119), Sensational Sweet Potato Casserole (page 123) or Garlic Red Skins (page 117) and a tossed salad.

Cinnamon-Kissed Chicken

This lightly sweetened chicken has a touch of orange and cinnamon flavor.

1/2	teaspoon ground cinnamon	1 pound skinless, boneless chicken breasts, cut into 1/2-inch-wide x 4-inch-long strips
1	tablespoon dark brown sugar	
1	teaspoon fresh orange zest*	
1/2	cup red wine vinegar salad dressing	

- In a large non-stick skillet mix the cinnamon, brown sugar, orange peel slivers, and salad dressing together.
- Add the chicken pieces and cook over medium heat for 3 to 4 minutes.
- Turn the chicken pieces over and cook an additional 2 to 3 minutes. Chicken will be white and not translucent when fully cooked.
- Serve warm.

*Note: To get orange zest, simply grate the peel of an orange with a vegetable peeler or paring knife. Use just the orange and not the white meaty part of the skin.

Yield: 4 servings

Calories: 154; Fat: 1g (9% fat); Cholesterol: 66mg; Carbohydrate: 7g; Dietary Fiber: 0g; Protein: 26g; Sodium: 485mg

Preparation time: 5 minutes
Cook time: 5 to 7 minutes
Total time: 15 minutes or less

Menu ideas: Eat as is or, if desired, pour the remaining sauce over cooked rice or baked sweet potatoes.

Honey Mustard Chicken

This dish is so simple, yet so scrumptious.

8	boneless, skinless chicken breasts, about 2 pounds	2	cups fat-free honey Dijon salad dressing

- Marinate the chicken in the salad dressing overnight or up to 2 days.
- Cook the chicken in a non-stick skillet or on a grill for 4 to 5 minutes over medium heat.
- Turn the chicken and continue cooking until the chicken is white in the center.
- In order to use the dressing you used as a marinade as a dipping sauce, you must bring it to a boil. Boil for 1 minute. Turn off heat. Let cool.
- Serve on the side for dipping the chicken pieces.

Yield: 8 (4-ounce) servings

Calories: 215; Fat: 1g (6% fat); Cholesterol: 66mg; Carbohydrate: 20g; Dietary Fiber: 2g; Protein: 26g; Sodium: 734mg

Preparation time: 5 minutes or less (not including marinating time)
Cooking time: 10 minutes
Total time: 15 minutes or less

Menu idea: Serve this with Tangy Tossed Salad (page 95) and Corn Casserole (page 113).

Spanish Tomatoes and Beef

It doesn't get any easier than this, folks.

1 (16-ounce) package ground meatless (I use MorningStar Farms.)	1 (18-ounce) can tomato paste
	1 (16-ounce) jar chunky salsa
1 (11-ounce) can white shoe peg corn	1 1/2 cups instant rice
	Shredded, fat-free cheddar cheese, optional
4 cups water	

- Put the ground meatless, corn, water, tomato paste, salsa, and rice into a large non-stick Dutch oven over medium heat, stirring constantly until well mixed.
- Bring to a boil. Cover, turn off the heat, and let the mixture simmer for a couple of minutes.
- Divide between four bowls and sprinkle with the cheese, if desired.
- Presto! You're done.

Note: If desired, you can substitute 1 pound cooked ground turkey breast without the skin.

Yield: 4 servings

Calories: 511;Fat: 0g (0% fat); Cholesterol: 0mg; Carbohydrate: 77g; Dietary Fiber: 9g; Protein: 40g; Sodium: 1783mg

Preparation time: 5 minutes or less
Cooking time: 10 minutes
Total time: 15 minutes or less

Menu idea: This complete one-skillet meal tastes good accompanied with corn bread, tossed salad, or steamed broccoli.

Spicy Ricey Vegetarian Dinner

You won't miss the meat in this hearty meal.

3 cups vegetable broth	1/4 cup fat-free Italian dressing
1 1/2 cups chunky salsa	3 cups instant rice
1 (15-ounce) can three-bean chili	

- In a large saucepot bring the broth, salsa, chili, and dressing to a boil. Reduce the heat.
- Add the rice. Let sit for 5 minutes.
- Serve hot.

Yield: 4 entrée servings

Calories: 417; Fat: 0g (0% fat); Cholesterol: 0mg; Carbohydrate: 74g; Dietary Fiber: 6g; Protein: 15g; Sodium: 1122mg

Preparation time: 5 minutes or less
Cooking time: 10 minutes
Total time: 15 minutes or less

Menu ideas: Eat as is or wrap in a warm, soft-flour tortilla. Serve with fresh tossed salad.

Zesty Sausage Sandwiches

These zesty sandwiches are full of flavor. They are perfect for anyone who would like to add a little spice and zip to an old favorite.

I (14-ounce) package fat-free smoked sausage	8 tablespoons fat-free mozzarella cheese
8 tablespoons honey Dijon barbecue sauce	8 hot dog buns

- You should have a total of four sausages. Cut each in half lengthwise to give you eight halves.
- Cover and microwave the sausages together in a carousel microwave on high for 3 minutes or until completely heated.
- While the sausages are cooking, spread 1 tablespoon barbecue sauce on the insides of each bun.
- Sprinkle 1 tablespoon mozzarella cheese on each sandwich over the barbecue sauce.
- Remove the warmed sausages from the microwave and place one sausage in each bun with the barbecue sauce and cheese.
- Return to the microwave and reheat for approximately 1 minute, or until the cheese is melted. The moisture from the barbecue sauce and the juices from the sausage will prevent the cheese from being rubbery.

Yield: 8 servings

Calories: 182; Fat: 0g (0% fat); Cholesterol: 23mg; Carbohydrate: 32g; Dietary Fiber: 1g; Protein: 13g; Sodium: 1062mg

Preparation time: 6 minutes or less
Cooking time: 4 minutes
Total time: 10 minutes or less

Menu ideas: During cold weather months, serve with a tomato soup and Angel Fluff (page 240). For warm weather serve with Zesty Summer Cottage Salad (page 88), Cucumber Dill Salad (page 90), or Orange Fluff (page 244) on top of sugar-free orange Jell-O.

Mexican Pasta

I hit gold when I created this. It's delicious hot as a main entrée or chilled as a pasta salad.

2 cups hot water
1 (16-ounce) jar chunky salsa
2 beef bouillon cubes
1 (8-ounce) box or 2 cups Mueller's brand elbow macaroni
1 (8-ounce) can whole kernel corn
1 (8-ounce) can kidney beans

- In a large non-stick skillet over high heat bring the water, salsa, and bouillon to a boil.
- Stir in the macaroni. Reduce the heat to low.
- Cover. Let simmer at a low boil for 10 minutes.
- Turn off the heat. Stir in the corn and beans.
- Cover. Let sit, covered, with the heat off for 2 minutes longer.

Yield: 6 (1-cup) servings

Calories: 214; Fat: 1g (5% fat); Cholesterol: 0mg; Carbohydrate: 41g; Dietary Fiber: 3g; Protein: 7g; Sodium: 765mg

Total time: 13 to 15 minutes

Menu ideas: Serve this as a hot entrée with a tossed salad, pita bread, and Jell-O or fruit salad. Also terrific to take to potlucks or chilled as a pasta salad.

Mexicali Chicken Burritos

I converted this high-fat recipe sent in by Grace Du Prey of California into a low-fat favorite made quickly.

1	pound boneless, skinless chicken breasts, all visible fat removed	1	(3-ounce) package fat-free cream cheese
1	(15-ounce) can beef chili	1/4	cup chunky mild salsa
		4	ounces shredded cheddar cheese
		8	fat-free flour tortillas

- In a large non-stick skillet cook the chicken over medium-high heat for 3 to 4 minutes.
- Turn the chicken over, and cook an additional 3 to 4 minutes or until fully cooked.
- Remove the chicken and cut it into $\frac{1}{4}$-inch-wide strips. Then cut the strips into $\frac{1}{2}$-inch lengths.
- Return the chicken to the skillet.
- Add the chili, cream cheese, and salsa and place over medium-low heat. Stir constantly until the cream cheese is completely dissolved.
- Sprinkle with the cheddar cheese.
- Cover and cook on medium-low for 2 to 3 minutes.
- Warm the tortillas by microwaving for 30 seconds.
- Divide the chicken mixture among the tortillas and roll them up.

Yield: 8 burritos

Calories: 252; Fat: 2g (6% fat); Cholesterol: 37mg; Carbohydrate: 32g; Dietary Fiber: 3g; Protein: 26g; Sodium: 668mg

Preparation time: 5 minutes
Cooking time: 15 minutes or less
Total time: 20 minutes or less

Menu ideas: Serve over cooked rice or with warm flour tortillas with taco sauce on the side. Also great with Mexican Chicken Salad (page 80).

Orange Roughy

This fish dish was submitted by Mable Jackson, one of my assistants.

1	pound orange roughy fillets	1	tablespoon Butter Buds, dry
1	medium onion	1/4	cup plain breadcrumbs
1	teaspoon lemon pepper		

- Spray a skillet with nonfat cooking spray and place the fillets in the skillet over medium heat.
- Slice the onion into thin strips and place them on top of the fish.
- Sprinkle just a little bit of lemon pepper evenly on top of the fish along with a few sprinkles of Butter Buds.
- Cook for 7 minutes. Turn over and cook for an additional 3 to 5 minutes. About the last 3 to 4 minutes of cooking time, sprinkle with the breadcrumbs.
- Fillets will be cooked when completely white throughout and they flake when cut with a fork.

Yield: 3 servings

Calories: 161; Fat: 2g (9% fat); Cholesterol: 30mg; Carbohydrate: 11g; Dietary Fiber: 1g; Protein: 24g; Sodium: 301mg

Preparation time: 5 minutes
Cooking time: 15 minutes or less, depending on thickness of fish
Total time: 20 minutes or less

Menu ideas: Delicious served with Garlic Red Skins (page 117), Spring Asparagus (page 118) or Tropical Passion Fruit Salad (page 89).

Chicken Fettuccine

Now this is some good eatin'.

I	(12-ounce) box fettuccine noodles	2	(26 1/2-ounce) jars spaghetti sauce with mushrooms
1 1/2	pounds boneless, skinless chicken breasts, cut into bite-size pieces		Nonfat grated Parmesan cheese, optional

- Cook the pasta as directed on the box.
- Over medium heat cook the chicken pieces in a large non-stick skillet until all pieces are fully cooked. The chicken will be completely white when fully cooked.
- Add the spaghetti sauce. Heat for about 4 to 5 minutes or until completely heated.
- Serve over hot pasta. If desired sprinkle with the Parmesan cheese.

Note: This dish is delicious reheated in the microwave. Simply stir the sauce in with the pasta and freeze or refrigerate until ready to use.

Yield: 8 (1-cup) servings

Calories: 289; Fat: 2g (7% fat); Cholesterol: 49mg; Carbohydrate: 39g; Dietary Fiber: 7g; Protein: 27g; Sodium: 518mg

Preparation time: 10 minutes
Cooking time: 20 minutes or less
Total time: 30 minutes or less

Menu idea: This is terrific served with a tossed salad, Green Beans Italiano (page 116), and Garlic Toast (page 61).

Pasta with Creamy Clam Sauce

This warm, satisfying, and delicious dish is perfect for making you feel all snugly and cozy on a chilly day.

1 (14^1/2-ounce) can fat-free, low-sodium chicken broth	1 (6^1/2-ounce) can minced clams, not drained
2 (2.8-ounce) packages chicken-flavor, baked Ramen noodle soup—Do not make as directed on package.	2 teaspoons minced garlic
	2 tablespoons fat-free margarine
	^{1}/4 cup cornstarch
	^{1}/2 cup skim milk

- In large saucepan bring the chicken broth to a boil. It will take about 3 minutes on high heat .
- Break the noodles into small pieces and drop them into the broth.
- Add the clams, garlic, and margarine. Simmer 3 minutes, stirring occasionally.
- While the noodles are cooking, in a small bowl dissolve the cornstarch in the milk by briskly stirring with a fork. Once the noodles are done, reduce the heat to low.
- Add the seasoning packets from the noodles and stir the milk/cornstarch mixture into the broth and noodles. Keep stirring until thick and creamy, about 2 to 3 minutes.
- Serve hot.

Yield: 4$\frac{1}{2}$ (1-cup) servings

Calories: 233; Fat: 1g (4% fat); Cholesterol: 16mg; Carbohydrate: 45g; Dietary Fiber: 1g; Protein: 10g; Sodium: 1327mg

Preparation time: 6 minutes or less
Cooking time: 9 minutes or less
Total time: 15 minutes or less

Menu idea: For a full meal serve this with steamed asparagus, crackers or French bread, and slices of fresh melon.

Cowboy Grub (Casserole)

This casserole is for the meat and potato lover and those who love barbecue. For extra fun serve on pie pans instead of plates.

1 **pound eye of round beef roast or steaks, cut into 1/4-inch cubes**	1/2 **cup chopped onion or frozen chopped onion for easier use**
1 **pound quick-cooking, shredded hash browns**	1/2 **cup brown sugar barbecue sauce**

- Spray a large non-stick skillet with nonfat cooking spray.
- Turn the heat on medium high.
- Place the meat on the bottom of the pan. Cover and cook for 3 to 4 minutes or until brown on the bottom.
- Turn the meat over and top with shredded hash browns and onion.
- Cover and cook 3 to 4 minutes or until the meat is no longer pink.
- Stir the entire dish. Cover and cook an additional 3 to 4 minutes, stirring occasionally.
- Turn the heat down to low. Add the barbecue sauce. Gently stir until well mixed.
- Serve immediately.

Note: You may substitute pork tenderloin for the beef.

Yield: 4 (10-ounce) servings

(with beef) Calories: 274; Fat: 6g (21% fat); Cholesterol: 61mg; Carbohydrate: 26g; Dietary Fiber: 2g; Protein: 28g; Sodium: 340mg
(with pork) Calories: 260; Fat: 5g (18% fat); Cholesterol: 74mg; Carbohydrate: 26g; Dietary Fiber: 2g; Protein: 27g; Sodium: 337mg

Preparation time: 3 minutes (derived from cutting meat into chunks)
Cooking time: 12 minutes or less
Total time: 15 minutes or less

Menu idea: Serve with Garlic Toast (page 61) and a tossed salad along with Crunchy Cucumbers with Cream (page 82).

Mexican Goulash

This flavorful dish is high in protein and flavor.

1 (15-ounce) can fat-free chili (I use Hormel turkey chili.)	1½ cups salsa
1 (16-ounce) can fat-free refried beans	4 ounces fat-free, shredded cheddar cheese
1 (12-ounce) can whole kernel corn, drained	5 (10-inch) flour tortillas

- Mix the chili, beans, corn, salsa, and cheese together until well blended.
- Spray a 2½-quart round microwavable casserole dish with a lid with nonfat cooking spray.
- Lay 1 tortilla flat on the bottom of the casserole dish.
- Top with one-fifth of the chili mixture.
- Continue layering the tortillas and chili mixture until all the ingredients are used.
- Cover and microwave on high in a carousel microwave for 10 minutes. If you don't have a carousel microwave rotate dish a ¼ turn every 2½ minutes to cook evenly.
- Let sit, covered, an additional 5 minutes before serving. Using a sharp knife (a steak knife works well) cut through all layers, making a checker board design on top. Each cut will be about one inch apart. The cut-up tortillas will taste a lot like pasta when the recipe is finished.
- With a large spoon stir the entire dish to mix the cut-up tortilla pieces. Serve in soup bowls.
- Sprinkle lightly with fat-free cheddar cheese, if desired.

Yield: 8 servings

Calories: 232; Fat: 2g (7% fat); Cholesterol: 7mg; Carbohydrate: 42g; Dietary Fiber: 7g; Protein: 11g; Sodium: 968mg

 **Preparation time:** 5 minutes or less
Cooking time: 10 minutes
Total time: 15 minutes or less

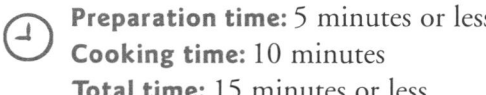 **Menu idea:** This is great with Mexican Chicken Salad (page 80) and corn bread.

Chicken Asparagus Casserole

This is great for a delicious, one-skillet casserole that is complete enough to eat as a meal by itself.

1 pound boneless, skinless chicken breasts, all visible fat removed	2 cups instant rice
1 (14½-ounce) can fat-free chicken broth	1 (14½-ounce) can asparagus, drained, or French-style cut green beans
¼ cup hot water	1 (10¾-ounce) can 98% fat-free cream of chicken soup
½ teaspoon dried thyme	

- In a large non-stick skillet cook the chicken breasts in the chicken broth and water over medium-high heat for 3 minutes, covered.
- Turn the chicken over and cook an additional 3 minutes, covered.
- Remove chicken breast and cut the chicken into ¼-inch thick strips. Return them to the broth.
- Reduce the heat to very low. Stir in the thyme and rice, making sure they are covered in broth.
- Gently stir in the drained asparagus and soup, stirring until well mixed. Do *not* cover. Continue cooking on low for 3 more minutes to thicken the sauce.
- Turn off the heat and let cool for a couple of minutes before serving.

Yield: 4 servings

Calories: 370; Fat: 4g (11% fat); Cholesterol: 75mg; Carbohydrate: 45g; Dietary Fiber: 2g; Protein: 35g; Sodium: 1123mg

Preparation time: 10 minutes
Cooking time: 15 minutes or less
Total time: 25 minutes or less

Menu ideas: A complete meal in itself. However, if desired, serve with a dinner roll and either fruit cocktail or frozen yogurt with sliced fruit.

Pizza Burritos

I hit a home run when I created these. All my fans (my family) cheer for more.

1	(16-ounce) can fat-free refried beans	1	(8-ounce) package fat-free mozzarella cheese
2	(14-ounce) jars pizza sauce	20	(10-inch) fat-free tortillas

- In a medium-size bowl mix the refried beans, pizza sauce, and cheese. Stir until well mixed.
- To soften, put the stack of tortilla shells in a carousel microwave on high for 1 minute.
- Take 1 tortilla and put 2 heaping tablespoons of the above mixture into the center.
- Roll up the tortilla and place in the microwave for 10 seconds.
- If desired, you can make numerous pizza burritos and multiply the number of burritos you have by 10 seconds each to figure out cooking time.

Yield: 20 servings

Calories: 215; Fat: 1g (2% fat); Cholesterol: 2mg; Carbohydrate: 41g; Dietary Fiber: 5g; Protein: 11g; Sodium: 900mg

Preparation time: 5 minutes
Cooking time: 5 to 7 minutes
Total time: 12 minutes or less

Menu idea: This goes well with salsa and fat-free tortilla chips, tossed salad, and frozen yogurt topped with fruit.

Steak & Potatoes Stir-Fry

This hearty stick-to-your-ribs-but-not-your-arteries dish will satisfy any meat-and-potatoes lover.

1	pound frozen, home-style, diced, quick-cooking potatoes (make sure the potatoes are pre-cooked)	1	(15-ounce) can whole kernel corn with juices, drained
1	pound beef tenderloin, fully cooked and cut into tiny pieces	1	teaspoon garlic salt
		1/2	teaspoon pepper, optional
		1/4	cup chopped fresh chives
		3	tablespoons fat-free margarine

- Spray a large non-stick skillet with nonfat cooking spray.
- Cook the potatoes on medium-high heat for approximately 5 to 6 minutes, without stirring, to brown. Turn the potatoes over and continue cooking until golden brown.
- Add the cooked beef, corn, garlic salt, pepper, chives, and margarine. Continue cooking until fully heated, approximately 3 to 4 minutes.

Yield: 5 servings

Calories: 316; Fat: 10g (28% fat); Cholesterol: 76mg; Carbohydrate: 28g; Dietary Fiber: 3g; Protein: 29g; Sodium: 627mg

Preparation time: less than 5 minutes
Cooking time: 10 minutes
Total time: 15 minutes or less

Menu ideas: You may want to serve ketchup or steak sauce on the side. Whole-wheat toast is a good accompaniment. Add a green vegetable as a side dish, and you have a complete meal.

Chicken & Green Bean Casserole

This one-skillet casserole dinner is just what the doctor ordered to fill your "I'm hungry, I'm tired, and I don't feel like cooking" hard-day blues.

1 **pound boneless, skinless chicken breasts or chicken breast pieces**	1 **($10^3/4$-ounce) can 98% fat-free cream of mushroom soup (add $1/2$ can water)**
2 **(15-ounce) cans green beans**	12 **reduced-fat crackers, crushed**
1 **chicken bouillon cube**	**Light soy sauce, optional**
1 **cup instant rice**	
1 **(4-ounce) package fresh sliced mushrooms**	

- Spray a large non-stick skillet with nonfat cooking spray.
- In the skillet on medium-high heat cook the chicken until the bottom is golden brown on both sides.
- Remove the chicken from the skillet.
- Pour 1 cup of liquid from the cans of beans into the skillet.
- Dissolve the chicken bouillon cube in the bean juice in the skillet.
- Add the rice to the juice and arrange the mushrooms on top of the rice.
- Drain the beans and arrange them on top of the mushrooms.
- Put the cooked chicken on top of the beans. Pour the can of mushroom soup over the casserole. Cover, turn off the heat, and let stand 5 minutes.
- Gently stir. Turn the heat back on to low and cook an additional 5 minutes. Sprinkle the crushed crackers on top of the casserole.
- Serve immediately with light soy sauce on the side, if desired.

Yield: 4 servings

Calories: 316; Fat: 3g (10% fat); Cholesterol: 66mg; Carbohydrate: 38g; Dietary Fiber: 3g; Protein: 33g; Sodium: 1096 mg

Preparation time: 5 minutes or less
Cooking time: 15 minutes
Total time: 20 minutes or less

Menu idea: A meal in itself. If desired, for dessert serve Black Forest Tortilla Stack (page 211).

Sweet & Sassy Entrée

If you like sweet and sour dishes, you'll like this one. Sometimes sweet and sour sauces can be sickeningly sweet and thick, but this one is perfect. The sauce combined with the pasta and vegetables is a twist my family really likes. This would be good with shrimp also, or eliminate the chicken for an excellent vegetarian entrée.

$^1/2$ cup fat-free raspberry salad dressing (I use T. Marzetti.)

1 teaspoon onion salt

$^1/2$ cup chicken broth

4 (4-ounce) skinless, boneless, honey-mustard-flavored chicken breasts, cut into bite-size pieces (or use chicken marinated in fat-free honey mustard salad dressing)

8 cups frozen vegetable and pasta combination (I use Flav-R-Pac brand: asparagus and linguine stir-fry with vegetable blend.)

- In a large non-stick skillet combine the salad dressing, onion salt and chicken broth together over medium heat until the salad dressing is dissolved.
- Increase the heat to medium-high. Add the chicken and vegetables.
- Cook for 7 to 9 minutes, stirring occasionally.

Yield: 4 (2$^1/2$-cup) servings

Calories: 368; Fat: 12g (28% fat); Cholesterol: 44mg; Carbohydrate: 44g; Dietary Fiber: 2g; Protein: 24g; Sodium: 1988mg

Preparation time: 5 minutes or less
Cooking time: 10 minutes or less
Total time: 15 minutes or less

Menu idea: Add Garlic Toast (page 61) and you have a complete meal.

Southwestern Fiesta

This recipe is an excellent source of protein.

1 pound ground turkey breast without skin	4 cups tomato sauce or tomato juice
1 (1¹/4-ounce) package taco seasoning mix	1 (15-ounce) can black beans, drained
2 cups salsa	2 cups instant rice

- Spray a large non-stick soup pan or Dutch oven with nonfat cooking spray.
- Cook the turkey and taco seasoning mix together in the prepared pan over medium heat, until fully cooked.
- Add the salsa, tomato sauce, and black beans. Bring to a boil.
- Add the rice, making sure the rice is covered with liquid.
- Turn off the heat and stir.
- Cover and let sit for 5 minutes.

Yield: 8 (10-ounce) servings

Calories: 252; Fat: 1g (4% fat); Cholesterol: 39mg; Carbohydrate: 38g; Dietary Fiber: 4g; Protein: 19g; Sodium: 1575mg

Yield: 26 (3-ounce) servings

Calories: 78; Fat: 0.5g (4% fat); Cholesterol: 12mg; Carbohydrate: 12g; Dietary Fiber: 1g; Protein: 6g; Sodium: 485mg

Preparation time: 5 minutes
Cooking time: 15 minutes or less
Total time: 20 minutes or less

Menu ideas: Eat as a main dish or as a dip. As a dip, serve with tortilla chips and fat-free sour cream. Some people like to sprinkle fat-free fancy shredded cheddar cheese on top. As a main dish, serve as is or wrapped in a warm, soft-flour tortilla. Add a fresh green salad.

Dilled Pork Steaks

These steaks are a creative way to quickly prepare a special and mouth-watering meal.

1 cup juice from dill pickles	Dried dill, optional
2 pounds pork tenderloin* with all visible fat removed, cut into steaks to make 8 (¹/4- pound) steaks	

- Marinate the steaks overnight in the pickle juice.
- Remove the meat from the marinade and discard the juice.
- Cook the steaks on a grill or in a non-stick skillet for 4 to 5 minutes. Turn over and continue cooking until the center is no longer pink.
- Sprinkle with dried dill before serving if desired.

Note: For dilled chicken or turkey steaks, substitute 2 pounds boneless, skinless chicken breast or turkey breast.

Yield: 8 (¹/4-pound) steaks

(Pork steaks) Calories: 132; Fat: 4g (28% fat); Cholesterol: 63mg; Carbohydrate: 0g; Dietary Fiber: 0g; Protein: 23g; Sodium: 107mg
(Chicken steaks) Calories: 126; Fat: 1g (11% fat); Cholesterol: 66mg; Carbohydrate: 0g; Dietary Fiber: 0g; Protein: 26g; Sodium: 198mg
(Turkey steaks) Calories: 127; Fat: 1g (8% fat); Cholesterol: 77mg; Carbohydrate: 0g; Dietary Fiber: 0g; Protein: 27g; Sodium: 174mg

Preparation time: 5 minutes
Cooking time: 10 minutes or less
Total time: 15 minutes or less

Menu ideas: Serve these steaks with Sassy Slaw (page 91), Corn Casserole (page 113), Sensational Sweet Potato Casserole (page 123), or Spring Asparagus (page 118).

Mexican Style Spaghetti

Sauce is boss in this creative combination. It's definitely a zesty twist to an old-time favorite.

16	ounces thin spaghetti, dry	4	ounces shredded fat-free cheddar cheese
1	(16-ounce) jar thick and chunky salsa	4	ounces fat-free shredded mozzarella cheese
2	(26-ounce) jars extra chunky garlic and onions pasta sauce		

- Cook the spaghetti as directed on the package. Drain.
- While the spaghetti is cooking, heat the salsa and pasta sauce together in a large saucepan over medium heat until it comes to a low boil. Reduce the heat. Simmer until spaghetti is done.
- Pour the sauce over the spaghetti. Sprinkle with both cheeses.
- Serve immediately.

Note: Do not overcook the sauce. All you need to do is heat the sauce. If you overcook it, the chunks will disappear.

Yield: 8 servings

Calories: 336; Fat: 1g (3% fat); Cholesterol: 4mg; Carbohydrate: 59g; Dietary Fiber: 5g; Protein: 19g; Sodium: 1134mg

Preparation time: 3 minutes
Cooking time: 10 minutes or less
Total time: 13 minutes or less

Menu idea: This is good served with Garlic Toast (page 61) and tossed salad.

Ham Kebabs

This is a great outdoor grill entrée.

2 **pounds extra lean ham, cut into 1½-inch cubes**	1 **(18-ounce) bottle honey Dijon barbecue sauce**
8 **kebab sticks**	

- Arrange the ham chunks on the sticks.
- Brush with the barbecue sauce.
- Cook over medium heat on a grill for 2 to 3 minutes. Turn. Continue cooking 2 to 3 minutes longer or until fully heated.

Note: For extra zing you can add 1½-inch cubes of fresh pineapple or onion pieces between the meat.

Yield: 8 kebabs

Calories: 237; Fat: 6g (22% fat); Cholesterol: 53mg; Carbohydrate: 24g; Dietary Fiber: 0g; Protein: 22g; Sodium: 2258mg

Preparation time: 10 minutes
Cooking time: 5 minutes
Total preparation time: 15 minutes or less

Menu ideas: This is great served with Sassy Slaw (page 91), Apple Cottage Salad (page 99), or Zesty Chilled Fruit Salad (page 101).

Beef Stroganoff

Who would have thought it could be this easy? There's only one pan to cleanup.

1	pound eye of round beef, cut into 1/2-inch cubes	2	teaspoons minced garlic
2	medium onions (or as a time saver use 1 pound frozen chopped onions)	3	cups beef broth or 3 beef bouillon cubes dissolved with 3 cups water
1	(4-ounce) can sliced mushroom stems and pieces, not drained	4	cups medium-size egg noodles
		1	cup fat-free sour cream
			Salt and pepper, optional

- Spray a large kettle or soup pot with nonfat cooking spray.
- Over medium heat cook the meat, onions, mushrooms, and garlic together. Stir occasionally.
- Once the meat is fully cooked, add the beef broth, egg noodles, and sour cream. Turn the heat to high.
- Once boiling, turn the heat down to low. *Do not cover.* Cook on low for 5 to 7 minutes until the pasta is to desired doneness. Stir occasionally.
- Remove from the heat. Let it sit for 4 to 5 minutes before serving. The broth will thicken as it sits. If desired sprinkle lightly with salt and pepper.

Note: For Chicken Stroganoff substitute 1 pound boneless, skinless chicken breasts cut into 1/2-inch cubes and use chicken broth instead of beef broth.

Yield: 7 (1-cup) servings

(with beef) Calories: 223; Fat: 3g (14% fat); Cholesterol: 60mg; Carbohydrate: 26g Dietary Fiber: 1g; Protein: 20g; Sodium: 494mg
(with chicken) Calories: 223; Fat: 3g (14% fat); Cholesterol: 60mg; Carbohydrate: 26g; Dietary Fiber: 1g; Protein: 20g; Sodium: 494mg

Preparation time: 5 minutes
Cooking time: 15 minutes or less
Total time: 20 minutes or less

Menu idea: Serve this with steamed broccoli, fat-free sourdough bread or rolls, and Spiced Apples (page 132).

Presto Ham Casserole

Easy is the name of this game, and it will score high points from your fans for being tasty.

1 (7.25-ounce) box macaroni and cheese—Do not make as directed on box.	1 pound extra lean ham, cut into 1/3-inch chunks
1 cup hot water	1 (15-ounce) can sweet peas, drained
1 (10³/4-ounce) can 98% fat-free cream of mushroom soup (add 1/2 can water)	

- Spray a 2-quart, covered, microwavable casserole dish with nonfat cooking spray.
- In the prepared dish mix the powdered cheese packet from the macaroni and cheese box with the hot water and soup until the cheese is completely dissolved.
- Stir in the chopped ham and the macaroni until well mixed.
- Cover. Cook in a carousel* microwave on high for 7 minutes. Very carefully remove the lid so you do not get a steam burn.
- Stir. Cover and continue cooking in the carousel microwave* for an additional 6 minutes.
- Stir in the drained peas. Cover and let sit 2 to 3 minutes before serving. If making ahead of time, freeze or refrigerate until needed. Microwave until warm.

*Note: If you do not have a carousel microwave, turn the dish a quarter turn every 2 minutes.

Yield: 5 servings

Calories: 341; Fat: 7g (18% fat); Cholesterol: 48mg; Carbohydrate: 41g; Dietary Fiber: 4g; Protein: 28g; Sodium: 1936mg

Preparation time: 5 minutes or less
Cooking time: 13 minutes
Total time: 18 minutes or less

Menu idea: This is good with a tossed salad and Jell-O with fruit.

Presto Sausage Casserole

It's hard to believe a casserole so good can be made so quickly.

1 (7.25-ounce) box macaroni and cheese—Do not make as directed on box.	1 pound fat-free smoked sausage, cut into bite-size pieces or 1 pound fat-free kielbasa, cut into bite-size pieces
1 cup hot water	
1 (10^3/4-ounce) can 98% fat-free cream of mushroom soup (add ^{1}/2 can water)	1 (15-ounce) can green beans, drained

- Spray a 2-quart, covered, microwavable casserole dish with nonfat cooking spray.
- In the casserole dish mix the powdered cheese packet from the macaroni and cheese box with the hot water and soup until the cheese is completely dissolved.
- Stir in the chopped sausage and macaroni until well mixed.
- Cover. Cook in a carousel* microwave on high for 7 minutes. Very carefully remove the lid, so you do not get a steam burn.
- Stir. Cover and continue cooking in the carousel microwave for an additional 6 minutes.
- Stir in the green beans. Cover and let sit 2 to 3 minutes before serving. If making ahead of time, freeze or refrigerate until needed. Microwave until warm.

Note: If you do not have a carousel microwave, turn the dish a quarter turn every 2 minutes.

Yield: 5 servings

Calories: 286; Fat: 2g (6% fat); Cholesterol: 45mg; Carbohydrate: 45g; Dietary Fiber: 2g; Protein: 23g; Sodium: 1710mg

Preparation time: 5 minutes or less
Cooking time: 13 minutes
Total time: 18 minutes or less

Menu idea: Serve with Mother's Day Salad (page 98) and Very Berry Fruit Salad (page 79).

Presto Poultry Casserole

This casserole is a great way to use leftover holiday turkey.

1 **(7.25-ounce) box macaroni and cheese—Do not make as directed on box.**	1 **pound leftover cooked chicken or turkey breast, cut into bite-size pieces**
1 **cup hot water**	1 **(15-ounce) can asparagus, drained**
1 **(10 3/4-ounce) can 98% fat-free cream of mushroom soup (add 1/2 can water)**	

- Spray a 2-quart, covered, microwavable casserole dish with nonfat cooking spray.
- In the casserole dish mix the powdered cheese packet from the macaroni and cheese box with the hot water and soup until the cheese is completely dissolved.
- Stir in the chopped chicken or turkey and macaroni until well mixed.
- Cover and cook in a carousel* microwave on high for 7 minutes. Very carefully remove the lid, so you do not get a steam burn.
- Stir. Cover and continue cooking in the carousel microwave for an additional 6 minutes.
- Stir in the asparagus. Cover and let sit 2 to 3 minutes before serving.
- If making ahead of time, freeze or refrigerate until needed. Microwave until warm.

*Note: If you do not have a carousel microwave, turn the dish a quarter turn every 2 minutes.

Yield: 5 servings

Calories: 348; Fat: 6g (17% fat); Cholesterol: 83mg; Carbohydrate: 34g; Dietary Fiber: 2g; Protein: 37g; Sodium: 732mg

Preparation time: 5 minutes or less
Cooking time: 13 minutes
Total time: 18 minutes or less

Menu ideas: This is good served with Warm Cran-Apple Salad (page 94) and Cucumber Dill Salad (page 90).

Mexican Casserole

This no-bake, no-boil casserole is the answer to satisfying hungry tummies quickly.

1	(1¼-ounce) packet taco seasoning mix	1	(15-ounce) can whole kernel corn, drained
2	cups hot water	1	pound ground meatless or cooked, ground, extra lean turkey breast
1	(7.25-ounce) box macaroni and cheese—Do not make as directed on box.	¾	cup fat-free sour cream
1	cup salsa		

- In a 2-quart, microwavable, covered casserole dish mix the taco seasoning, hot water, macaroni and cheese, salsa, corn and ground meatless until well mixed and the dry cheese mixture (from the macaroni box) is dissolved.
- Cover and cook for 8 minutes on high in a carousel* microwave.
- Carefully remove the casserole lid so you don't get burned from the steam. Mix well.
- Cover and continue cooking on high in the carousel microwave for an additional 6 minutes.
- Stir in the sour cream. Cover and let sit for 2 to 3 minutes before serving.

Note: If you do not have a carousel microwave, turn the dish a quarter turn every 2 minutes.

Yield: 6 servings

Calories: 363; Fat: 2g (5% fat); Cholesterol: 10g; Carbohydrate: 55g; Dietary Fiber: 6g; Protein: 30g; Sodium: 1657mg

Preparation time: 5 minutes or less
Cooking time: 13 minutes plus 2 minutes sitting time
Total time: 20 minutes or less

Menu idea: A taco salad, sliced cucumbers, and sliced cantaloupe or melon make this a nice meal.

Shrimp Rice Casserole

This delectable dish is good to the last bite.

8 cups water	1 (2.8-ounce) jar bacon pieces
4 cups long-grain rice	1 (12-ounce) bottle teriyaki baste and glaze sauce (I use Kikkoman.)
8 beef-flavored bouillon cubes	
2 pounds frozen, fully cooked, and ready-to-eat shrimp, 60 to 80 per-pound size	

- In a large Dutch oven or big saucepan bring the water, rice, bouillon cubes, shrimp, and bacon pieces to a full boil.
- Turn the heat down to low and cover.
- Simmer for 10 minutes or until all the water is absorbed.
- Stir in the teriyaki sauce.
- Serve hot.

Yield: 18 (1-cup) servings

Calories: 252; Fat: 2g (7% fat); Cholesterol: 102mg; Carbohydrate: 41g; Dietary Fiber: 1g; Protein: 16g; Sodium: 1190mg

Preparation time: 5 minutes
Cooking time: 15 minutes or less
Total time: 20 minutes or less

Menu idea: Sassy Slaw (page 91) and Broccoli Parmesan (page 124) are great served with this casserole.

Apricot Chicken and Rice

Rice-A-Roni never tasted so good.

1 package beef flavored Rice-A-Roni	**1½** pounds boneless, skinless chicken breasts
4 medium onions, cut in quarters with the layers of onions in each quarter separated	**½** cup Knott's Berry Farm Light Apricot-Flavored Fruit Syrup
	1 teaspoon garlic salt

- Prepare the Rice-A-Roni as directed on the box, adding the onions to the rice.
- Meanwhile, in a large non-stick skillet arrange the chicken breast pieces. Pour the apricot syrup over the breasts and sprinkle with garlic salt.
- Cover and cook on medium heat for 7 minutes.
- Turn the chicken pieces over.
- Cover and cook until the chicken is completely white, about 5 to 10 minutes, depending on the thickness.
- Remove the chicken pieces and pour the sauce from the chicken into the cooked Rice-A-Roni and stir until well mixed.
- Serve the chicken over the rice.

Yield: 4 servings

Calories: 464; Fat: 3g (7% fat); Cholesterol: 100mg; Carbohydrate: 60g; Dietary Fiber: 3g; Protein: 45g; Sodium: 1514mg

Preparation time: 5 minutes
Cooking time: 20 minutes
Total time: 25 minutes

Menu idea: This is good served with Crunchy Cucumbers with Cream (page 82) and steamed broccoli.

Zesty Sausage Skillet Dinner

The one-dish skillet dinner that'll add zip to your day.

> 1 (14-ounce) fat-free smoked sausage, quartered and cut into bite-size pieces
>
> 1 (20-ounce) package seasoned, diced, potato home fries, thawed
>
> 2/3 cup honey-Dijon barbecue sauce

- Spray a large non-stick skillet with nonfat cooking spray.
- Put the sausage, potatoes, and barbecue sauce in the skillet and cook over medium heat. Stir until all the ingredients are well coated with the sauce.
- Cover and reduce the heat to medium-low. Cook without stirring for 10 minutes.
- With a pancake turner, turn the mixture over. The bottom will be caramelized and brown.
- Cover and cook an additional 5 minutes or until the other side is caramelized.

Yield: 4 large servings

Calories: 359; Fat: 6g (15% fat); Cholesterol: 51mg; Carbohydrate: 57g; Dietary Fiber: 3g; Protein: 19g; Sodium: 1652mg

Preparation time: 5 minutes
Cooking time: 15 minutes
Total time: 20 minutes or less

Menu idea: Tossed salad, green beans, and sugar-free Jell-O for dessert round out this zesty skillet dinner.

Beef and Broccoli Skillet Casserole

Just what busy people need—a great tasting one-dish dinner made quickly and easily with very little cleanup. This is a unique blend between sweet and sour and stir-fry without all the yucky fat.

1 pound eye of round steak or roast with all visible fat removed, cut into ½-inch cubes	3 cups hot water
1 (1-pound) bag frozen broccoli florets, cut into 1-inch pieces	1 envelope onion soup mix, dry
	3 cups instant rice
	¾ cup fat-free French salad dressing

- In a large non-stick skillet cook the beef on high for 3 to 4 minutes or until the bottom is cooked.
- Turn the beef over and pour the broccoli, water, and onion soup mix over the beef. Stir until the soup mix is dissolved.
- Cover and cook on high for 6 minutes.
- Add the rice and stir until the rice is covered with the liquid.
- Turn off the heat, cover, and let it sit for 5 minutes.
- Stir in the dressing.
- Serve immediately with light soy sauce on the side if desired.

Note: Pork tenderloin can be substituted for eye of round beef if desired. It tastes just as good.

Yield: 6 (1-cup) servings

(with beef) Calories: 345; Fat: 3g (8% fat); Cholesterol: 39mg; Carbohydrate: 54g; Dietary Fiber: 3g; Protein: 23g; Sodium: 781mg
(with pork) Calories: 339; Fat: 3g (8% fat); Cholesterol: 42mg; Carbohydrate: 54g; Dietary Fiber: 3g; Protein: 21g; Sodium: 776mg

Preparation time: 3 minutes
Cooking time: 15 minutes or less
Total time: 18 minutes or less

Menu idea: Any green vegetable complements this casserole, and a fortune cookie makes a great dessert.

Mexican Pork Tenderloin with Rice

This is a zesty entrée that'll add zip to any blah day.

4	pork tenderloin steaks, about 1 pound total, with all visible fat removed
1	(16-ounce) jar chunky salsa
1	(8-ounce) can red kidney beans, not drained
1	(8-ounce) can whole kernel corn, not drained
1/2	cup instant enriched long grain rice
1	(4-ounce) can mild green chili peppers, chopped, optional
2	to 3 dashes Tabasco sauce, optional

- In a large non-stick skillet that has been sprayed with nonfat cooking spray cook the pork steaks and salsa over medium heat for 5 to 7 minutes.
- Turn the steaks over and cook for 5 to 7 minutes or until they are no longer pink in the center. Remove the meat from the skillet.
- Add to the skillet the kidney beans, corn, and rice. Stir until well mixed. Bring to a boil.
- Put the cooked meat on top of the rice.
- Remove from the heat, cover, and let sit for 5 minutes.
- Serve with taco sauce on the side if desired.

Note: This can also be made days ahead of time, refrigerated, and reheated in the microwave. Or freeze and reheat.

Yield: 4 servings (1 pork steak and 1 cup rice per serving)

Calories: 296; Fat: 5g (30% fat); Cholesterol: 63mg; Carbohydrate: 31g; Dietary Fiber: 4g; Protein: 27g; Sodium: 818mg

Preparation time: 10 minutes or less
Cooking time: 15 minutes
Total time: 25 minutes or less

Menu ideas: This is a complete meal in itself. If desired serve with a fresh green salad or green beans.

Hearty Barbecue Skillet Dinner

This is a meat-and-potato lover's meal.

2 pounds red potatoes	1/2 cup packed dark brown sugar
2 medium onions, chopped	1 (14-ounce) low-fat smoked
1 beef bouillon cube dissolved in 1 cup water	sausage, chopped into bite-size pieces
1 (15-ounce) can tomato sauce	

- Poke the potatoes with a fork numerous times and microwave them on high until cooked (about 10 minutes). They will be soft to the touch when fully cooked.
- In the meantime, in a large non-stick skillet cook the chopped onions, dissolved beef bouillon, tomato sauce, and brown sugar, and sausage over medium heat, stirring occasionally.
- Cut the cooked potatoes into bite-size pieces. Stir them into the pan with the other ingredients, covering all the ingredients with the sauce.
- The recipe is completely cooked when the onions are tender and everything is fully heated.

Note: This meal can be made days in advance and easily reheated.

Yield: 6 servings

Calories: 303; Fat: 2g (6% fat); Cholesterol: 24mg; Carbohydrate: 59g; Dietary Fiber: 3g; Protein: 13g; Sodium: 1140mg

Preparation time: 15 minutes or less
Cooking time: 20 minutes
Total time: 25 minutes or less

Menu idea: This is good served with Cucumber Dill Salad (page 90), sliced tomatoes, and applesauce.

Potato Puffs

This recipe is entirely different.

1/2 teaspoon garlic powder	1 (5-ounce) can white chicken in water, drained
1 3/4 cups fat-free chicken broth	
1 1/2 cups instant mashed potatoes	1 cup home fries, thawed
1/2 cup Egg Beaters or 4 egg whites, beaten	2 tablespoons fat-free margarine

- Preheat the oven to 400 degrees.
- Line 2 cookie sheets with foil. Spray the foil with nonfat cooking spray.
- In a bowl mix the garlic powder, chicken broth, potatoes, Egg Beaters, chicken, home fries, and margarine until well blended.
- Drop by rounded tablespoon onto the prepared cookie sheets.
- Bake for 12 to 14 minutes or until slightly brown on edges.

Note: For beef puffs substitute 4-ounces dried chipped beef and fat-free beef broth for the chicken.

Yield: 4 servings

(with chicken) Calories: 265; Fat: 2g (6% fat); Cholesterol: 11mg; Carbohydrate: 50g; Dietary Fiber: 4g; Protein: 12g; Sodium: 346mg
(with beef) Calories: 272; Fat: 2g (7% fat); Cholesterol: 10mg; Carbohydrate: 50g; Dietary Fiber: 4g; Protein: 13g; Sodium: 910mg

Preparation time: 10 minutes or less
Cooking time: 14 minutes or less
Total time: 24 minutes or less

Menu idea: Great as an entrée. Serve with Pepperidge Farms Fat-Free Chicken Gravy on top, Tomato Biscuits (page 59), and Broccoli Parmesan (page 124).

Au Gratin Casserole Dinner

If you like cheesey broccoli, au gratin potatoes, and ham, you'll like this one-dish entrée.

1 (5¹/2-ounce) box au gratin potatoes—Do not make as directed on box.	12 ounces extra lean ham or turkey ham, cut into bite-size pieces
1 (12-ounce) can fat-free evaporated milk	1 (16-ounce) bag frozen broccoli pieces
1¹/2 cups hot water	

- In a 2-quart, microwavable, casserole dish, mix the potatoes and seasoning cheese packet from the box mix with the milk and water until the powdered cheese is completely dissolved.
- Stir in the ham pieces.
- Cover with wax paper. Cook in a carousel* microwave on high for 5 minutes.
- Stir in the broccoli pieces. Cover and continue cooking in the carousel microwave on high for an additional 15 minutes, stirring occasionally.
- Remove the wax paper and let it sit for 3 to 5 minutes before serving.

*Note: If you do not have a carousel microwave, turn the dish a quarter turn every 2 minutes.

Yield: 4 servings

Calories: 336; Fat: 6g (15% fat); Cholesterol: 44mg; Carbohydrate: 46g; Dietary Fiber: 5g; Protein: 30g; Sodium: 2170mg

Preparation time: 5 minutes or less
Cooking time: 20 minutes
Total time: 25 minutes or less

Menu idea: A complete meal in itself; however, Spiced Apples (page 132) also taste delicious with this entrée.

Chicken Cheesey Pizza

This is a tasty twist to that old-time favorite, traditional pizza.

1 (10-ounce) can Pillsbury pizza dough	1/4 cup nonfat grated Parmesan cheese topping
1 fresh boneless, skinless chicken breast, approximately 1/2 pound	1/2 cup fat-free ranch dressing
1/8 to 1/4 teaspoon ground pepper	1 (8-ounce) package shredded fat-free mozzarella cheese
1/4 cup light whipped salad dressing	

- Preheat the oven to 425 degrees.
- Press the dough onto a jelly roll pan (a cookie sheet with 1-inch sides) that has been sprayed with nonfat cooking spray.
- Cook the chicken breast in a microwave for about 2 minutes until no pink is visible.
- Drain the juice. Cut the cooked chicken breast into tiny 1/4-inch pieces.
- Sprinkle with the pepper.
- Mix the whipped dressing, grated topping, and ranch dressing together. Spread the mixture over the pizza crust.
- Sprinkle the mozzarella cheese over the mixture. Top with the peppered chicken pieces.
- Bake for 12 to 15 minutes or until the crust is golden brown.

Note: Red or green pepper slices would also taste good on top of the pizza before baking.

Yield: 4 entrée-size pieces

Calories: 440; Fat: 6g (13% fat); Cholesterol: 52mg; Carbohydrate: 54g; Dietary Fiber: 3g; Protein: 40g; Sodium: 1696mg

Preparation time: 10 minutes or less
Cooking time: 15 minutes or less
Total time: 25 minutes or less

Menu idea: This is good served with a tossed salad and Green Beans Italiano (page 116).

Mexican Pizza

A flavorful twist to an old-time favorite.

1 pound ground meatless (I use Morningstar Farms.)	8 ounces shredded nonfat cheddar cheese
1 (1¹/4-ounce) package taco seasoning mix	1 large fresh tomato, chopped
³/4 cup hot water	¹/2 red onion, sliced into thin rings
2 (7¹/2-ounce) cans Pillsbury buttermilk biscuits	1 medium fresh green pepper, sliced into very thin slices

- Cook the ground meatless with the taco seasoning mix and hot water over medium to low heat for about 10 minutes, stirring occasionally.
- While the ground meatless is cooking, spray two 8 x 8-inch pans with nonfat cooking spray.
- Press 8 of the biscuits into the bottom of each pan, pinching the dough together to make a crust. Make sure the dough covers the entire bottom of the pans all the way to the edges.
- Preheat the oven to 425 degrees.
- Spread half of the taco-seasoned meatless mixture over each crust.
- Top with half of the shredded cheese on each pizza.
- Divide the chopped tomato, thinly sliced onion rings, and green pepper slices between the two crusts and place on top of the cheese.
- Bake for 12 minutes. Let it cool for 2 minutes before serving.

Yield: 8 servings

(with ground meatless) Calories: 287; Fat: 11g (32% fat); Cholesterol: 95mg; Carbohydrate: 17g; Dietary Fiber: 2g; Protein: 34g; Sodium: 428mg

Preparation time: 15 minutes or less
Cooking time: 12 minutes or less
Total time: 27 minutes or less

Menu ideas: If desired, serve with salsa, fat-free sour cream, and crushed low-fat baked tortilla chips. Also serve a tossed salad on the side and Zesty Corn (page 136).

Chicken (or Turkey) Casserole

I converted a high-fat, time-consuming casserole sent in by Carolyn Green from southern Ohio into this fast and easy-to-prepare dish that is every bit as tasty.

1 cup elbow macaroni, uncooked	1 cup chicken broth, from a can or made with chicken bouillon
1 (10-ounce) can premium chunk chicken in water or 10 ounces cooked turkey breast, drained	$^1/2$ cup chopped onion, fresh or frozen
1 (10$^3/4$-ounce) can 98% fat-free cream of mushroom soup (add $^1/2$ can water)	1 (4-ounce) can sliced mushrooms, drained

- Spray a 2-quart, covered casserole dish with nonfat cooking spray.
- Combine the macaroni, chicken or turkey, soup, broth, onion, and mushrooms in the prepared dish and mix well.
- Cook covered in a carousel* microwave for 17 to 20 minutes, or until the pasta is tender.
- Let sit for 3 minutes before removing the lid. Be very careful when taking off the lid, because the steam is extremely hot.

Note: If you don't have a carousel microwave, turn the pasta several times during cooking.

Yield: 4 servings

(with chicken) Calories: 220; Fat: 2g (9% fat); Cholesterol: 30mg; Carbohydrate: 29g; Dietary Fiber: 2g; Protein: 19g; Sodium: 879mg
(with turkey) Calories: 258; Fat: 3g (12% fat); Cholesterol: 48mg; Carbohydrate: 29g; Dietary Fiber: 2g; Protein: 27g; Sodium: 647mg

Preparation time: 5 minutes or less
Cooking time: 20 minutes
Total time: 25 minutes or less

Menu ideas: Serve with green beans along with a tossed salad and fat-free sliced bread on the side. If desired, serve sugar-free Jell-O for dessert or Brownie Cookies (page 219).

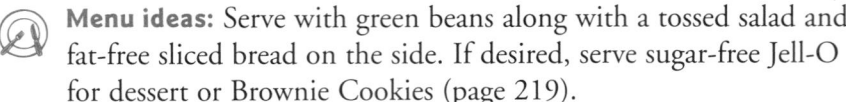

Sausage or Ham Casserole

This recipe idea came from the Chicken (or Turkey) Casserole. If you like that, you're sure to like this.

I cup elbow macaroni, uncooked	I cup beef broth
7 ounces fat-free smoked sausage or extra lean ham, chopped	1/2 cup chopped onion, fresh or frozen
I (10³/4-ounce) can 98% fat-free cream of mushroom soup (add 1/2 can water)	1/2 cup chopped green pepper, fresh or frozen

- Spray a 2-quart, covered casserole dish with nonfat cooking spray.
- Combine the macaroni, sausage (or ham), soup, broth, onion, and green pepper in the prepared dish and mix well.
- Cook covered in a carousel* microwave for 17 to 20 minutes, or until the pasta is tender.
- Let sit for 3 minutes before removing the lid. Be very careful when taking off the lid, because the steam is extremely hot.

Note: If you don't have a carousel microwave, turn the pasta several times during cooking.

Yield: 4 servings

(with sausage) Calories: 197; Fat: 1g (4% fat); Cholesterol: 21mg; Carbohydrate: 34g; Dietary Fiber: 1g; Protein: 13g; Sodium: 992mg
(with ham) Calories: 211; Fat: 3g (15% fat); Cholesterol: 23mg; Carbohydrate: 29g; Dietary Fiber: 1g; Protein: 15g; Sodium: 1119mg

Preparation time: 5 minutes or less
Cooking time: 20 minutes
Total time: 25 minutes or less

Menu ideas: Serve with fat-free rolls, steamed broccoli, and, if desired for dessert, Apple Oatmeal Cookies (page 234) to curb your sweet tooth.

Eight-Layer Chili Casserole

If only all vegetarian dishes could be this satisfying and hearty.

1	medium onion, chopped	1	(8-ounce) jar mild taco sauce
1	(16-ounce) can fat-free refried beans	1	(11-ounce) package flour tortillas, approximately 10 inches in size
1	(15-ounce) mild vegetarian fat-free chili with black beans		

- Spray a 2½-quart, round, microwavable casserole dish with a lid with nonfat cooking spray.
- In a medium-size bowl, microwave the onions, covered, for 2 minutes.
- Stir into the onions the refried beans, chili, and taco sauce until well blended.
- Tear two of the tortillas into small pieces. These will be used to fill in the outer space between the tortilla layer and casserole dish. Lay one tortilla flat on the bottom of the casserole dish. If needed use the torn tortilla to fill in the space between the casserole dish and the edge.
- Top with ¾ cup of the chili mixture. Top the chili with the tortilla.
- Continue layering the chili mixture, ¾ cup at a time, and the tortillas until all ingredients are used.
- Cover and microwave on high for 10 minutes. Let sit for 5 minutes before serving.
- Cut with a sharp knife—a steak knife works well—cutting through all layers as you would a pie.

Yield: 8 servings

Calories: 214; Fat: 0g (0% fat); Cholesterol: 0mg; Carbohydrate: 44g; Dietary Fiber: 7g; Protein: 9g; Sodium: 852mg

Preparation time: 10 minutes or less
Cooking time: 15 minutes
Total time: 25 minutes or less

Menu idea: This casserole is good with a tossed salad and crackers or corn bread.

Quickie Meal

This dish reminds me of a hamburger helper, one-dish meal but made with rice. Great for on-the-run days when you need a quickie meal.

1 **pound extra-lean ground turkey breast**	1 **(4-ounce) can mushroom pieces and stems with juice**
3 **cups beef broth**	1 **cup rice**
1 **(14^1/2-ounce) can diced tomatoes, roasted garlic flavor with onion and oregano**	**Pepper**

- Cook the turkey with a little of the broth in a large non-stick skillet over medium heat until fully cooked.
- Remove the turkey. Bring the remaining broth, tomatoes, and mushrooms with juice to a boil. Add the rice. Stir well. Reduce the heat to a low boil, cover, and cook 10 minutes.
- Meanwhile crumble the cooked turkey into tiny pieces. Stir them into the rice mixture.
- Cook another 5 minutes.
- Turn off the heat. Cover. Let simmer 2 to 3 minutes. Serve hot.
- If desired top with ground pepper and light soy sauce.

Yield: 5 servings

Calories: 279; Fat: 2g (6% fat); Cholesterol: 62mg; Carbohydrate: 36g; Dietary Fiber: 2g; Protein: 28g; Sodium: 1136mg

Preparation time: 5 minutes or less
Cooking time: 20 minutes
Total time: 25 minutes or less

Menu idea: Oriental Vegetables (page 130) and fruit cocktail will make this a scrumptious meal.

Breaded Pork Tenderloins

Move over, old-fashioned fried pork tenderloin. This winner is a frequent request that tastes every bit as delicious.

1 pound pork tenderloin roast, cut crosswise into 6 pieces with all visible fat removed	3/4 cup Italian breadcrumbs
1/3 cup all-purpose flour	2 egg whites, beaten
1 teaspoon seasoned salt	2 tablespoons skim milk

- Preheat the oven to 400 degrees.
- Spray a cookie sheet with nonfat cooking spray.
- Pound the pork into ¼- to ⅛-inch thickness.
- In a small bowl stir together the flour, seasoned salt, and breadcrumbs.
- In a separate small bowl beat together the egg whites and skim milk. Coat the meat in the flour/breadcrumbs mixture.
- Dip the coated meat in the egg mixture, and then dip again in the flour/breadcrumbs mixture.
- Place the prepared meat on the cookie sheet.
- Spray the top of the breaded meat with nonfat cooking spray.
- Bake for 10 minutes.
- Turn the meat over. Spray the top with nonfat cooking spray. Bake for an additional 10 minutes. The breading will be crispy and slightly golden brown when done.

Yield: 6 servings

Calories: 175; Fat: 3g (18% fat); Cholesterol: 42mg; Carbohydrate: 16g; Dietary Fiber: 1g; Protein: 19g; Sodium: 519mg

Preparation time: 10 minutes or less
Cooking time: 20 minutes
Total time: 30 minutes or less

Menu idea: If desired, serve with the Spring Salad (page 103) Mashed Potatoes Deluxe (page 119), and California Garlic Blend (page 120).

Christmas Chicken & Rice Dinner

This colorful combination of red and green gives this flavorful entrée its distinguished name.

1/3 cup pineapple-orange juice frozen concentrate	2 tablespoons cornstarch
4 ounces fat-free margarine	1 red pepper, cut into 1/4-inch strips
1/2 teaspoon garlic salt, optional	1 green pepper, cut into 1/4-inch strips
1 pound boneless, skinless chicken breasts, cut into 1/2-inch pieces	

- In a large non-stick skillet cook together the pineapple-orange concentrate, margarine, garlic salt, and chicken over medium heat until the chicken is fully cooked, stirring occasionally.
- Remove 1/3 cup of the sauce. Stir the cornstarch into the sauce until dissolved. Add the mixture back into the chicken mixture.
- Stir well until the chicken pieces are well coated with the sauce and the sauce thickens. Add the sliced red and green peppers.
- Continue cooking 5 minutes with the lid on over medium heat. The peppers will be tender yet slightly crunchy.
- Serve plain or over rice.

Yield: 5 servings (not including rice)

Calories: 178; Fat: 1g (7% fat); Cholesterol: 53mg; Carbohydrate: 18g; Dietary Fiber: 1g; Protein: 22g; Sodium: 174mg

Preparation time: 10 minutes or less
Cooking time: 15 minutes
Total time: 25 minutes or less

Menu idea: This is great served with a tossed salad, wild or white rice, and steamed asparagus.

Manhandler Meatloaves

As one little girl once said after being questioned about the large amount she was eating, "I just can't help myself, Aunt Dawn. It's so good. I just can't stop eating it."

1 (6-ounce) box pork-flavored stuffing	2 pounds ground eye of round beef
1 (8-ounce) carton egg substitute (I use Egg Beaters.)	**Glaze:**
1 cup mild thick and chunky salsa	1/4 cup grape jelly
1/2 cup honey barbecue sauce	1/2 cup honey barbecue sauce
2 (14-ounce) packages fat-free smoked sausage	2 tablespoons salsa

- Preheat the oven to 350 degrees.
- With a blender grind the breadcrumbs of the stuffing mix for approximately 20 seconds until finely ground.
- In a large bowl combine the egg substitute, salsa, barbecue sauce, breadcrumbs, and the seasoning packet from the stuffing mix. Stir until well combined.
- Cut the sausage lengths into 1-inch pieces and grind in a blender until the sausage becomes "ground sausage."
- Combine the sausage and eye of round with the egg mixture. (It is easiest to combine together with your hands.)
- To make the glaze, microwave the jelly for a few seconds to help the jelly dissolve. Mix together the jelly with the barbecue sauce and salsa until there are no chunks of jelly remaining. Choose a cooking method below to prepare the meatloaf.

Microwave:
- Divide the meatloaf mixture into half and mold each half into a ring with your hands and place each on a microwavable plate that has been sprayed with nonfat cooking spray.
- Microwave each one for 12 to 13 minutes in a carousel microwave.
- Let them stand for 3 to 4 minutes before serving.

Bake:

- Preheat the oven to 350 degrees.
- Spray two 8 x 4 x 2-inch loaf pans with nonfat cooking spray and mold the meatloaf mixture into the prepared pans.
- Bake in the oven for 50 minutes.
- Spread half the glaze over one loaf and the other half over the other loaf and continue baking for an additional 10 minutes.

Slow Cooker:

- Form the meatloaf mixture into a round loaf and place in a slow cooker. (For an easy cleanup, line the slow cooker with foil. Spray the foil with nonfat cooking spray before cooking.)
- Cook on low for 8½ to 9 hours, or on high for 4 hours.
- Put half the glaze on the meatloaf after removing it from the slow cooker. Let the meatloaf sit for 3 to 4 minutes before serving.

Note: Remember this recipe makes two meatloaves. Make sure you divide the meatloaf and glaze into two portions. If desired, cook one meatloaf and freeze the second to cook later.

Yield: 16 (4-ounce) servings (makes two meatloaves)

Calories: 214; Fat: 2g (10% fat); Cholesterol: 51mg; Carbohydrate: 23g; Dietary Fiber: 0g; Protein: 23g; Sodium: 1086mg

Preparation time: 20 minutes or less
Cooking time: Depends on method of cooking

Menu ideas: This is especially good with either Mushroom, Onion & Bacon Green Bean Casserole (page 115) or Carrots with a Light, Buttery Caramel Glaze (page 121) and Mashed Potatoes Deluxe (page 119).

Farmer's Casserole

You won't believe how flavorful and easy this casserole is.

1¹/2 pounds extra lean ham, cut into bite-size pieces	cream of mushroom soup (add ¹/2 can water)
1 (20-ounce) package seasoned diced potatoes, home fries	¹/2 cup chopped red onion or frozen chopped regular onions
1 (4-ounce) can mushroom stems and pieces, juices drained	1 (14¹/2-ounce) can green beans, drained
1 (10³/4-ounce) can 98% fat-free	

Microwave:

- Spray a 2-quart microwavable casserole dish with nonfat cooking spray.
- Put the ham, potatoes, mushrooms, soup, onions, and beans into the prepared dish. Mix until well blended.
- Cover and cook on high for 7 to 8 minutes stirring once. (Turn the dish several times during cooking.)

Slow Cooker:

- Spray a slow cooker with nonfat cooking spray.
- Put the ham, potatoes, mushrooms, soup, onions, and beans into the slow cooker and mix until well blended.
- Cover and cook on low for 4 hours.

Yield: 6 to 7 servings

Calories: 278; Fat: 9g (28% fat); Cholesterol: 50mg; Carbohydrate: 26g; Dietary Fiber: 3g; Protein: 23g; Sodium: 1732mg

Preparation time: 8 minutes or less
Cooking time: Varies depending on cooking method

Menu ideas: A complete meal in itself, or serve cooked asparagus, fat-free bread with jam on the side, along with Oreo Mousse (page 246).

Swiss Steak and Potatoes

What a wonderful, warm, and mouth-watering meal to come home to on a cold or chilly day.

1 (14¹/2-ounce) can stewed, sliced tomatoes, not drained	1 pound bag fresh mini carrots
	2 medium onions, quartered
1 (12-ounce) jar fat-free beef-flavored gravy	1 pound eye of round, cut into ¹/2-inch-thick steaks
¹/4 teaspoon dried thyme	4 medium potatoes, washed

- Spray a slow cooker with nonfat cooking spray.
- In a large bowl combine the tomatoes, gravy, thyme, carrots, and onions together until well mixed.
- Place the meat into the mixture, making sure the meat is completely covered with the sauce.
- Place the potatoes on top.
- Cover and cook on high for 4 hours or on low for 8 hours. The recipe is completely cooked after documented time; however, the meal can remain in the slow cooker for up to 1 hour longer without burning.

Yield: 4 servings

Calories: 345; Fat: 4g (10% fat); Cholesterol: 47mg; Carbohydrate: 53g; Dietary Fiber: 7g; Protein: 27g; Sodium: 630mg

Preparation time: 20 minutes or less
Cooking time: 4 hours
Total time: 4 hours 20 minutes

Menu ideas: This is a complete meal in itself. However, you may want to round it off with Sweet & Sour Fresh Vegetable Garden Salad (page 83), Pinwheel Dinner Rolls (page 64), and Punchbowl Cake (page 207) for dessert.

Cowboy Chow

Cowboys of the olden days could only wish it would have tasted this good. For fun, serve in pie pans instead of plates.

1   (14-ounce) package low-fat smoked sausage, cut into bite-size pieces
1   cup thick and chunky salsa
1   cup original western barbecue sauce
1   (10-ounce) can whole kernel corn, drained
1   (15^{1}/2-ounce) can dark red kidney beans, drained
1   (53-ounce) can pork and beans, drained, all visible chunks of fat removed
^{1}/2   cup chopped onion or frozen chopped onions

Microwave:
- Spray a 3-quart microwavable bowl with nonfat cooking spray.
- In the bowl combine the sausage, salsa, barbecue sauce, corn, kidney beans, pork and beans, and onion until well mixed.
- Cover and place in a carousel microwave. (If you don't have a carousel microwave, rotate dish a quarter turn every 2 minutes.)
- Cook on high for 5 to 6 minutes or until completely heated.

Stovetop:
- Spray a large saucepan with nonfat cooking spray.
- In the saucepan combine the sausage, salsa, barbecue sauce, corn, kidney beans, pork and beans, and onion until well mixed.
- Bring to a boil. Reduce heat to low. Cover and simmer for 5 minutes.

Slow Cooker:

- Spray a slow cooker with nonfat cooking spray.
- In the slow cooker combine the sausage, salsa, barbecue sauce, corn, kidney beans, pork and beans, and onion until well mixed.
- Cover and cook on low for 3 hours. (If needed it can cook up to 6 hours.)

Yield: $9\frac{1}{2}$ (1-cup) servings

Calories: 293; Fat: 4g (11% fat); Cholesterol: 24mg; Carbohydrate: 51g; Dietary Fiber: 11g; Protein: 17g; Sodium: 1528mg

Preparation time: 5 minutes or less
Cooking time: varies depending on cooking method used

Menu idea: Serve with cornbread and sliced cucumbers on the side along with a chilled light fruit cocktail for dessert.

Chicken and Potato Stew

One of my assistants, Robin Friend, who loves to eat rich foods, gave me this recipe.

1 **pound boneless, skinless chicken breasts, cut into bite-size pieces**	2 **(16-ounce) packages frozen vegetables for stew**
1 **(10³/4-ounce) can 98% fat-free cream of mushroom soup (add ¹/2 can water)**	2 **tablespoons fat-free margarine**

- In a slow cooker layer the chicken, soup, frozen vegetables, and margarine.
- Cover and cook on low for 4 to 5 hours.

Yield: 6 servings

Calories: 199; Fat: 1g (6% fat); Cholesterol: 44mg; Carbohydrate: 24g; Dietary Fiber: 1g; Protein: 20g; Sodium: 289mg

Preparation time: 5 minutes or less
Cooking time: 4 to 5 hours on low
Total time: 5 hours or less

Menu idea: Serve with biscuits or sourdough bread for a complete meal.

Smothered Steak

Each succulent bite is as tasty as the one before.

1 pound beef tenderloin, whole	8 ounces fresh mushrooms, sliced
2 large onions, quartered and separated	1/4 cup Butter Buds, dry
2 large green peppers, cut into 3/4-inch strips	1/2 cup water
	1 teaspoon celery salt or garlic salt

- Spray a slow cooker with nonfat cooking spray.
- Place the beef in the bottom and top it with the onions, peppers, and mushrooms. In a bowl mix the Butter Buds, water, and garlic or celery salt together until the Butter Buds dissolve. Pour over the vegetables. Gently toss the vegetables to distribute the seasonings.
- Cover. Cook on high for 4 to 5 hours. Or cook on low for 8 to 9 hours.
- Cut the beef into 4 ($\frac{1}{4}$-pound) steaks. Arrange on a platter.
- Toss the vegetables in the juices before pouring the juices and vegetables over the beef.
- Serve hot.

Preparation time: 7 minutes or less
Cooking time: 4 to 5 hours on high or 8 to 9 hours on low

Yield: 4 servings

Calories: 263; Fat: 9g (29% fat); Cholesterol: 72mg; Carbohydrate: 19g; Dietary Fiber: 4g; Protein: 28g; Sodium: 491mg

Menu ideas: If there is room in your slow cooker, place 12 small, red-skin potatoes on top. If not, microwave the potatoes or serve with Garlic Red Skins (page 117) and Creamed Spinach (page 114).

California Medley Stew

This stew is a twist to an old-time favorite.

4	medium potatoes with skins on, cut in 1/2-inch cubes	1	pound California blend frozen vegetables (fresh or frozen)
1	medium onion, chopped	2	(14 1/2-ounce) cans fat-free chicken broth
2	(14-ounce) packages low-fat smoked sausage, cut into 1/2-inch pieces	1/2	cup cornstarch
2	(1-ounce) envelopes Butter Buds, dry or 2 tablespoons Butter Buds Sprinkles	1	teaspoon garlic salt, optional

- Spray a slow cooker with nonfat cooking spray.
- Put the potatoes and onion in first, and then top with the sausage, Butter Buds, vegetables, and broth.
- Cover and cook on low for 8 to 10 hours.
- Drain the broth from the slow cooker. Put the broth (reserve 1 cup) in a large non-stick skillet over high heat. With a whisk, mix the 1 cup of the broth with the cornstarch and garlic salt.
- Once the cornstarch is completely dissolved, stir it into the remaining broth in the skillet. With a whisk, keep stirring until thick, about 4 to 5 minutes.
- Gently stir in the meat and vegetables from the cooker into the thickened gravy.
- Serve immediately.

Yield: 8 (10-ounce) servings

Calories: 245; Fat: 3g (10% fat); Cholesterol: 35mg; Carbohydrate: 40g; Dietary Fiber: 3g; Protein: 17g; Sodium: 1190mg

Preparation time: 10 minutes or less
Cooking time: 8 to 10 hours.

Menu idea: Serve with sourdough bread for a complete meal.

Caribbean Rice

Mexico inspired me to create this flavorful dish. A terrific meal to make before leaving home for work, errands, church, etc. How comforting it is to come home to the flavorful aroma of a delicious meal awaiting you.

1	(9½-ounce) bottle Lawry's Teriyaki Sauce with Ginger and Sesame Chicken Sauté	1	pound cooked, peeled, and deveined frozen shrimp, 26- to 30-count per pound
1	(20-ounce) can crushed pineapple in its juices, not drained	3	cups instant long grain rice
1	(15-ounce) can sweet peas, drained, or 1 cup chopped green peppers	3	cups beef broth or 3 beef bouillon cubes dissolved in 3 cups of water

- Spray a slow cooker with nonfat cooking spray.
- Put the Chicken Sauté, pineapple, peas or peppers, and shrimp into the cooker. Very gently stir until well mixed.
- Cover and cook on high for 3½ to 4 hours or on low for 7 to 8 hours.
- Ten minutes before it's time to eat, prepare the rice as directed below.
- Bring the beef broth to a boil in a medium saucepan.
- Stir in the rice. Cover and remove from the heat. Let it stand for 5 minutes.
- Gently stir the cooked rice into the slow cooker.
- Serve immediately with light soy sauce on the side if desired.

Yield: 8 entrée servings

Calories: 291; Fat: 1g (3% fat); Cholesterol: 111mg; Carbohydrate: 48g; Dietary Fiber: 2g; Protein: 19g; Sodium: 2002mg

Preparation time: 15 minutes
Cooking time: Depends on temperature (3½ to 8 hours)

Menu idea: This is good with cooked asparagus and French bread.

Herbed Beef Tenderloin with Seasoned Potatoes & Buttered Mushrooms

Put the ingredients into a slow cooker before a long day away and come home to a mouth-watering aroma that's delicious and ready to eat.

2 pounds beef tenderloin with all visible fat removed	1 (1-pound) bag frozen seasoned diced potatoes
1¹/2 teaspoons dried thyme	2 tablespoons plus 1 tablespoon fat-free margarine
1¹/2 teaspoons dried basil	
1 teaspoon garlic salt	6 ounces fresh sliced mushrooms

- Spray a slow cooker with nonfat cooking spray.
- Sprinkle all sides of the beef with the thyme, basil, and garlic salt.
- Place the tenderloin around the outer rim edge of the slow cooker.
- Take two pieces of foil about 18 inches long. Fold the seams together along the side. Spray the foil with nonfat cooking spray.
- Place the potatoes in the center of the foil. Spread 2 tablespoons of the margarine over the potatoes. Fold the foil to seal in the flavor.
- Place the potatoes in the center of the slow cooker.
- Spray another 18 inches of foil with nonfat cooking spray.
- Place the mushrooms in the foil in a stack. Dab 1 tablespoon of the margarine on top of the mushrooms. Sprinkle lightly with garlic salt if desired. Fold the foil, as you did for the potatoes, to seal in the flavor.
- Place the mushrooms on top of the beef and potatoes.
- Cover and cook on low for 8 to 10 hours or cook on high for 4 to 5 hours. Serve the juices in the bottom of the cooker on the side.

Yield: 6 servings

Calories: 307; Fat: 11g (32% fat); Cholesterol: 95mg; Carbohydrate: 17g; Dietary Fiber: 2g; Protein: 34g; Sodium: 428mg

Preparation time: 10 minutes or less
Cooking time: 8 to 10 hours on low; 4 to 5 hours on high

Menu idea: Serve this with Broccoli Parmesan (page 124), Carrots with a Light Buttery Caramel Glaze (page 121), and Garlic Toast (page 61) for a wonderfully complete meal.

Beanie Baby Stew

This is a breeze to put together and a crowd pleaser every time.

1	(24-ounce) jar Great Northern beans	1	(7-ounce) can diced green chilies
2	(10-ounce) cans white chicken chunks in water	1	pound frozen diced potatoes used for hash browns
1	(49½-ounce) can chicken broth with all visible fat removed	½	cup cornstarch
1	(12-ounce) bag frozen chopped onions	½	cup water
			Fat-free mozzarella cheese, optional

- Put the beans, chicken, broth, onions, chilies, and potatoes into a slow cooker.
- Cover and cook on high for 4 hours or low for 8 to 9 hours.
- With a ladle or strainer remove as much of the cooked ingredients as possible and put into a large bowl. With a potato masher, smash the cooked mixture for about 1 minute. This will make the broth thicker.
- Combine the cornstarch with the cold water. Stir briskly until the cornstarch is completely dissolved.
- Stir the dissolved cornstarch into the broth in the cooker. Stir until well mixed.
- Return the mashed, cooked vegetables to the cooker.
- Stir and turn the cooker to high. Cover and cook for another 20 to 30 minutes. The stew will have a thick and creamy consistency when done.
- If desired, lightly sprinkle each bowl with fat-free mozzarella cheese just before eating.

Yield: 14 (1-cup) servings

Calories: 185; Fat: 4g (18% fat); Cholesterol: 25mg; Carbohydrate: 23g; Dietary Fiber: 4g; Protein: 15g; Sodium: 540mg

Preparation time: 5 minutes or less
Cooking time: 8 to 9 hours on low; 4 hours on high

Menu idea: Tossed salad and Sweet Corn Bread (page 60) taste yummy with this stew.

Ham & Cabbage Dinner

As a child this was one of my favorite meals. It's great to prepare when camping, if you're fortunate enough to have electricity when you camp. Some people like to put fresh peeled carrots and chunks of onions in this dish.

2 tablespoons Butter Buds Sprinkles, dry	1 head cabbage with core removed, cut into 6 wedges
1 (14^1/2-ounce) can fat-free, low-sodium chicken broth	1^1/2 pounds extra lean ham
	^{1}/4 cup fat-free butter spread

- In a slow cooker stir the Butter Buds with the chicken broth until dissolved.
- Put the cabbage wedges in the bottom of the cooker. Don't worry if the broth does not cover the cabbage.
- Place the chunk of ham on top of the cabbage.
- Cover and cook on low for 8 to 10 hours or on high for 4 hours. (Don't worry about overcooking.)
- Cut the ham into 6 slices.
- Stir the cooked cabbage wedges in the broth before removing from the cooker. With a slotted spoon remove the cabbage and place it in a pretty serving bowl.
- Toss with the butter spread. If desired, sprinkle lightly with light salt.
- Serve immediately with extra butter spread and salt and pepper on the side.

Yield: 6 servings

Calories: 207; Fat: 6g (26% fat); Cholesterol: 53mg; Carbohydrate: 13g; Dietary Fiber: 3g; Protein: 25g; Sodium: 1905mg

Preparation time: 10 minutes or less
Cooking time: 8 to 10 hours on low; 4 hours on high

Menu idea: This is great with cooked red potatoes and sliced fat-free wheat bread. A mousse of any flavor is a rich and satisfying dessert that is easy to prepare and complements this meal.

Lemon Pepper Pork Tenderloin with Lemon Kissed Potatoes

Put in right before leaving for church. There's nothing like coming home to a delicious home-cooked meal.

2 pounds pork tenderloin with all visible fat removed	8 medium potatoes, diced into 1/2-inch cubes
2 medium lemons cut into quarters, seeds discarded	1 cup water
1 teaspoon ground pepper	1 teaspoon cream of tartar
1 teaspoon garlic salt	1 teaspoon dried parsley

- With a knife cut the pork tenderloin down the center lengthwise to divide it in half. With a knife cut 1/4-inch-deep cuts all over the pork. Squeeze the lemon juice on the tenderloin.
- Sprinkle lightly with the pepper and garlic salt. Put the meat around the sides and bottom of a slow cooker.
- Put the diced potatoes in a bowl with 1 cup of water and 1 teaspoon cream of tartar, and let it soak for 1 minute. This will keep the potatoes from turning brown or discoloring while cooking.
- Put the potatoes on top of the meat in the pot. Sprinkle with dried parsley. Arrange what remains of the lemon quarters on top.
- Cook on high for 2 1/2 to 3 hours or cook on low 5 to 6 hours. Remove the lemons before serving.
- Serve on a large plate. If desired, you can sprinkle the potatoes lightly with salt and more dried parsley.

Yield: 8 servings

Calories: 236; Fat: 4g (14% fat); Cholesterol: 63mg; Carbohydrate: 27g; Dietary Fiber: 3g; Protein: 27g; Sodium: 272mg

Preparation time: 10 minutes or less
Cooking time: 5 to 6 hours on low; 2 1/2 to 3 hours on high

Menu ideas: Serve with Sassy Slaw (page 91) or Tangy Tossed Salad (page 95).

Beef and Potatoes with Mushroom and Onion Gravy

Beef doesn't get more tender than this. Forget the knife; it just falls apart.

1	plus 1 (1-ounce) envelope dry onion soup mix	1	(12-ounce) bag frozen chopped onions
1	cup water	2	(7-ounce) cans mushrooms stems and pieces, not drained
2½	pounds eye of round roast cut into ¼-inch to ⅓-inch thin slices	8	medium potatoes
		⅓	cup cornstarch

- In a slow cooker dissolve 1 envelope soup mix in the water.
- In the slow cooker layer the ingredients as follows: beef, soup mix, onions, and mushrooms until all used up.
- Cover and cook on low for 9 to 10 hours. Cook the potatoes in the microwave while cooking the beef.
- Remove the meat onto a serving platter.
- Set aside 1 cup of the liquid. Put the remaining juices, mushrooms, and onions into a large non-stick skillet over high heat and bring to a boil. (This will happen within a minute.)
- In the meantime briskly stir the cornstarch into the 1 cup of liquid set aside. Once dissolved, with a whisk, briskly stir the mixture into the boiling liquid. Constantly stir until thick, about 1 minute.

Note: Partially thaw the eye of round the night before and it will be easier to cut.

Yield: 8 servings

Calories: 406; Fat: 5g (12% fat); Cholesterol: 74mg; Carbohydrate: 51g; Dietary Fiber: 5g; Protein: 37g; Sodium: 648mg

Preparation time: 20 minutes or less
Cooking time: 9 to 10 hours

Menu idea: Tossed salad with sliced fresh tomatoes topped with fat-free Italian dressing and French bread make this a complete meal.

Banana Butterscotch Drops

These sweet drops will curb any sweet tooth. If you like banana bread and butterscotch cookies, you'll like this unusual cookie combination.

3	ripe medium bananas, mashed	2	cups old-fashioned oats
1	(18.25-ounce) box yellow cake mix (I use Betty Crocker Super Moist.)	1	cup butterscotch baking chips

- Preheat the oven to 350 degrees.
- Line the cookie sheets with foil for easier cleanup. Spray cookie sheets with a nonfat cooking spray.
- Mash the bananas with a mixer on medium speed, mix the bananas for 1 minute. Add the cake mix and continue mixing for $1\frac{1}{2}$ to 2 minutes, until all the ingredients are well blended.
- With a wooden spoon stir in the oatmeal and butterscotch baking chips. Stir until well blended.
- With a measuring teaspoon, drop rounded teaspoonfuls of cookie dough onto the prepared cookie sheet.
- Bake for 14 to 15 minutes or until the bottoms are golden brown.

Yield: 6 dozen cookies

Calories: 53; Fat: 1g (17% fat); Cholesterol: 0mg; Carbohydrate: 10g; Dietary Fiber: 0g; Protein: 1g; Sodium: 49mg

Preparation time: 10 minutes or less
Baking time: 15 minutes or less
Total time: 25 minutes or less

Butterfinger Trifle

This is rich.

2	plus 2 cups skim milk	I	(12-ounce) fat-free pound cake
2	(4-serving-size) boxes sugar-free vanilla instant pudding	I	(4-serving-size) box sugar-free chocolate instant pudding mix
I6	ounces fat-free whipped topping	I	(4-serving-size) box sugar-free butterscotch instant pudding mix
1½	plus ½ (2.1-ounce) Butterfinger candy bars		

- With a whisk beat 2 cups of the milk and the vanilla pudding mixes together for 1 minute.
- Stir in 8 ounces whipped topping and 1½ of the candy bars, crushed. Save the remaining half candy bar for later. Gently stir in the cake pieces.
- With a whisk beat the remaining 2 cups milk and chocolate- and butterscotch-flavored puddings together for 1 minute. Stir in the remaining 8 ounces whipped topping.
- In the bottom of a large glass bowl spread half of the chocolate-butterscotch pudding mixture.
- Top with half of the cake mixture.
- Smooth on the remaining chocolate-butterscotch mixture.
- Spread the remaining cake mixture on top.
- Sprinkle with the remaining crushed candy bar.
- Keep chilled until ready to serve.

Yield: 16 servings

Calories: 187; Fat: 2g (9% fat); Cholesterol: 1mg; Carbohydrate: 36g; Dietary Fiber: 0g; Protein: 4g; Sodium: 427mg

Preparation time: 10 minutes or less
Chilling time: 45 minutes or less
Total time: 55 minutes or less

Punchbowl Cake

This recipe was given to me by Pat Paydo of Birmingham, Alabama. It is absolutely wonderful—fast, easy, delicious, and very pretty.

1 (13^{1}/2-ounce) angel food cake	2 medium bananas, sliced and quartered
1 (21-ounce) can strawberry or blueberry pie filling	1 (8-ounce) container fat-free whipped topping

- Cut the cake into three layers. Tear one of the layers into tiny pieces.
- Mix the pie filling with quartered banana slices until well blended.
- Put one layer of cake on the bottom of a punch bowl. Use the torn pieces of cake to fill in any gaps.
- Spread half of the fruit mixture over the cake.
- Place the second layer of the cake on top of the fruit filling. Use the torn pieces to fill in any gaps.
- Spread the remaining fruit mixture on top of the cake.
- Frost with the whipped topping evenly on the top.

Yield: 12 servings

Calories: 188; Fat: 0g (0% fat); Cholesterol: 0mg; Carbohydrate: 42g; Dietary Fiber: 2g; Protein: 3g; Sodium: 264mg

Total time: 10 minutes or less

Apple Berry Bake

This is one of my favorite creations, and it is absolutely delicious. If you like apple crisp and cranberries, you'll like this creative combination as much as I do. It's a guaranteed winner.

1/4	ounce fat-free margarine	1	teaspoon ground cinnamon
1	(8-ounce) package apple-cinnamon crisp mix	1	large apple, peeled and chopped into 1/4-inch pieces, approximately 1 cup
1	(16-ounce) can whole-berry cranberry sauce		

- Preheat the oven to 400 degrees.
- Spray a 9 x 9-inch cake pan or a 9-inch pie pan with nonfat cooking spray.
- With a fork mix together well the margarine and apple-cinnamon crisp.
- Set in the freezer. (The dough will be "doughy," not crumbly.)
- Mix the cranberries, cinnamon, and chopped apple together until well combined.
- Pour this cranberry/apple mixture into the pan.
- With two forks arrange the pieces of dough on top of the cranberry-apple mixture. There may be some spots where the dough has not completely covered the cranberry/apple mixture.
- Bake for 27 minutes or until the top of the dough is golden brown and the fruit is bubbly hot.
- Let cool for 4 to 5 minutes before serving.

Yield: 9 servings

Calories: 185; Fat: 1g (7% fat); Cholesterol: 0mg; Carbohydrate: 43g; Dietary Fiber: 2g; Protein: 2g; Sodium: 126mg

Preparation time: 8 minutes or less
Baking time: 27 minutes
Total time: 35 minutes or less

Strawberry Squares

$^1/_2$ cup applesauce	I (4-serving-size) box sugar-free, strawberry-flavored gelatin mix, dry
$^1/_2$ cup strawberry preserves	
$^3/_4$ plus $^1/_4$ cup Egg Beaters	I cup powdered sugar
I (18.25-ounce) yellow cake mix (I use Betty Crocker Super Moist.)	I (8-ounce) container fat-free cream cheese, softened

- Preheat the oven to 350 degrees.
- Spray a 9 x 15-inch jelly roll pan with nonfat cooking spray.
- Mix the applesauce, strawberry preserves, $^1/_4$ cup of the Egg Beaters, and the cake mix together with a mixer on medium speed. Beat for 2 minutes.
- Spread the batter into the prepared pan.
- With the mixer beat together the dry gelatin mix, powdered sugar, and cream cheese with the remaining Egg Beaters on medium speed for 2 minutes. Pour over the cake batter.
- Bake for 22 to 25 minutes or until a knife inserted in the center comes out clean.

Yield: 24 servings

(Nutritional Information per square)
Calories: 144; Fat: 2g (11% fat); Cholesterol: 2mg; Carbohydrate: 28g; Dietary Fiber: 0g; Protein: 3g; Sodium: 221mg

Preparation time: 10 minutes or less
Baking time: 25 minutes or less
Total time: 35 minutes or less

Swiss Chocolate Almond Ice Cream Cake

Oh, man! This is too good.

2	quarts Swiss chocolate almond low-fat frozen yogurt	6	reduced-fat fudge sandwich cookies
5	fat-free chocolate brownies	1	(11½-ounce) jar fat-free hot fudge

- Let the frozen yogurt sit out to soften, about 5 minutes.
- Spray a 9 x 13-inch pan with nonfat cooking spray.
- Put the brownies and cookies in a food processor. Turn it on for about 30 to 40 seconds until they are a coarse, crumbly consistency.
- With the palm of your hand, press the brownie-cookie mixture on the bottom of the prepared pan.
- Spoon the frozen yogurt over the brownie/cookie crust. With a spatula spread the yogurt to look smooth.
- Heat the hot fudge in a microwave. Quickly spread the hot fudge over the yogurt. The hot fudge will melt the yogurt. That's okay.
- Freeze overnight. (This can be made days in advance.)
- Cut into 15 squares.

Yield: 15 servings

Calories: 241; Fat: 2g (9% fat); Cholesterol: 5mg; Carbohydrate: 51g; Dietary Fiber: 2g; Protein: 6g; Sodium: 199mg

🕐 **Preparation time:** 15 to 20 minutes

Black Forest Tortilla Stack

It doesn't get any easier or any faster than this, folks.

I	(1.4-ounce) box chocolate sugar-free, instant pudding mix, dry	7	(10-inch) fat-free flour tortillas
2	cups skim milk	I	(21-ounce) can cherry pie filling
		1/4	cup fat-free hot fudge

- Mix pudding and skim milk together, stirring briskly for 2 minutes.
- Lay one tortilla on a cake plate. Spread ½ cup chocolate pudding over the tortilla. Lay the second tortilla on top of the pudding. Spread one-third of the can of cherry pie filling over the tortilla. Lay the third tortilla on top of the pie filling. Repeat the layering process with the remaining four tortillas.
- Microwave the hot fudge for 15 seconds on high or until fully heated.
- Drizzle the hot fudge over the pudding and let it drizzle over the sides.
- Keep refrigerated until ready to serve.

Yield: 12 servings

Calories: 199; Fat: 0g (0% fat); Cholesterol: 1mg; Carbohydrate: 43g; Dietary Fiber: 2g; Protein: 5g; Sodium: 461mg

🕐 **Total preparation time:** 5 minutes or less

Mint Mousse

This rich, thick dessert is fabulous.

1/2	teaspoon mint extract	1	(4-serving-size) box sugar-free
1	(12-ounce) container fat-free whipped topping		vanilla instant pudding, dry
		6	drops green food coloring, optional

- Mix together the extract, whipped topping, pudding, and food coloring, if using.
- Keep stirring for 2 minutes.
- Spoon the mixture into dessert cups. For a fancier look, spoon into wide-mouth wine glasses instead of dessert cups.
- Ready to serve as is, or refrigerate until ready to eat.

Note: During Christmas place a small candy cane into each dessert or crush 1 candy cane into tiny pieces and sprinkle it on top. For St. Patrick's Day set a spearmint candy leaf on top of each dessert.

Yield: 5 servings

(without garnish) Calories: 132; Fat: 0g (0% fat); Cholesterol: 0mg; Carbohydrate: 27g; Dietary Fiber: 0g; Protein: 0g; Sodium: 272mg

Total preparation time: 5 minutes or less

Pumpkin Fluff (Pumpkin Fluff Pie)

This creamy, fluffy dessert is "just right" after a heavy meal.

I¹/2 cups canned pumpkin
I   teaspoon ground cinnamon
¹/2 cup Splenda that measures like sugar
I   tablespoon light maple syrup

I   (12-ounce) container fat-free whipped topping
I   (1.3-ounce) box sugar-free vanilla pudding, dry

- Mix the pumpkin, cinnamon, Splenda, and maple syrup together until well blended.
- In a different bowl, mix the whipped topping and pudding together until well blended.
- Combine the pumpkin mixture with the pudding mixture. Stir until well mixed.
- Sprinkle the top lightly with cinnamon if desired.
- Keep refrigerated until ready to eat. Serve chilled.

Yield: 8 servings

Calories: 111; Fat: 0g (0% fat); Cholesterol: 0mg; Carbohydrate: 24g; Dietary Fiber: 2g; Protein: 1g; Sodium: 248mg

★ **For Pumpkin Fluff Pie:** Use a prepared graham cracker reduced-fat piecrust. Simply prepare the pumpkin fluff as directed and put the mixture into the piecrust. Sprinkle the top with cinnamon if desired.

Yield: 8 servings

Calories: 212; Fat: 3g (15% fat); Cholesterol: 0mg; Carbohydrate: 40g; Dietary Fiber: 2g; Protein: 2g; Sodium: 344mg

🕐 **Preparation time:** 10 minutes or less

Blueberry Fluff Cups

Fun, fast, and fabulous for the Fourth of July.

---

1 1/2 cups fat-free whipped topping
3 tablespoons blueberry spreadable fruit jam
1 (4 1/2-ounce) package shortcakes

1 cup fresh blueberries sprinkled lightly with Splenda if needed

---

- Mix the whipped topping and blueberry jam together until well blended.
- Spoon the mixture evenly onto each shortcake. If desired, put a dab of whipped topping on top.
- Top the shortcake with blueberries. Cover and keep chilled until ready to eat.
- For a prettier, more elegant presentation, put each dessert onto its own pretty dessert plate before serving.

Yield: 4 servings

Calories: 185; Fat: 2g (11% fat); Cholesterol: 15mg; Carbohydrate: 36g; Dietary Fiber: 2g; Protein: 1g; Sodium: 141mg

Total preparation time: 5 minutes or less

Apricot Cake

This is always an appreciated afternoon delight.

Cake:
1   (17-ounce) can apricot halves in heavy syrup
1   (18.25-ounce) yellow cake mix, dry (I use Betty Crocker Super Moist.)
1   cup apricot preserves

Frosting:
1   (4-serving-size) box sugar-free instant vanilla pudding and pie filling mix, dry
1   (12-ounce) container fat-free whipped topping

- Preheat the oven to 350 degrees.
- Spray a 9 x 13-inch pan with nonfat cooking spray.
- In the blender purée the apricots with the syrup until there are no apricot chunks and the consistency is thick.
- With a mixer, mix the dry cake mix in a medium-size bowl with the puréed apricots on medium speed for 2 minutes.
- Spread the cake batter into the prepared pan.
- Bake for 33 to 35 minutes, or until the cake is golden brown and edges are loose from the pan.
- Let the cake cool for approximately 10 minutes. Spread $\frac{1}{3}$ cup of the apricot preserves over the cake.
- For the frosting, in a medium bowl with a mixer stir together the remaining $\frac{2}{3}$ cup apricot preserves with the dry pudding mix and whipped topping. Mix on low for about 1 minute or until well mixed.
- This cake is delicious served warm from the oven with a dab of this frosting, or let the cake cool completely and frost the entire cake with the frosting.

Yield: 15 servings

Calories: 266; Fat: 3g (10% fat); Cholesterol: 0mg; Carbohydrate: 58g; Dietary Fiber: 1g; Protein: 1g; Sodium: 324mg

Preparation time: 8 minutes or less
Baking time: 33 to 35 minutes
Total time: 43 minutes or less

Frozen Cheesecake Dessert

If you like cheesecake-flavored ice cream, you're gonna love this. This recipe was originally sent in by Tami Heiss of Toledo, Ohio. I think you'll love it.

³/4 **cup graham cracker crumbs (prepared crumbs are easy)**	¹/3 **cup Splenda that measures like sugar**
1 **(12-ounce) container fat-free whipped topping**	1 **(21-ounce) can cherry or blueberry pie filling**
2 **(8-ounce) containers fat-free cream cheese**	

- Spray a 9 x 13-inch pan with nonfat cooking spray.
- Sprinkle graham cracker crumbs in the bottom of the pan.
- In a large bowl with a mixer, mix the whipped topping, cream cheese, and Splenda together on medium speed for 2 minutes.
- Spread into the prepared pan.
- Top with the pie filling. Freeze for 2 hours to set.
- Let sit 10 minutes before cutting.

Yield: 15 servings

Calories: 150; Fat: 0g (0% fat); Cholesterol: 5mg; Carbohydrate: 28g; Dietary Fiber: 0g; Protein: 5g; Sodium: 195mg

Preparation time: 10 to 12 minutes
Freezing time: 2 hours
Total time: 2 hours 20 minutes

Banana Split Tortilla Stack

This dessert is a creative twist to an American favorite.

1	(20-ounce) can crushed pineapple in its juices	7	(10-inch) fat-free flour tortillas
7	ice cubes	1	(21-ounce) can cherry pie filling
1	(1-ounce) box sugar-free instant vanilla pudding, dry	2	medium bananas, cut into slices
		2	tablespoons light chocolate syrup

- Squeeze out as much pineapple juice as possible into a measuring cup.
- Add up to the 7 ice cubes to make 2 cups of liquid.
- Pour the juice and ice cubes into a medium-size mixing bowl.
- Add the pudding mix and stir briskly for 2 minutes.
- Remove any ice cubes that have not dissolved.
- Add the drained pineapple to the pudding mixture. Stir until well mixed.
- Lay one tortilla on a cake plate. Spread ½ cup of the pineapple pudding over the tortilla. Lay the second tortilla on top of the pudding. Spread one-third of the can of cherry pie filling over the tortilla. Press one-third of the banana slices into the pie filling. Lay the third tortilla on top of the pie filling. Repeat the steps for the remaining 4 tortillas.
- Spread ½ cup pudding on the top layer. There will be ½ cup pudding left that you can discard.
- Drizzle the chocolate syrup over the top layer.
- Ready to eat as is. If desired, you can garnish top with 6 individual dabs of the whipped topping and garnish the top with 1 maraschino cherry. Keep chilled until ready to serve.

Yield: 12 servings

Calories: 207; Fat: 0g (0% fat); Cholesterol: 0mg; Carbohydrate: 47g; Dietary Fiber: 3g; Protein: 4g; Sodium: 382mg

Total preparation time: 10 minutes or less.

Sand, Rocks & Candy

For fun, decorate this by placing a child's small plastic sand bucket with the little sand shovel next to the bucket on top and into the dessert. Great for beachside picnics and cookouts.

2	(2-ounce) Chick-O-Sticks (or substitute Butterfinger candy bars with the chocolate scraped off)
2	(1.7-ounce) boxes butterscotch-flavored, sugar-free pudding mix, dry
4	cups skim milk
1 1/2	cups graham cracker crumbs

- Keep the wrapper on and crush the candy by hitting it with a rolling pin.
- Briskly stir together the dry pudding mix and skim milk for 2 minutes. Stir 1 crushed Chick-O-Stick into the pudding.
- Sprinkle half of the graham cracker crumbs on the bottom of a 9 x 13-inch pan.
- Spread the pudding over the graham cracker crumbs.
- Sprinkle the remaining graham cracker crumbs over the pudding.
- Sprinkle the second crushed Chick-O-Stick over the crumbs.
- Serve immediately or cover and keep chilled until ready to serve.

Yield: 12 servings

Calories: 141; Fat: 2g (14% fat); Cholesterol: 2mg; Carbohydrate: 26g; Dietary Fiber: 0g; Protein: 4g; Sodium: 457mg

Total preparation time: 6 minutes or less

Brownie Cookies

This scrumptious cookie mix is very versatile. Many different cookies can be made from this base, and they're all terrific.

1/4	cup brown sugar	2	tablespoons flour
3	tablespoons applesauce	1	(10.25-ounce) package brownie mix
1	egg white		

- Preheat the oven to 350 degrees.
- Line two cookie sheets with foil and spray with nonfat cooking spray.
- Mix together the brown sugar, applesauce, and egg white until well blended. Stir in the flour and brownie mix until well mixed.
- Drop by rounded teaspoonfuls onto the prepared cookie sheets. With a damp fork press the cookies down into 1½-inch circles.
- Bake for 10 minutes.

Yield: 2 dozen cookies

(Nutritional Information per cookie)
Calories: 66; Fat: 2g (21% fat); Cholesterol: 4mg; Carbohydrate: 12g; Dietary Fiber: 0g; Protein: 1g; Sodium: 39mg

Preparation time: 5 minutes or less
Baking time: 10 minutes
Total time: 15 minutes or less

★ **Brownie Sandwich Cookies:** Once the cookies are done and are cool, spread 2 teaspoons marshmallow creme on the bottom of a cookie. Place a second cookie on top of the marshmallow creme and press together.

Yield: 16 cookies.

(Nutritional Information per cookie)
Calories: 151; Fat: 3g (19% fat); Cholesterol: 8mg; Carbohydrate: 29g; Dietary Fiber: 1g; Protein: 2g; Sodium: 81mg

Boston Cream Cake

I got this idea from our local bakery. Of course their version was at least three times more fattening. This recipe makes two 8-inch round cakes.

Cakes:
- 6 egg whites
- 1/2 cup applesauce
- 1 (18.25-ounce) box yellow cake mix, dry (I use Betty Crocker Super Moist.) Do not make as directed on box.

Filling:
- 1 (1-ounce) box sugar-free, fat-free instant vanilla pudding, dry—Do not make as directed on box.
- 1 1/2 cups skim milk
- 1/3 plus 1/3 cup fat-free hot fudge topping

- Preheat the oven to 350 degrees.
- Spray four 8-inch round pans with nonfat cooking spray.
- With a mixer, beat the egg whites for 30 seconds. Add the applesauce and beat 10 seconds. Gradually add the cake mix. Do not pour in all at once. Once the entire cake mix is added, beat on high for 2 minutes.
- Divide and spread the batter evenly into the prepared pans.
- Bake for 15 minutes or until a knife inserted in the center comes out clean.
- Cool in the pans for 10 minutes. Remove from the pans and cool completely. They cool more quickly on cooling racks.
- For the filling, with the mixer on lowest speed, mix the dry pudding mix and milk together for 2 minutes. Refrigerate.
- To assemble, when cakes are cooled, put one cake layer on a cake plate. Spread half of the cream mixture on the cake. Put the second cake layer on top of the creamed mixture. Spread 1/3 cup hot fudge topping on top of the cake.
- Repeat for the second cake.

Yield: 16 servings (8 per cake)

Calories: 187; Fat: 1g (4% fat); Cholesterol: 0mg; Carbohydrate: 42g ; Dietary Fiber: 0g; Protein: 4g; Sodium: 353mg

Preparation time: 12 minutes
Baking time: 15 minutes
Total time: 35 minutes or less

Spice Cookies

Not only does this very versatile cookie satisfy your sweet tooth, but when they're baking, the fragrant aroma of potpourri fills your home with a warm and cozy feeling.

2	cups whole wheat flour	1/2	cup applesauce
1	cup sugar	1/2	teaspoon ground cloves
1	teaspoon baking soda	1	teaspoon ground cinnamon
4	egg whites		

- Preheat the oven to 350 degrees.
- Line 2 cookie sheets with foil. Spray the foil with nonfat cooking spray.
- In a large mixing bowl mix together the flour, sugar, soda, egg whites, applesauce, cloves, and cinnamon with a spatula until well mixed.
- Drop the cookie dough by rounded teaspoonfuls onto the prepared cookie sheets.
- Bake for 6 to 7 minutes or until the bottoms are lightly browned.

Yield: 6 dozen cookies

(Nutritional information per cookie)
Calories: 24; Fat: 0g (0% fat); Cholesterol: 0mg; Carbohydrate: 5g; Dietary Fiber: 0g; Protein: 1g; Sodium: 21mg

Preparation time: 10 minutes or less
Baking time: 18 to 21 minutes
Total time: 31 minutes or less

★ **Chocolate Chip Spice Cookies:** Press 3 chocolate chips on top of each cookie before baking.

Yield: 6 dozen cookies

(Nutritional information per cookie)
Calories: 39; Fat: 1g (22% fat); Cholesterol: 0mg; Carbohydrate: 7g; Dietary Fiber: 1g; Protein: 1g; Sodium: 21mg

Apple Spice Cookies

When baking these delicious cookies, your home with will smell like heaven.

2	cups whole wheat flour	1/2	teaspoon ground cloves
1	cup sugar	1	teaspoon ground cinnamon
1	teaspoon baking soda	2	Rome Beauty apples (Golden Delicious or Granny Smith will work), cut into 1/4-inch pieces
4	egg whites		
1/2	cup applesauce		

- Preheat the oven to 350 degrees.
- Line cookie sheets with foil. Spray the foil with nonfat cooking spray.
- In a large mixing bowl mix together the flour, sugar, soda, egg whites, applesauce, cloves, and cinnamon with a spatula until well mixed.
- Stir the apples into the prepared dough.
- Drop the cookie dough by rounded teaspoonfuls onto the prepared cookie sheets.
- Bake for 6 to 7 minutes or until the bottoms are lightly browned.

Yield: 6 dozen cookies

(Nutritional Information per cookie)
Calories: 26; Fat: 0g (0% fat); Cholesterol: 0mg; Carbohydrate: 6g; Dietary Fiber: 1g; Protein: 1g; Sodium: 21mg

★ **Apple-Walnut Cookies:** Not using more than 1/2 cup finely chopped walnuts for the entire recipe, sprinkle the walnuts on top of the cookies before baking.

Yield: 6 dozen cookies

(Nutritional Information per cookie)
Calories: 32; Fat: 1g (17% fat); Cholesterol: 0mg; Carbohydrate: 6g; Dietary Fiber: 1g; Protein: 1g; Sodium: 21mg

Preparation time: 10 minutes or less
Baking time: 18 to 21 minutes
Total time: 31 minutes or less

Raisin Spice Cookies

These are perfect cookies for a cool afternoon. The spicy scent fills your home with warmth and love.

2 cups whole wheat flour	1/2 teaspoon ground cloves
1 cup sugar	1 teaspoon ground cinnamon
1 teaspoon baking soda	3/4 cup raisins
4 egg whites	1/4 cup confectioners' sugar
1/2 cup applesauce	

- Preheat the oven to 350 degrees.
- Line 2 cookie sheets with foil. Spray the foil with nonfat cooking spray.
- In a large mixing bowl mix together the flour, sugar, soda, egg whites, applesauce, cloves, cinnamon, and raisins with a spatula until well mixed.
- Drop the cookie dough by rounded teaspoonfuls onto the prepared cookie sheets.
- Bake for 6 to 7 minutes or until the bottoms are lightly browned.
- Sprinkle the confectioners' sugar evenly over the tops of the cooled cookies.

Yield: 6 dozen cookies

(Nutritional Information per cookie)
Calories: 31; Fat: 0g (0% fat); Cholesterol: 0mg; Carbohydrate: 7g; Dietary Fiber: 1g; Protein: 1g; Sodium: 21mg

★ **Craisin Cookies:** Stir in 3/4 cup chopped, dried cranberries into the prepared dough.

Yield: 6 dozen cookies

(Nutritional Information per cookie)
Calories: 28; Fat: 0g (0% fat); Cholesterol: 0mg; Carbohydrate: 6g; Dietary Fiber: 1g; Protein: 1g; Sodium: 21mg

Preparation time: 10 minutes or less
Baking time: 18 to 21 minutes
Total time: 31 minutes or less

Carrot Cookies

These are wonderful cookies that have a warm spicy aroma and a healthy tasting of carrots.

2 cups whole wheat flour	1/2 teaspoon ground cloves
1 cup sugar	1 teaspoon ground cinnamon
1 teaspoon baking soda	1 1/2 cups finely grated carrot
4 egg whites	1/4 cup confectioners' sugar
1/2 cup applesauce	

- Preheat the oven to 350 degrees.
- Line 2 cookie sheets with foil. Spray the foil with nonfat cooking spray.
- In a large mixing bowl mix together the flour, sugar, soda, egg whites, applesauce, cloves, cinnamon, and carrot with a spatula until well mixed.
- Drop the cookie dough by rounded teaspoonfuls onto the prepared cookie sheets.
- Bake for 6 to 7 minutes or until the bottoms are lightly browned.
- Sprinkle the confectioners' sugar evenly over the tops of the cooled cookies.

Yield: 6 dozen cookies

(Nutritional Information per cookie)
Calories: 26; Fat: 0g (0% fat); Cholesterol: 0mg; Carbohydrate: 6g; Dietary Fiber: 1g; Protein: 1g; Sodium: 22mg

Preparation time: 10 minutes or less
Baking time: 18 to 21 minutes
Total time: 31 minutes or less

Peppermint Cream Pudding Cake

This cool, creamy dessert cake satisfies even the most discriminating taste.

2 plus I peppermint candy canes, finely crushed in the blender	I (12-ounce) container fat-free whipped topping
1 1/2 cups skim milk	I (10 1/2-ounce) angel food cake
I (3 1/2-ounce) box French vanilla instant pudding, dry	

- Mix 2 of the candy canes, the milk, and pudding together in a bowl for about 2 minutes by hand with a whisk. Add the whipped topping and keep stirring until well blended, smooth, and creamy.
- Cut the cake into four thin layers. Line the bottom of a 9 x 13-inch pan with the cake pieces. You will need to tear some of the pieces of cake so you can line the entire bottom of the pan.
- Frost the cake with the cream mixture.
- Sprinkle the remaining crushed candy on top. Eat as is, or keep chilled until ready to eat.

Yield: 12 servings

Calories: 180; Fat: 0g (0% fat); Cholesterol: 1mg; Carbohydrate: 40g; Dietary Fiber: 0g; Protein: 3g; Sodium: 353 mg

Preparation time: 5 to 10 minutes

Perfect Pineapple Cookies

It's hard to eat just one. If you like pineapple upside-down cake, you'll love these cookies.

1/4 cup dark brown sugar	1 (18.25-ounce) box yellow cake mix (I use Betty Crocker Super Moist.) Do not make as directed on box.
1 (20-ounce) can crushed pineapple in natural juices, drained, 1 cup juice discarded	
3 egg whites	1/2 cup graham cracker crumbs

- Preheat the oven to 350 degrees.
- Line 4 cookie sheets with foil and spray with nonfat cooking spray.
- With a spatula or spoon, mix together the brown sugar, pineapple, and egg whites until well mixed and the sugar is dissolved.
- Add the cake mix and graham cracker crumbs. Continue stirring until well mixed.
- Drop by teaspoonfuls onto prepared cookie sheets. Dip your fingers in water and press the tops of the cookies down to 1½-inch circles.
- Bake at 350 degrees for 11 to 12 minutes or until the bottoms are golden brown.

Yield: 7 dozen cookies

(Nutritional information per cookie)
Calories: 33; Fat: 0.5g (0% fat); Cholesterol: 0mg; Carbohydrate: 7g; Dietary Fiber: 0g; Protein: 0g; Sodium: 50mg

Preparation time: 5 minutes or less
Baking time: 12 minutes or less per dozen
Total time: 51 minutes or less for 7 dozen

Double Chocolate Oatmeal Cookies

For the chocolate lover.

3/4 cup applesauce	I	(18.25-ounce) box Devil's Food cake mix, dry (I use Betty Crocker Super Moist.) Do not make as directed on box.
1/2 cup dark brown sugar		
1 1/2 cups quick-cooking oats	I	cup semi-sweet chocolate chips

- Preheat the oven to 350 degrees.
- Line 2 cookie sheets with foil. Spray the foil with nonfat cooking spray.
- In a large bowl mix the applesauce and brown sugar with a spatula until well mixed.
- Stir in the oats and dry cake mix. Continue stirring until well mixed.
- Stir in the chocolate chips until well mixed and chips are evenly distributed throughout the dough.
- Drop the cookie dough onto the prepared cookie sheets by the rounded teaspoonful.
- Dip a fork into water and press the dough down to about 1 1/2-inch circles.
- Bake for 12 to 13 minutes.

Yield: 5 dozen cookies

(Nutritional information per cookie)
Calories: 62; Fat: 1g (18% fat); Cholesterol: 0mg; Carbohydrate: 12g; Dietary Fiber: 1g; Protein: 1g; Sodium: 79mg

Preparation time: 5 minutes or less
Baking time: 13 minutes or less for 2 dozen
Total time: 41 to 44 minutes for 5 dozen

Double Chocolate Creme-Filled Sandwich Cookies

This is especially good for those who love chocolate.

3/4 cup applesauce
1/2 cup dark brown sugar
11/2 cups quick-cooking oats
1 (1pound 21/4-ounce) box reduced-fat Devil's Food cake mix, dry (I use Betty Crocker Super Moist.) Do not make as directed on box.
1 cup semi-sweet chocolate chips
11/4 cup marshmallow creme

- Preheat the oven to 350 degrees.
- Line 2 cookie sheets with foil. Spray the foil with nonfat cooking spray.
- In a large bowl mix the applesauce and brown sugar with a spatula until well mixed.
- Stir in the oats and dry cake mix. Continue stirring until well mixed.
- Stir in the chocolate chips until well mixed and chips are evenly distributed throughout the dough.
- Drop the cookie dough onto the prepared cookie sheets by the rounded teaspoonful.
- Dip a fork into water and press the dough down to about 1½-inch circles.
- Bake for 12 to 13 minutes.
- Once cooled, place 2 teaspoons marshmallow creme on top of half of the cookies. Place the bare cookies on top of the ones with topping to make a sandwich.

Yield: 2½ dozen cookies

Calories: 142; Fat: 3g (16% fat); Cholesterol: 0mg; Carbohydrate: 30g; Dietary Fiber: 1g; Protein: 2g; Sodium: 154mg

Preparation time: 5 minutes or less
Baking time: 13 minutes or less for 2 dozen
Total time: 29 to 31 minutes for 2½ dozen

Chocolate Pecan Cookies

These are perfect for the chocolate lover nut.

3/4 cup applesauce	mix, dry (I use Betty Crocker Super Moist.) Do not make as directed on box.
1/2 cup dark brown sugar	
1 1/2 cups quick-cooking oats	1 cup semi-sweet chocolate chips
1 (I pound 2 1/4-ounce) box reduced-fat Devil's Food cake	1 1/4 cup chopped pecans

- Preheat the oven to 350 degrees.
- Line cookie sheets with foil. Spray the foil with nonfat cooking spray.
- In a large bowl mix the applesauce and brown sugar with a spatula until well mixed.
- Stir in the oats and dry cake mix. Continue stirring until well mixed.
- Stir in the chocolate chips until well mixed and chips are evenly distributed throughout the dough.
- Drop the cookie dough onto the prepared cookie sheets by the rounded teaspoonful.
- Dip a fork into water and press the dough down to about 1 1/2-inch circles.
- Sprinkle each cookie lightly with the chopped pecans.
- Bake for 12 to 13 minutes.

Yield: 5 dozen cookies

(Nutritional Information per cookie)
Calories: 68; Fat: 2g (25% fat); Cholesterol: 0mg; Carbohydrate: 13g; Dietary Fiber: 1g; Protein: 1g; Sodium: 75mg

Preparation time: 5 minutes or less
Baking time: 13 minutes or less for 2 dozen
Total time: 41 to 44 minutes for 5 dozen

Chocolate Pecan Creme-Filled Sandwich Cookies

These are an extra special treat for those chocolate nuts out there.

3/4 cup applesauce	1 cup semi-sweet chocolate chips
1/2 cup dark brown sugar	1 1/4 cup chopped pecans
1 1/2 cups quick-cooking oats	1 1/4 cup marshmallow creme
1 (1 pound 2 1/4-ounce) box reduced-fat Devil's Food cake mix, dry (I use Betty Crocker Super Moist.) Do not make as directed on box.	

- Preheat the oven to 350 degrees.
- Line cookie sheets with foil. Spray the foil with nonfat cooking spray.
- In a large bowl mix the applesauce and brown sugar with a spatula until well mixed.
- Stir in the oats and dry cake mix. Continue stirring until well mixed.
- Stir in the chocolate chips until well mixed and chips are evenly distributed throughout the dough.
- Drop the cookie dough onto the prepared cookie sheets by the rounded teaspoonful.
- Dip a fork into water and press the dough down to about 1 1/2-inch circles.
- Sprinkle each cookie lightly with the chopped pecans.
- Bake for 12 to 13 minutes.
- Once cooled, place 2 teaspoons marshmallow creme on top of half of the cookies. Place the bare cookies on top of the ones with topping to make a sandwich.

Yield: 2 1/2 dozen cookies

(Nutritional Information per cookie)
Calories: 156; Fat: 4g (22% fat); Cholesterol: 0mg; Carbohydrate: 30g; Dietary Fiber: 1g; Protein: 2g; Sodium: 154mg

Preparation time: 5 minutes or less
Baking time: 13 minutes or less for 2 dozen
Total time: 29 to 31 minutes for 2 1/2 dozen

Hot Fudge Cake

This mouth-watering, delicious dessert is just what the tummy ordered.

1	(18.25-ounce) devil's food cake mix (I use Betty Crocker Super Moist.) Do not make as directed on box.	6	egg whites
1^1/3 cups water		1	half-gallon fat-free, frozen vanilla yogurt, slightly thawed
3	tablespoons applesauce	1	(11^1/2-ounce) jar fat-free hot fudge
		1	(8-ounce) container fat-free whipped topping

- Preheat the oven to 350 degrees.
- Spray two 9 x 13-inch pans with nonfat cooking spray.
- With a mixer beat the cake mix, water, applesauce, and egg whites on low speed for 30 seconds. Beat on medium speed 2 minutes longer.
- Divide the batter between the prepared pans.
- Bake for 15 minutes.
- Let the cakes cool for 10 minutes.
- Spread the frozen yogurt evenly over one of the cakes.
- Place the second cake on top of the frozen yogurt. At this point you can eat the cake or freeze it to eat later. Cover with plastic wrap or foil before freezing.
- To serve, cut into sixteen pieces. Place each individual piece on a serving plate.
- Microwave the hot fudge 30 to 45 seconds in the jar it comes in. Stir. Drizzle 1 tablespoon hot fudge on each serving.
- Top with a dab of whipped topping. Top that with a maraschino cherry if desired.
- Serve immediately.

Yield: 16 servings

Calories: 311; Fat: 1g (4% fat); Cholesterol: 2mg; Carbohydrate: 67g; Dietary Fiber: 1g; Protein: 8g; Sodium: 426mg

Preparation time: 5 minutes
Baking time: 15 minutes
Total time: 30 minutes including cooling time

Chocolate Cheese Squares

Fast and easy to prepare. Needs time to bake and cool.

1 (17½-ounce) double chocolate chunk cookie mix, dry—Do not make as directed on package.	2 (8-ounce) packages fat-free cream cheese, softened
6 plus 3 egg whites	¼ cup chocolate-flavored powdered sugar
½ cup sugar	

- Set aside 1 cup of the dry cookie mix. In a large bowl combine the remaining cookie mix with 3 of the egg whites.
- Spray a 9¼ x 13¼-inch cookie sheet with edges, also known as a jelly roll pan, with nonfat cooking spray.
- With a spatula spread the cookie mixture on the bottom of the pan evenly. This layer will be thin.
- Beat together the sugar, cream cheese, the remaining 6 egg whites, and reserved cookie mix. Beat on medium speed for 1½ minutes or until well blended. Pour over the batter in the prepared pan.
- Bake for 40 minutes or until the center is firm.
- Let cool 10 minutes. Cut into 24 squares approximately 2½ x 2½ inches.
- Sift powdered sugar over the squares. If desired you can arrange the squares on a serving plate. They will chill faster if removed from the baking pan and separated. Do not stack. Cover with foil. Refrigerate at least 30 minutes to chill before serving. Keep refrigerated. Best served chilled.

Yield: 24 servings

(Nutritional Information per square)
Calories: 150; Fat: 5g (30% fat); Cholesterol: 3mg; Carbohydrate: 21g; Dietary Fiber: 0g; Protein: 5g; Sodium: 174mg

Preparation time: 10 minutes or less
Baking time: 40 minutes
Total time: 50 minutes or less

Pumpkin Apple Bake

This dessert is wonderful served warm with a dab of fat-free whipped topping or serve chilled. Although I use no eggs, it reminds me a lot of a thick pumpkin custard with apples in it. Definitely a good replacement during the holidays for pumpkin pie.

I plus $\frac{1}{2}$ cup pancake mix	I (20-ounce) can apple pie filling
$I^{1}/3$ plus $\frac{1}{3}$ cups fat-free sweetened condensed milk	I tablespoon pumpkin pie spice
I (29-ounce) can pumpkin	I cup packed dark brown sugar

- Preheat the oven to 350 degrees.
- Spray a 9 x 13-inch pan with nonfat cooking spray.
- In a microwavable small bowl mix $\frac{1}{2}$ cup of the pancake mix and $\frac{1}{3}$ cup of the sweetened condensed milk until well mixed.
- Mix the remaining pancake mix and milk with the pumpkin, apple pie filling, pie spice, and brown sugar together. Spread the mixture into the prepared pan.
- Microwave the dough mixture for a few seconds, until bubbly. Drizzle the bubbly, hot dough mixture over the pumpkin mixture.
- Bake for 50 minutes. Top will be toasty brown in color when done.
- Let sit 5 minutes before cutting. Refrigerate unused portions.

Note: If desired, try adding $\frac{1}{2}$ cup raisins also.

Yield: 15 servings

Calories: 228; Fat: 0g (0% fat); Cholesterol: 1mg; Carbohydrate: 55g; Dietary Fiber: 3g; Protein: 4g; Sodium: 141mg

Preparation time: 5 minutes
Baking time: 50 minutes
Total time: 55 minutes

Apple Oatmeal Cookies

These soft, chewy cookies don't last long in our home. This is one of my best recipes ever.

3/4 cup applesauce
1/2 cup dark brown sugar
1 1/2 cups quick-cooking oats
1 (18.25-ounce) box yellow cake mix (I use Betty Crocker Super Moist.) Do not make as directed on box.

1 1/2 teaspoons cinnamon
1/2 cup raisins
1 cup peeled and finely chopped apple, Jonathan or McIntosh

- Preheat the oven to 350 degrees.
- Line 2 cookie sheets with foil. Spray the foil with nonfat cooking spray.
- In a large bowl mix well the applesauce and brown sugar.
- Stir in the oats, cake mix, cinnamon, raisins, and apples. Continue stirring until well mixed and the dough is smooth.
- Drop the cookie dough onto the prepared cookie sheets by rounded teaspoonfuls.
- Dip a fork into water and press the dough down to about 1 1/2-inch circles.
- Bake for 10 to 12 minutes or until lightly golden on bottom.

Yield: 6 dozen cookies

(Nutritional information per cookie)
Calories: 44; Fat: 0g (0% fat); Cholesterol: 0mg; Carbohydrate: 10g; Dietary Fiber: 0g; Protein: 1g; Sodium: 48mg

Preparation time: 10 minutes
Baking time: 12 minutes or less per 2 dozen
Total time: 40 to 46 minutes for 6 dozen

Very Berry Cheesecake Trifle

This beautiful trifle is super rich. A little bit goes a long way. It always gets wonderful comments such as "Ooh! Aah! How pretty!" when I serve it.

2 **(8-ounce) packages fat-free cream cheese, softened**	1 **(8-ounce) container fat-free whipped topping**
3/4 **cup powdered sugar**	1 **(10½-ounce) angel food cake, torn into bite-size pieces**
1 **teaspoon imitation vanilla, butter & nut flavor extract (This is the name of one extract, not three different extracts. If you don't have it, you can substitute 1 teaspoon almond extract.)**	1 **(21-ounce) can strawberry pie filling**
	1 **(21-ounce) can blueberry pie filling**

- In a large bowl with a mixer on low, beat the softened cream cheese, powdered sugar, and extract for 2 minutes until well blended.
- Add the whipped topping and continue mixing for another minute or until well blended. Clean the beaters of the mixer.
- With a spatula stir in the cake pieces.
- Using a large glass bowl spread the strawberry pie filling evenly over the bottom of the bowl.
- Spread the cream cheese/cake mixture evenly over the strawberry pie filling. This is the middle layer of the trifle.
- Spread the blueberry pie filling evenly over the cream cheese/cake mixture.
- Ready to serve as is, or refrigerate until ready to eat.
- Refrigerate any unused portions.

Yield: 15 servings

Calories: 218; Fat: 0g (0% fat); Cholesterol: 5mg; Carbohydrate: 45g; Dietary Fiber: 1g; Protein: 6g; Sodium: 328mg

🕐 **Total preparation time:** 15 minutes or less

Zucchini Snack Cake

This versatile snack cake is as nutritious as it is delicious.

1¹/2 teaspoons ground cinnamon	1 cup applesauce
6 egg whites	3 cups finely shredded fresh zucchini
1 (18.25-ounce) yellow cake mix (I use Betty Crocker Super Moist.) Do not make as directed on package.	¹/2 cup raisins

- Preheat the oven to 350 degrees.
- Spray four 8-inch round cake pans with nonfat cooking spray.
- In a large bowl with a spatula, mix the cinnamon, egg whites, cake mix, and applesauce until well blended, about 2 minutes.
- Gently stir in the zucchini and raisins until well mixed.
- Divide the batter evenly into the prepared pans.
- Bake at 350 degrees for 20 minutes. Cool 10 minutes.
- Cut each cake into six pieces.

Yield: 24 pieces

Calories: 102; Fat: 1g (5% fat); Cholesterol: 0mg; Carbohydrate: 23g; Dietary Fiber: 1g; Protein: 2g; Sodium: 155mg

Preparation time: 20 minutes or less
Baking time: 20 minutes
Total time: 40 minutes or less

★ **Four-layer Zucchini Cake:** While the cakes are baking, with a mixer on medium speed beat together 1 (8-ounce) package fat-free cream cheese and 1 cup marshmallow creme for 1 minute or until well mixed. Once the cakes are cooled, spread the cream cheese mixture evenly on the top of the cake layers. Stack the cakes four layers high.

Yield: 12 servings

Calories: 263; Fat: 1g (4% fat); Cholesterol: 3mg; Carbohydrate: 57g; Dietary Fiber: 1g; Protein: 7g; Sodium: 410mg

Pineapple-Carrot Snack Cake

A very delicious and healthy snack cake.

Cakes:

6 egg whites
3/4 cup applesauce
3 teaspoons cinnamon
I (8¹/4-ounce) can crushed pineapple in heavy syrup, not drained
I (18.25-ounce) reduced rat yellow cake mix, dry (I use Betty Crocker Super Moist.)
2 cups coarsely grated carrots, approximately 3 to 4 carrots
¹/2 cup raisins

Frosting:

I (8¹/4-ounce) can crushed pineapple
I (8-ounce) container fat-free whipped topping
I (1.7-ounce) box sugar-free vanilla pudding, dry

- Preheat the oven to 350 degrees.
- Spray four 8-inch cake pans with nonfat cooking spray.
- With a mixer on medium speed, beat together the egg whites, applesauce, cinnamon, and pineapple, with its juice, for 30 seconds.
- Add the cake mix. Beat on high speed for 2 minutes.
- With a wooden spoon stir in the carrots and raisins until well blended. Divide the batter into the prepared pans.
- Bake for 20 minutes or until a knife inserted in the center of the cake comes out clean. Let cool 10 minutes before removing from the pans.
- To make the frosting, stir the pineapple, whipped topping, and pudding together for 1 minute.
- Spread the mixture between the layers only.
- Stack the cake layers. Cover and keep the frosted cake refrigerated until ready to use.

Yield: 16 servings

Calories: 153; Fat: 1g (4% fat); Cholesterol: 0mg; Carbohydrate: 28g; Dietary Fiber: 0g; Protein: 1g; Sodium: 143mg

Preparation time: 20 minutes
Baking time: 20 minutes
Total preparation time: 40 minutes

Banana Split Ice Cream Cake

This is a real hit with children.

1 cup crushed pretzel sticks (approximately 1½ cups)	1 (8-ounce) container fat-free whipped topping
½ gallon deluxe banana split fat-free ice cream, slightly thawed	¼ cup light chocolate syrup

- Spray a 9 x 13-inch pan with nonfat cooking spray.
- Sprinkle the pretzel crumbs onto the bottom of the pan. There will not be enough pretzels to cover entire bottom of pan. You will see the pan in some places.
- Spoon the ice cream on top of the pretzels. Spread the whipped topping over the ice cream.
- Drizzle the chocolate syrup over the whipped topping.
- Keep frozen until ready to serve.
- Cut into 15 squares.

Yield: 15 servings

Calories: 208; Fat: 0g (0% fat); Cholesterol: 5mg; Carbohydrate: 44g; Dietary Fiber: 0g; Protein: 4g; Sodium: 172mg

Preparation time: 10 minutes or less

Jammin' Snack Cake Bars

Turn up the radio and "JAM" while baking these tasty treats.

5 egg whites	1 (9-ounce) box yellow cake mix
1 (8-ounce) package fat-free cream cheese, softened	1/2 cup strawberry jam, or your favorite
1/3 cup powdered sugar	

- Preheat the oven to 350 degrees.
- Spray a 9 x 13-inch pan with nonfat cooking spray.
- With a mixer beat the egg whites, cream cheese, and powdered sugar together for about 1 minute on medium speed.
- Add the cake mix slowly. Beat on high for 2 minutes.
- Spread the mix into the prepared pan.
- Bake for 15 minutes.
- While the cake is still hot, spread 1/2 cup jam on top.

Yield: 15 servings

Calories: 126; Fat: 2g (16% fat); Cholesterol: 2mg; Carbohydrate: 22g; Dietary Fiber: 0g; Protein: 4g; Sodium: 214mg

Preparation time: 10 minutes or less
Baking time: 15 minutes
Total time: 25 minutes or less

Angel Fluff

This recipe is quick and easy to prepare. Tastes best if prepared a few days ahead of time to give the creamy mixture time to absorb the Jell-O flavoring.

2 (8-ounce) containers fat-free cream cheese	1 tablespoon plus 1 teaspoon sugar-free, strawberry-flavored gelatin
1 (16-ounce) container fat-free sour cream	1 (10-ounce) angel food cake, torn into bite-size pieces
1½ cups marshmallow creme	1 (21-ounce) can cherry pie filling

- With a mixer combine the cream cheese, sour cream, marshmallow creme, and gelatin powder on high speed until well mixed.
- Spread half the cream cheese mixture on the bottom of a large glass bowl. Arrange half the torn cake pieces on top. Smooth half the pie filling over the cake.
- Repeat the layering of the cream cheese mixture, cake pieces, and pie filling.
- Chill.

Yield: 15 servings

Calories: 210; Fat: 0g (0% fat); Cholesterol: 10mg; Carbohydrate: 42g; Dietary Fiber: 1g; Protein: 8g; Sodium: 347mg

Total preparation time: 15 minutes or less

Butterscotch Blitz

The bonus is you can whip it up quickly.

I	cup skim milk	I	(12-ounce) container fat-free whipped topping
I	(1.7-ounce) butterscotch-flavored, sugar-free instant pudding, dry	15	graham crackers
		2	tablespoons butterscotch chips

- Briskly mix the milk and butterscotch pudding together for 1 minute with a spoon. Stir in the whipped topping.
- Arrange 7½ graham crackers on the bottom of a 9 x 13-inch pan. Spread half the butterscotch mixture over the crackers.
- Arrange the second layer of 7 ½ graham crackers on top of the butterscotch mixture. Spread the remaining butterscotch mixture on the second layer of graham crackers.
- Finely chop the butterscotch chips. Sprinkle over the dessert. Keep chilled and covered until ready to eat.
- Eat within 2 days.

Yield: 6 servings

Calories: 301; Fat: 5g (15% fat); Cholesterol: 1mg; Carbohydrate: 56g; Dietary Fiber: 1g; Protein: 4g; Sodium: 599mg

Total preparation time: 10 minutes or less

Peppermint Chocolate Cheesecake

This is one of my favorite creations. At a ritzy restaurant I ate an extremely high-fat version of this creation, which got my creative wheels turning. I think you'll agree that this dessert tastes unbelievably sinful. Thank the good Lord it's not.

12 peppermint disk candies	1/2 cup chocolate-flavored powdered sugar
2 (8-ounce) packages fat-free cream cheese, softened	6 reduced-fat Oreo cookies
1 cup marshmallow creme	3 low-fat chocolate cupcakes with creamy filling

- Spray a 9 x 9-inch pan with nonfat cooking spray.
- Put the peppermint disks in a blender and crush them into a fine powder. Set aside 1 teaspoon of the peppermint powder for later use.
- With a mixer combine the remaining crushed peppermint powder, cream cheese, marshmallow creme, and powdered sugar together on high for 1 minute.
- Crush the Oreos into tiny pieces. Set aside one-quarter of them.
- Cut the cupcakes into tiny pieces. Mix three-fourths of the crushed Oreos and all of the cupcake pieces together and press with your hands the cupcake/Oreo mixture onto the bottom of the prepared pan.
- Spread the cream cheese mixture on top of the crust. Mix the reserved peppermint with the remaining crushed Oreos and sprinkle this mixture on top of the cake.
- Serve as is, or keep refrigerated until ready to eat.

Yield: 9 servings

Calories: 241; Fat: 1g (5% fat); Cholesterol: 9mg; Carbohydrate: 46g; Dietary Fiber: 1g; Protein: 8g; Sodium: 391mg

⊝ **Total preparation time:** 15 minutes or less

Mint Mousse Cake

An easy icebox delight. The key to this fast and easy dessert is to keep all the ingredients chilled and move quickly to return them to the refrigerator when finished.

2	(8-ounce) containers fat-free whipped topping, very cold	1	(12-ounce) fat-free chocolate pound cake, chilled
1/2	cup well-chilled, fat-free, chocolate mint syrup	8	maraschino cherries, optional

- Combine the whipped topping with the syrup in a chilled bowl. Gently stir together until well combined into a smooth, creamy, light mousse.
- Remove the cake from the refrigerator and cut horizontally into three slices.
- Lightly spread the layers of the cake with the mousse, and then frost the top and sides of the cake. *You will not use all of the mousse.*
- Garnish with the maraschino cherries. Cover and refrigerate immediately. Keep chilled until ready to serve.
- When ready to serve, top each slice of cake, once on its own plate, with a dab of the remaining mint mousse.

Yield: 8 servings

Calories: 260; Fat: 0g (0% fat); Cholesterol: 0mg; Carbohydrate: 58g; Dietary Fiber: 0g; Protein: 2g; Sodium: 189mg

Preparation time: 10 minutes or less
Total time: 10 minutes or less

Orange Fluff

Excellent by itself or as a topping on a pound cake, angel food cake, or plain Jell-O.

1 (8-ounce) fat-free sour cream	1 (11-ounce) can mandarin orange segments in light syrup, drained
1 (0.35-ounce) box sugar-free orange gelatin dessert, dry	
1 (8-ounce) container fat-free whipped topping	

- Stir the sour cream, gelatin, and whipped topping together until well mixed.
- Gently fold in the orange segments.
- Serve chilled.

Yield: 5 servings

Calories: 149; Fat: 0g (0% fat); Cholesterol: 7mg; Carbohydrate: 29g; Dietary Fiber: 0g; Protein: 4g; Sodium: 106mg

Total preparation time: 5 minutes or less

Strawberry-Banana Cream Dessert

This recipe is fast and easy to prepare; however it takes time to set. I like to make this the night before. This can be made up to two days in advance.

1 (0.7-ounce) box sugar-free raspberry gelatin	1/2 (10-ounce) angel food cake, cut into 1/2-inch pieces
3 cups boiling water	3 medium-size bananas, sliced into thin slices
1 (10-ounce) package frozen sliced strawberries in sugar, thawed	1 cup fat-free whipped topping

- Spray a 9 x 13-inch pan with nonfat cooking spray.
- Dissolve the gelatin in the boiling water in a medium-size bowl. Set aside 1 cup of the gelatin mix.
- Add the strawberries and the cut-up cake pieces to the remaining 2 cups of gelatin in a bowl. Stir until well mixed.
- Evenly spread the prepared cake mixture into the prepared pan. Evenly arrange the banana slices on top of the cake mixture.
- Stir the remaining 1 cup of gelatin with the whipped topping until a smooth, creamy consistency is reached.
- Pour the whipped topping evenly over the sliced bananas and cake. Make sure all the banana slices are covered, because if not, the bananas will turn dark.
- Refrigerate for at least 2 hours.

Yield: 15 servings

Calories: 87; Fat: 0g (0% fat); Cholesterol: 0mg; Carbohydrate: 20g; Dietary Fiber: 1g; Protein: 2g; Sodium: 131mg

Preparation time: 20 minutes or less
Refrigeration time: 2 hours

Oreo Mousse

It's hard to believe this thick, rich, creamy mousse is fat-free.

1 (1.5-ounce) sugar-free chocolate instant pudding mix, dry—Do not prepare as directed on package.	1 (12-ounce) container fat-free whipped topping 3 plus 1 reduced-fat Oreos, crushed

- Mix the pudding and whipped topping together for about 2 minutes by hand with a spatula until well mixed.
- Stir in the cookie crumbs of 3 cookies
- Put into individual dessert cups. If you don't have dessert cups, wide-mouth wine glasses work great.
- Sprinkle the remaining cookie crumbs on top.
- Serve chilled.

Yield: 6 servings

Calories: 146; Fat: 1g (5% fat); Cholesterol: 0mg; Carbohydrate: 30g; Dietary Fiber: 0g; Protein: 0g; Sodium: 366mg

Preparation time: 10 minutes or less
Total time: 10 minutes or less

Zebras

Lions and tigers will love this mixture of brownies and ice cream. Fast, low-fat, and special.

1 **(10.25-ounce) package fudge brownie mix**	1/2 **gallon caramel-praline crunch fat-free ice cream**
1/2 **cup applesauce**	12 **teaspoons light chocolate syrup**

- Preheat the oven to 350 degrees.
- Spray a 12-muffin tin with nonfat cooking spray.
- Stir the brownie mix with the applesauce until well blended. Divide the batter evenly into the muffin tin previously prepared.
- Bake for 17 minutes.
- Once the brownies are in the oven, take the ice cream out of the freezer to soften.
- Let the brownies cool 4 to 5 minutes. Leave the brownies in the muffin tin.
- Spoon 1/4 cup of the ice cream on top of each warm brownie. Cover with plastic wrap and freeze for 2 hours.
- Dip a sharp steak knife into hot water. Run the knife along the outside edge of each cup.
- Remove the dessert.
- Drizzle each Zebra lightly with chocolate syrup, about 1 teaspoon each.

Yield: 12 brownies

Calories: 319; Fat: 3g (9% fat); Cholesterol: 15mg; Carbohydrate: 64g; Dietary Fiber: 1g; Protein: 5g; Sodium: 184mg

Preparation time: 5 minutes
Baking time: 17 minutes
Total time: 22 minutes

Butterscotch Fluff

This smooth, silky, rich dessert tastes totally fattening. Don't worry; it isn't.

I (1.34-ounce) box sugar-free butterscotch pudding mix, dry— Do not prepare according to directions on box.	I (12-ounce) container fat-free whipped topping

- Mix the pudding mix and whipped topping together with a spatula until well blended, about 2 minutes.
- Spoon into individual dessert cups. If you don't have dessert cups, wide-mouth wine glasses work well.
- Serve chilled.

Yield: 6 servings

Calories: 114; Fat: 0g (0% fat); Cholesterol: 0mg; Carbohydrate: 24g; Dietary Fiber: 0g; Protein: 0g; Sodium: 293mg

Preparation time: 5 minutes or less

Banana Cream Cake

Banana cream pie lovers will love this.

1 (18.25-ounce) white cake mix with pudding in the mix (I use Betty Crocker Super Moist.)	1 cup skim milk
2 egg whites	1 (1.35-ounce) box sugar-free instant vanilla pudding
3 plus 1 bananas cut into bite-size slices, about 1/4-inch thick	1 (8-ounce) container fat-free whipped topping

- Preheat oven to 350 degrees.
- Spray a 9 x 13-inch pan with nonfat cooking spray.
- Beat the egg whites on medium with a hand-held mixer.
- Add three-fourths of the banana slices and beat until well mixed.
- Add the cake mix. Continue mixing for approximately 1 minute. Spread into the prepared pan.
- Bake for 30 minutes.
- In the meantime, while the cake is baking make the cream topping. With a mixer combine the milk and pudding mix together on medium speed for 2 minutes.
- Add the whipped topping and keep mixing until well blended and cream is of consistent color. Set the cream aside.
- Let the cake cool for 10 minutes.
- Arrange the remaining banana slices on top of the cake. Spread the cream mixture over the banana slices, covering the entire cake.
- Serve warm or cover and refrigerate for serving later.

Yield: 15 servings

Calories: 216; Fat: 3g (15% fat); Cholesterol: 0mg; Carbohydrate: 43g; Dietary Fiber: 1g; Protein: 3g; Sodium: 359mg

Preparation time: 12 minutes or less
Baking time: 30 minutes
Total time: 42 minutes or less

Caramel/Apple Dessert

This recipe was sent to me by Lou Ann Hartman.

1	(5-ounce) bag Snack Well Caramel Nut Clusters	1	(8-ounce) container fat-free whipped topping
1	(2.1-ounce) box sugar-free instant vanilla pudding	3	Granny Smith apples, chopped into tiny pieces
1	cup skim milk		

- Cut each piece of candy into six pieces.
- Mix the pudding with the milk, and add the whipped topping, chopped apples, and candy pieces.
- Mix all together well. Refrigerate.
- Stir before serving.

Yield: 6 servings

Calories: 238; Fat: 3g (15% fat); Cholesterol: 0mg; Carbohydrate: 43g; Dietary Fiber: 1g; Protein: 3g; Sodium: 359mg

Preparation time: 10 to15 minutes or less

Pineapple Snack Cake

A tasty, light, healthy snack cake.

1 (18.25-ounce) reduced-fat yellow cake mix, dry (I use Betty Crocker Super Moist.)	$^2/_3$ cup firmly packed dark brown sugar
1 (20-ounce) can crushed, unsweetened pineapple in its juice, not drained	

- Preheat the oven to 350 degrees.
- Spray a 11 x 17-inch jelly roll pan (a cookie sheet with a $^1/_2$-inch rim) with nonfat cooking spray.
- With a spatula combine the dry cake mix with the crushed pineapple and its juice.
- Stir until well mixed.
- Spread the batter thinly in the prepared pan. For easier spreading you may want to spray a spatula with nonfat cooking spray before using it to spread the batter.
- With your fingers, sprinkle the brown sugar evenly and lightly over the batter.
- Bake for 25 minutes or until sides are golden brown.
- Let cool before cutting into 24 square bars. If stacking, put wax paper between layers.

Yield: 24 square bars

Calories: 117; Fat: 1g (4% fat); Cholesterol: 0mg; Carbohydrate: 28g; Dietary Fiber: 0g; Protein: 1g; Sodium: 143mg

Preparation time: 10 minutes or less
Baking time: 25 minutes
Total time: 35 minutes or less

Pineapple Fluff

Mmmmm, this is oh, so-o-o-o good!

1 (1.7-ounce) sugar-free vanilla pudding mix, dry—Do not prepare according to directions on box.	1 (12-ounce) container fat-free whipped topping
	1/2 cup very finely chopped celery, about 1 large stem
1 (20-ounce) can crushed pineapple in natural juice, no sugar added, not drained	2 medium bananas, sliced into thin slices
	1/2 (10-ounce) angel food cake, torn into bite-size pieces

- Mix the pudding and pineapple with juices and whipped topping until the pudding is dissolved and well mixed, about 2 minutes.
- Stir in the celery and bananas. Stir until well coated.
- Stir the torn cake pieces into the dessert. Keep stirring until well coated.
- Serve chilled.

Yield: 14 (1/2-cup) servings

Calories: 118; Fat: 0g (0% fat); Cholesterol: 0mg; Carbohydrate: 27g; Dietary Fiber: 1g; Protein: 1g; Sodium: 236mg

Preparation time: 12 minutes or less

Maraschino Chocolate Cherry Cream Pie

This baby is rich. Watch out!

29 reduced-fat Chocolate Nilla Wafers by Nabisco	1/2 plus 1/2 teaspoon almond extract
1 (10-ounce) jar maraschino cherries, cut in half, juice drained, save 5 tablespoons	12 plus 12 ounces fat-free whipped topping (2 containers)
1 (1.7-ounce) box sugar-free chocolate pudding mix—Do not prepare according to directions on box.	2 tablespoons reduced-fat chocolate chips, finely chopped

- Line a 9-inch pie pan with wafers.
- Set aside 9 cherries to decorate the top.
- Mix the dry pudding mix, ½ teaspoon of the almond extract and 12 ounces of whipped topping together until well blended, about 2 minutes.
- Stir the cherries into the chocolate mixture. Spread in the pie pan over the cookies.
- Measure 5 tablespoons cherry juice and stir in with the remaining 12 ounces whipped topping and the remaining ½ teaspoon almond extract until well mixed, about 1 minute.
- Smooth the whipped topping mixture over the chocolate mixture in the pie pan.
- Sprinkle the chocolate pieces around the perimeter of the pie pan.
- Decorate with the 9 reserved cherries.
- Cover. Keep refrigerated until ready to eat.

Yield: 8 servings

Calories: 275; Fat: 2g (7% fat); Cholesterol: 0mg; Carbohydrate: 59g; Dietary Fiber: 0g; Protein: 1g; Sodium: 390mg

Total preparation time: 20 minutes or less

Perfect Pineapple Cake

What can I say? Aunt Diane says it's perfect.

Cake:
- (18.25-ounce) box yellow cake mix (I use Betty Crocker.) Do not make as directed on box.
- (20-ounce) can crushed pineapple in its natural juice

Frosting:
- 1/2 cup dark brown sugar
- (8-ounce) can crushed pineapple in its natural juice, (discard 1/2 cup of juice)
- (1.7-ounce) box instant sugar-free vanilla pudding mix, dry
- (12-ounce) container fat-free whipped topping

- Preheat the oven to 350 degrees.
- Line a 9 x 13-inch pan with foil for easier cleanup. Spray the lined pan with nonfat cooking spray.
- With a mixer beat together the cake mix and the 20-ounce can of pineapple with juice for 1 minute or until well mixed. Spread into the prepared pan.
- Bake for 30 minutes or until a knife inserted in the center comes out clean.
- For the frosting, in a microwavable bowl mix together the brown sugar and drained 8-ounce can of pineapple. Microwave on high for 30 to 40 seconds, just enough to dissolve the sugar with the pineapple when mixed together but not enough to cook it.
- Add the dry pudding mix and whipped topping to the pineapple mixture. Stir until well mixed. Keep refrigerated until ready to frost the cake.
- Frost the cooled cake and serve.
- Keep the cake refrigerated.

Note: If desired you can serve the cake warm without frosting it. Instead just put a dab of frosting on each piece.

Yield: 15 servings

Calories: 233; Fat: 1g (3% fat); Cholesterol: 0mg; Carbohydrate: 54g; Dietary Fiber: 0g; Protein: 2g; Sodium: 373mg

Preparation time: 10 minutes or less
Baking time: 30 minutes
Total time: 40 minutes or less not including cooling time for cake

Peaches & Cream Trifle

As beautiful as it is delectable.

1	(29-ounce) can sliced peaches, drained	1	(21-ounce) can peach pie filling
2	tablespoons sugar	1	(8-ounce) container fat-free whipped topping
1	(10-ounce) store-bought angel food cake	2	tablespoons finely chopped walnuts

- After draining the juice from the peaches, while peaches are still in the can take a sharp knife and cut the peaches into $\frac{1}{4}$- to $\frac{1}{2}$-inch pieces. Stir in the sugar.
- Cut the cake into three layers. Cut the top layer of the cake into $\frac{1}{2}$-inch pieces.
- In a large glass bowl, lay the bottom layer of the cake in the bowl. Fill in the empty spots with half of the cut-up cake pieces.
- Spread half the can of pie filling over the cake. Spread half the can of cut peaches over the pie filling.
- Spread half the container of whipped topping over the peaches.
- Place the second layer of the cake over the whipped topping. Fill in any empty spots with the remaining cut-up cake pieces.
- Repeat the layering with the remaining pie filling, peaches, and whipped topping.
- Sprinkle the walnuts on top.
- Serve as is, or cover and keep chilled until ready to use.

Yield: 15 servings

Calories: 139; Fat: 1g (5% fat); Cholesterol: 0mg; Carbohydrate: 31g; Dietary Fiber: 1g; Protein: 2g; Sodium: 158mg

🕐 **Preparation time:** 10 minutes or less

Drinks

Orange Lemonade

My husband created this, and we really like it. It's not too sweet or too tart, but like Goldilocks would say, "It's just right."

Juice of 4 lemons		1/2	cup sugar
Juice of 2 oranges		2	quarts cold water

- Mix together the lemon juice, orange juice, sugar, and water.
- Serve chilled on ice.

Yield: 8 servings

Calories: 63; Fat: 0g (0% fat); Cholesterol: 0mg; Carbohydrate: 17g; Dietary Fiber: 0g; Protein: 0g; Sodium: 0mg

Preparation time: 5 minutes or less

Fruity Freeze Drink

An invigorating drink for summer festivities.

1	cup fat-free frozen yogurt, your favorite flavor	1	cup Diet Sprite, chilled
		7	ice cubes

- Put the yogurt, Sprite, and ice cubes in a blender on high for 45 seconds or until the ice cubes are crushed.
- Serve in tall glasses.

Yield: 2 drinks

Calories: 81; Fat: 0g (0% fat); Cholesterol: 0mg; Carbohydrate: 18g; Dietary Fiber: 0g; Protein: 3g; Sodium: 40mg

Preparation time: 5 minutes or less

Sherbet Breeze

A refreshment for those lazy summer days.

1	cup frozen sherbet, your favorite flavor	1	cup Diet Sprite, chilled
		7	ice cubes

- Put the sherbet, Sprite, and ice cubes in a blender on high for 45 seconds or until the ice cubes are crushed.
- Serve in glasses.

Yield: 2 drinks

Calories: 121; Fat: 0g (0% fat); Cholesterol: 0mg; Carbohydrate: 28g; Dietary Fiber: 0g; Protein: 0g; Sodium: 35mg

Preparation time: 5 minutes or less

Berry Fruit Freeze Drink

Cool and refreshing for those hot summer days.

2	cups Diet Sprite or Diet 7-Up	1	cup raspberry sherbet
10	ice cubes	1/2	cup blackberries or blueberries

- Put the Sprite or 7-Up, ice cubes, sherbet, and berries in a blender, cover, and turn on highest speed for 10 to 15 seconds. Turn off. Repeat.
- Pour into cups.
- Serve immediately.

Yield: 4 (1-cup) servings

Calories: 71; Fat: 0g (0% fat); Cholesterol: 0mg; Carbohydrate: 16g; Dietary Fiber: 1g; Protein: 0g; Sodium: 18mg

Preparation time: 5 minutes or less

Tropical Fizz Slushy

I love virgin, frozen Piña Coladas, but they're so fattening that I decided to give this recipe a try. My version is delicious, and a fraction of the cost of those at expensive restaurants.

3 to 3¹/2 cups ice	1¹/2 cups non-alcoholic Piña Colada mix
2 (12-ounce cans) Diet Sprite	

- Put the ice, Sprite, and Piña Colada mix in a blender. Ingredients will come about ¹/2 to ³/4 inch from the top of a 5-cup blender.
- Put the blender on high speed (ice crush speed) for about 30 seconds. The ice will be completely crushed, and the drink will be slushy when ready.
- Pour into tall, 12-ounce glasses. Garnish with a fresh slice of pineapple if desired.

Yield: 4 (12-ounce) servings

Calories: 97; Fat: 2g (16% fat); Cholesterol: 0mg; Carbohydrate: 20g; Dietary Fiber: 0g; Protein: 0g; Sodium: 6mg

Preparation time: 5 minutes or less

Fruity Frothy

This smooth, frothy drink is as refreshing as it is easy to make.

20 ice cubes	1 cup Piña Colada mix
3¹/2 cups juice, a combination of orange, strawberry, and banana	

- Put the ice cubes, juice, and Piña Colada mix in a blender on high for 30 seconds to 1 minute until the ice is crushed and the drink is smooth.
- Serve immediately.

Yield: 4 (10-ounce) servings

Calories: 160; Fat: 1g (6% fat); Cholesterol: 0mg; Carbohydrate: 37g; Dietary Fiber: 0g; Protein: 1g; Sodium: 8mg

Total preparation time: 5 minutes or less

Spiced Tea

This is wonderful to drink warm or chilled over ice. A terrific drink for all seasons.

1	gallon hot water	$1/2$	cup brown sugar
8	tea bags	2	teaspoons ground cinnamon
2	tablespoons cinnamon candies (Red Hots)	$1/2$	teaspoon ground allspice

- Put the water, tea bags, Red Hots, sugar, cinnamon, and allspice into a large kettle or soup pot.
- Stir until the seasonings are dissolved.
- Bring to a boil.
- Turn off the heat. Stir again.
- Remove the tea bags. Ready to drink as is or serve over ice.

Yield: 16 (1-cup) servings

Calories: 34; Fat: 0g (0% fat); Cholesterol: 0mg; Carbohydrate: 9g; Dietary Fiber: 0g; Protein: 0g; Sodium: 3mg

Total time: 5 minutes or less

Tootie-Fruity Frozen Drink

The fruity texture of the pineapple gives this otherwise creamy, smooth drink a unique texture and flavor.

4	cups low-fat frozen peach yogurt	1	cup canned crushed pineapple in its own juice
1	cup orange juice	1	small orange, sliced into 6 slices, optional

- Put the yogurt, orange juice, and pineapple in a blender. For short periods of time, 5 seconds, turn the blender off and on. You may need to rearrange the ingredients in the blender with a long spoon when the blender is off to be sure that all ingredients are well blended. Repeat 4 or 5 times.
- Pour into pretty cups. If desired put a slit into the rind of each orange slice.
- Set an orange slice on the rim of each cup for an eye-appealing effect.

Yield: 6 (1-cup) servings

Calories: 150; Fat: 0g (0% fat); Cholesterol: 1mg; Carbohydrate: 35g; Dietary Fiber: 0g; Protein: 4g; Sodium: 54mg

Total preparation time: 5 minutes or less

Christmas Punch

The deep redness of this full-bodied punch gives this special holiday drink its name.

1	gallon apple juice	1/2	cup cinnamon candies (Red Hots)
2	liters Diet Mountain Dew	1/3	cup lemon juice, fresh or bottled

- In a large pot, bring the apple juice, Mountain Dew, and Red Hots to a boil. Reduce the heat. Keep stirring until all the Red Hots are dissolved.
- Add the lemon juice. Stir well.
- Serve warm or chilled in pretty Christmas glasses or cups.

Yield: 24 (1-cup) servings

Calories: 99; Fat: 0g (0% fat); Cholesterol: 0mg; Carbohydrate: 25g; Dietary Fiber: 0g; Protein: 0g; Sodium: 13mg

Total preparation time: 10 minutes or less
Menu ideas: Serve with your favorite Christmas meal. The punch is also delicious served at showers, birthday parties, and graduations.

Index

A

Angel Fluff, 238

Apple

    Apple Berry Bake, 206

    Apple Cottage Salad, 99

    Apple Oatmeal Cookies, 232

    Apple Spice Cookies, 220

    Caramel/Apple Dessert, 248

    Christmas Punch, 262

    Cran-Apple Oatmeal, 28

    Cranberry Apple Salad, 92

    Pumpkin Apple Bake, 231

    Spiced Apples, 132

    Warm Cran-Apple Salad, 94

Apple Berry Bake, 206

Apple Cottage Salad, 99

Apple Oatmeal Cookies, 232

Apple Spice Cookies, 220

Apricot Cake, 213

Apricot Chicken and Rice, 171

Asparagus

    Chicken Asparagus Casserole, 156

    Mushroom-Asparagus Casserole, 129

    Spring Asparagus, 118

Au Gratin Casserole Dinner, 177

B

Bacon

    Bacon, Lettuce, and Tomato Salad, 96

    "Fake Bacon," 30

    Manhandler Breakfast Bake, 34

    Mushroom, Onion, and Bacon Green Bean Casserole, 115

Bacon, Lettuce, and Tomato Salad, 96

Banana

    Banana Butterscotch Drops, 203

    Banana Cream Cake, 247

    Banana Cream Oatmeal, 29

    Banana Split Ice Cream Cake, 236

    Banana Split Tortilla Stack, 215

    Strawberry-Banana Cream Dessert, 243

Barbecue

    Cowboy Chow, 190

    Hearty Barbecue Skillet Dinner, 175

    Manhandler Meatloaves, 186

    Party Poppers, 51

    Zesty Sausage Sandwiches, 148

Beans

    Beanie Baby Stew, 197

    "B.B.B." (Best Baked Beans), 134

Beans (cont.)

    Cowboy Chow, 190

    Eight-Layer Chili Casserole, 182

    Hawaiian-Style Baked Beans, 137

    Mexican Goulash, 155

    Mexican Pasta, 149

    Mexican Pork Tenderloin with Rice, 174

    Pizza Burritos, 157

    Smokey Bean Soup, 69

    Southwestern Fiesta, 161

    Southwestern Three Bean Salad, 81

    Spicy Thick Vegetarian Chili, 75

Beanie Baby Stew, 197

"B.B.B." (Best Baked Beans), 134

Beef

    B.B.B." (Best Baked Beans), 134

    Beef and Broccoli Skillet Casserole, 173

    Beef and Potatoes with Mushroom and Onion Gravy, 200

    Beef Stroganoff, 165

    Cowboy Grub (Casserole), 154

    Herbed Beef Tenderloin with Seasoned Potatoes & Buttered Mushrooms, 196

    Manhandler Meatloaves, 186

    Mexicali Chicken Burritos, 150

    Popeye's Favorite Salad, 100

    Smothered Steak, 193

    Spanish Tomatoes and Beef, 146

    Steak & Potato Cattlemen's Soup, 67

    Steak & Potatoes Stir-Fry, 158

    Swiss Steak and Potatoes, 189

Beef and Broccoli Skillet Casserole, 173

Beef and Potatoes with Mushroom and Onion Gravy, 200

Beef Stroganoff, 165

Berry Fruit Freeze Drink, 257

Best Baked Beans, "B.B.B.," 134

Black Forest Tortilla Stack, 209

Blueberry

    Berry Fruit Freeze Drink, 257

    Blueberry Crumb Cake, 40

    Blueberry Custard Bake, 36

    Blueberry Fluff Cups, 212

    Very Berry Cheesecake Trifle, 233

    Very Berry Fruit Salad, 79

Boston Cream Cake, 218

Breaded Pork Tenderloins, 184

Breakfast Burrito, 35

Breakfast Fruit-Filled Pockets, 41

Broccoli

    Beef and Broccoli Skillet Casserole, 173

    Broccoli & Cauliflower Salad, 102

    Broccoli & Ham Salad, 85

    Broccoli, Ham & Cheese Frittata, 39

    Broccoli Parmesan, 124

Brownie Cookies, 217

Butterfinger Trifle, 204

Buttermilk Ranch Dressing, 53

Butterscotch Blitz, 239

Butterscotch Fluff, 246

C

Calico Corn, 112

California Garlic Blend, 120

California Medley Soup, 70

California Medley Stew, 194

Caramel/Apple Dessert, 248

Caribbean Chicken Salad Sandwiches, 107

Caribbean Rice, 195

Carrot

Carrot Cookies, 222

Carrot with a Light, Buttery Caramel Glaze, 121

Mashed Potatoes and Carrots, 133

Pineapple-Carrot Snack Cake, 235

Cheese

Apple Cottage Salad, 99

Au Gratin Casserole Dinner, 177

Broccoli, Ham & Cheese Frittata, 39

Broccoli Parmesan, 124

Cheese Biscuits, 63

Chicken & Onion Cheese Spread, 46

Chicken Cheesy Pizza, 178

Chocolate Cheese Squares, 230

Ham & Cheese Potato Salad, 93

Ham & Cheese Spread, 45

Mexican Cheese Moons, 55

Mexican Pizza, 179

Peppermint Chocolate Cheesecake, 240

Pizza Burritos, 157

Very Berry Cheesecake Trifle, 233

Zesty Summer Cottage Salad, 88

Cheese Biscuits, 63

Cherry

Cherry Oatmeal, 26

Cherry Pizza, 38

Maraschino Chocolate Cherry Pie, 251

Chicken

Apricot Chicken & Rice Dinner, 171

Caribbean Chicken Salad Sandwiches, 107

Chicken & Green Bean Casserole, 159

Chicken & Onion Cheese Spread, 46

Chicken and Potato Stew, 192

Chicken Asparagus Casserole, 156

Chicken Cheesy Pizza, 178

Chicken Corn Chowder, 74

Chicken Fettuccine, 152

Chicken Nuggets, 141

Chicken Onion Dip, 50

Chicken (or Turkey) Casserole, 180

Christmas Chicken & Rice Dinner, 185

Cinnamon-Kissed Chicken, 144

Creamed Peppery Chicken, 143

Honey Mustard Chicken, 145

Mexicali Chicken Burritos, 150

Mexican Chicken Salad, 80

Mother-Daughter Salad, 97

Oriental Chicken Soup, 76

Presto Poultry Casserole, 168

Sour Cream Chicken Pasta Salad, 126

Southwestern Chicken Soup, 68

Spring Salad with Chicken, 104

Sweet & Sassy Entrée, 160

Chicken & Green Bean Casserole, 159

Chicken & Onion Cheese Spread, 46

Chicken and Potato Stew, 192

Chicken Asparagus Casserole, 156

Chicken Cheesy Pizza, 178

Chicken Corn Chowder, 74

Chicken Fettuccine, 152

Chicken Nuggets, 141

Chicken Onion Dip, 50

Chicken (or Turkey) Casserole, 180

Chili

    Spicy Thick Vegetarian Chili, 75

    Mexican Goulash, 155

    Eight-Layer Chili Casserole, 182

Chocolate Cheese Squares, 230

Chocolate Pecan Cookies, 227

Chocolate Pecan Cream-Filled Sandwich
   Cookies, 228

Christmas Chicken & Rice Dinner, 185

Christmas Punch, 262

Cinnamon Drops, 31

Cinnamon-Kissed Chicken, 144

Cinnamon Rolls (minisize), 37

Coconut Cream Oatmeal, 25

Corn

    Calico Corn, 112

    Chicken Corn Chowder, 74

    Corn Casserole, 113

    Corn Chowder, 73

    Cowboy Chow, 190–191

    Mexican Casserole, 169

    Mexican Goulash, 155

    Southwestern Corn Muffins, 62

    Sweet Corn Bread, 60

    Zesty Corn, 136

Corn Casserole, 113

Corn Chowder, 73

Cowboy Chow, 190

Cowboy Grub (Casserole), 154

Cran-Apple Oatmeal, 28

Cranberry

    Apple Berry Bake, 206

    Cran-Apple Oatmeal, 28

    Cranberry Apple Salad, 92

    Cranberry Orange Scones, 33

    Warm Cran-Apple Salad, 94

Creamed Green Beans with Ham, 111

Creamed Peppery Chicken, 143

Creamed Spinach, 114

Crunchy Cucumbers with Cream, 82

Cucumber

    Cucumber Dill Salad, 90

    Cucumber Sandwiches, 57

    Crunchy Cucumbers with
      Cream, 82

D

Deviled Eggs, 47

Dijon Mayo Spread for Sandwiches, 56

Dilled Pork Steaks, 162

Dip

    Chicken Onion Dip, 50

    Mild Mustard/Dill Dipping
      Sauce, 54

    Ruby Raspberry Fruit Drip, 52

    Vegetable Dip, 48

Double Chocolate Cream-Filled
   Sandwich Cookies, 226

Double Chocolate Oatmeal Cookies, 225

E

Egg (or egg substitute)
    Blueberry Custard Bake, 36

Breakfast Burrito, 35

Deviled Eggs, 47

Manhandler Breakfast Bake, 34

Popeye's Favorite Salad, 100

Spring Salad, 103

Spring Salad with Chicken, 104

Zesty Egg-Salad Sandwiches, 108

Eight-Layer Chili Casserole, 182

F

"Fake Bacon," 30

Farmer's Casserole, 188

Fish

Orange Roughy, 151

Tuna Pasta Salad, 127

Frozen Cheesecake Dessert, 214

Fruit (Mixed)

Berry Fruit Freeze Drink, 257

Breakfast Fruit-Filled Pockets, 41

Fruity Freeze Drink, 256

Fruity Frothy, 259

Mother's Day Salad, 98

Polynesian Fruit Salad, 78

Punchbowl Cake, 205

Tootie-Fruity Frozen Drink, 261

Tropical Passion Fruit Salad, 89

Very Berry Fruit Salad, 79

Zesty Chilled Fruit Salad, 101

Fruity Freeze Drink, 256

Fruity Frothy, 259

G

Garlic Red Skins, 117

Garlic Toast, 61

Green Beans

Chicken & Green Bean
Casserole, 159

Creamed Green Beans with
Ham, 111

Green Beans Italiano, 116

Home-Style Green Beans and
Potatoes, 135

Mushroom, Onion, and Bacon Green
Bean Casserole, 115

Savory Sausage and Green Bean
Casserole, 122

H

Ham

Au Gratin Casserole Dinner, 177

Broccoli & Ham Salad, 85

Broccoli, Ham, & Cheese
Frittata, 39

(turkey ham)

Creamed Green Beans with
Ham, 111

"Fake Bacon," 30

Farmer's Casserole, 188

Ham & Cabbage Dinner, 198

Ham & Cheese Potato Salad, 93

Ham & Cheese Spread, 45

Ham Kabobs, 164

Harvest Ham Steaks, 142

Hawaiian-Style Baked Beans, 137

Presto Ham Casserole, 166

Sausage or Ham Casserole, 181

Tangy Tossed Salad, 95
(turkey ham)

Ham & Cabbage Dinner, 198

Ham & Cheese Potato Salad, 93

Ham & Cheese Spread, 45
Ham Kabobs, 164
Harvest Ham Steaks, 142
Hawaiian-Style Baked Beans, 137
Hearty Barbecue Skillet Dinner, 175
Herbed Beef Tenderloin with Seasoned
    Potatoes & Buttered Mushrooms, 196
Home-Style Green Beans and
    Potatoes, 135
Honey Mustard Chicken, 145
Hot Fudge Cake, 229

I
Italian Dunkers, 58

J
Jammin' Snack Cake Bars, 237

L
Lemon
    Lemon Pepper Pork Tenderloin
        with Lemon-Kissed
        Potatoes, 199
    Orange Lemonade, 256
Lettuce
    Bacon, Lettuce, and Tomato
        Salad, 96
    Mexican Chicken Salad, 80
    Mother's Day Salad, 98
    Spring Salad, 103
    Spring Salad with Chicken, 104
    Tangy Tossed Salad, 95

M
Manhandler Breakfast Bake, 34
Manhandler Meatloaves, 186

Maraschino Chocolate Cherry Cream
    Pie, 251
Mashed Potatoes and Carrots, 133
Mashed Potatoes Deluxe, 119
Mexicali Chicken Burritos, 150
Mexican Casserole, 169
Mexican Cheese Moons, 55
Mexican Chicken Salad, 80
Mexican Goulash, 155
Mexican Pasta, 149
Mexican Pizza, 179
Mexican Pork Tenderloin with Rice,
    174
Mexican-Style Spaghetti, 163
Mild Mustard/Dill Dipping Sauce, 54
Mint Mousse, 210
Mint Mousse Cake, 241
Mm!, 32
Mother-Daughter Salad, 97
Mother's Day Salad, 98
Mushroom
    Beef and Potatoes with Mushroom
        and Onion Gravy, 200
    Herbed Beef Tenderloin with
        Seasoned Potatoes & Buttered
        Mushrooms, 196
    Mushroom-Asparagus
        Casserole, 129
    Mushroom, Onion, and Bacon
        Green Bean Casserole, 115

O
Onion
    Beef and Potates with Mushroom
        and Onion Gravy, 200

Chicken & Onion Cheese
    Spread, 46
Chicken Onion Dip, 50
Mushroom, Onion, and Bacon
    Green Bean Casserole, 115
Smothered Steak, 193
Orange
    Cranberry Orange Scones, 33
    Orange Fluff, 242
    Orange Lemonade, 256
    Orange Roughy, 151
Oreo Mousse, 244
Oriental Chicken Soup, 76
Oriental Vegetables, 130

P

Party Poppers, 51
Pasta
    Chicken Fettuccine, 152
    Mexican Pasta, 149
    Mexican Style Spaghetti, 163
    Mother-Daughter Salad, 97
    Pasta with Creamy Clam Sauce, 153
    Sausage Pasta Salad, 128
    Seafood Pasta Salad, 87
    Sour Cream Chicken Pasta
        Salad, 126
    Sour Cream Pasta Salad, 125
    Sweet & Sassy Entrée, 160
    Tuna Pasta Salad, 127
Pasta with Creamy Clam Sauce, 153
Peaches & Cream Gelatin Salad, 77
Peaches & Cream Oatmeal, 27
Peaches & Cream Trifle, 253
Peppered Potato Salad, 105

Peppermint Chocolate Cheesecake, 240
Peppermint Cream Pudding Cake, 223
Perfect Pineapple Cake, 252
Perfect Pineapple Cookies, 224
Pineapple
    Caribbean Chicken Salad
        Sandwiches, 107
    Caribbean Rice, 195
    Hawaiian-Style Baked Beans, 137
    Perfect Pineapple Cake, 252
    Perfect Pineapple Cookies, 224
    Pineapple-Carrot Snack Cake, 235
    Pineapple Fluff, 250
    Pineapple Snack Cake, 249
Pinwheel Dinner Rolls, 64
Pizza
    Cherry Pizza, 38
    Chicken Cheesey Pizza, 178
    Mexican Pizza, 179
    Pizza Burritos, 157
Polynesian Fruit Salad, 78
Popeye's Favorite Salad, 100
Pork
    Au Gratin Casserole Dinner, 177
        Breaded Pork Tenderloins, 184
    Broccoli & Ham Salad, 85
    Creamed Green Beans with
        Ham, 111
    Dilled Pork Steaks, 162
    "Fake Bacon," 30
    Farmer's Casserole, 188
    Ham & Cabbage Dinner, 198
    Ham & Cheese Potato Salad, 93
    Ham & Cheese Spread, 45
    Ham Kabobs, 164

Pork (cont.)

    Harvest Ham Steaks, 142

    Hawaiian-Style Baked Beans, 137

    Lemon Pepper Pork Tenderloin with Lemon-Kissed Potatoes, 199

    Mexican Pork Tenderloin with Rice, 174

    Presto Ham Casserole, 166

    Sausage or Ham Casserole, 181

Potato

    Au Gratin Casserole Dinner, 177

    Beef and Potatoes with Mushroom and Onion Gravy, 200

    California Medley Stew, 194

    Chicken and Potato Stew, 192

    Farmer's Casserole, 188

    Garlic Red Skins, 117

    Ham & Cheese Potato Salad, 93

    Hearty Barbecue Skillet Dinner, 175

    Herbed Beef Tenderloin with Seasoned Potatoes & Buttered Mushrooms, 196

    Home-Style Green Beans and Potatoes, 135

    Lemon Pepper Pork Tenderloin with Lemon-Kissed Potatoes, 199

    Mashed Potatoes and Carrots, 133

    Mashed Potatoes Deluxe, 119

    Peppered Potato Salad, 105

    Potato Puffs, 176

    Sensational Sweet Potato Casserole, 123

    Steak & Potato Soup, 67

    Steak & Potatoes Stir-Fry, 158

    Swiss Steak and Potatoes, 189

    Twice Baked Potatoes, 131

    Zesty Potato Salad, 106

Potato Puffs, 176

Pumpkin Apple Bake, 231

Pumpkin Fluff, 211

Punchbowl Cake, 205

Presto Ham Casserole, 166

Presto Poultry Casserole, 168

Presto Sausage Casserole, 167

Q

Quickie Meal, 183

R

Raisin Spice Cookies, 221

Rice

    Apricot Chicken and Rice, 171

    Caribbean Rice, 195

    Christmas Chicken & Rice Dinner, 185

    Mexican Pork Tenderloin with Rice, 174

    Shrimp Rice Casserole, 170

    Spicy Ricey Vegetarian Dinner, 147

Ruby Raspberry Fruit Dip, 52

S

Sand, Rocks & Candy, 216

Sandwich

    Caribbean Chicken Salad Sandwiches, 107

    Cucumber Sandwiches, 57

    Dijon Mayo Spread for Sandwiches, 56

    Zesty Egg-Salad Sandwiches, 108

    Zesty Sausage Sandwiches, 148

Sassy Slaw, 91

Sausage

Cowboy Chow, 190

Hearty Barbecue Skillet Dinner, 175

Manhandler Meatloaves, 186

Party Poppers, 51

Presto Sausage Casserole, 167

Sausage or Ham Casserole, 181

Sausage Pasta Salad, 128

Sausage (or Ham) Casserole, 181

Sausage Pasta Salad, 128

Savory Sausage and Green Bean Casserole, 122

Zesty Sausage Sandwiches, 148

Zesty Sausage Skillet Dinner, 172

Sausage or Ham Casserole, 181

Sausage Pasta Salad, 128

Sausage (or Ham) Casserole, 181

Sausage Pasta Salad, 128

Savory Sausage and Green Bean Casserole, 122

Seafood

Orange Roughy, 151

Pasta with Creamy Clam Sauce, 153

Seafood Pasta Salad, 87

Seafood Salad, 86

Seaside Salad, 84

Tuna Pasta Salad, 127

Sensational Sweet Potato Casserole, 123

Sherbet Breeze, 257

Shrimp Rice Casserole, 170

Smokey Bean Soup, 69

Smothered Steak, 193

Sour Cream Pasta Salad, 125

Sour Cream Chicken Pasta Salad, 126

Southwestern Chicken Soup, 68

Southwestern Corn Muffins, 62

Southwestern Fiesta, 161

Southwestern Three Bean Salad, 81

Southwestern Vegetable Soup, 72

Spanish Tomatoes and Beef, 146

Spice Cookies, 219

Spiced Apples, 132

Spiced Tea, 260

Spicy Ricey Vegetarian Dinner, 147

Spicy Thick Vegetarian Chili, 75

Spinach

Creamed Spinach, 114

Popeye's Favorite Salad, 100

Spring Asparagus, 118

Spring Salad, 103

Spring Salad with Chicken, 104

Steak & Potato Cattlemen's Soup, 67

Steak & Potatoes Stir-Fry, 158

Strawberry

Mm!, 32

Strawberry-Banana Cream Dessert, 243

Strawberry Squares, 207

Sweet Corn Bread, 60

Sweet & Sassy Entrée, 160

Sweet & Sour Fresh Vegetable Garden Salad, 83

Sweet & Sour Teenie Weenies, 49

Swiss Chocolate Almond Cream Cake, 208

Swiss Steak and Potatoes, 189

T

Taco Vegetable Soup, 71

Tangy Tossed Salad, 95
Tomato
  Bacon, Lettuce, and Tomato
    Salad, 96
  Seaside Salad, 84
  Spanish Tomatoes and Beef, 146
  Tomato Biscuits, 59
Tootie-Fruity Frozen Drink, 261
Tropical Fizz Slushy, 258
Tropical Passion Fruit Salad, 89
Tuna Pasta Salad, 127
Turkey
  Broccoli, Ham & Cheese
    Frittata, 39 (turkey ham)
  Chicken (or Turkey) Casserole, 180
  Mexican Casserole, 169
  Mexican Goulash, 155
    (turkey chili)
  Quickie Meal, 183
  Southwestern Fiesta, 161
  Tangy Tossed Salad, 95
    (turkey ham)
Twice Baked Potatoes, 131

V

Vegetable Dip, 48
Vegetables (Mixed)
  California Garlic Blend, 120
  California Medley Soup, 70
  California Medley Stew, 194
  Oriental Vegetables, 130
  Southwestern Vegetarian Soup, 72
  Sweet & Sassy Entrée, 160
  Sweet & Sour Fresh Vegetable
    Garden Salad, 83

Very Berry Fruit Salad, 79
Very Berry Cheesecake Trifle, 233

W

Warm Cran-Apple Salad, 94

Z

Zebras, 245
Zesty Chilled Fruit Salad, 101
Zesty Corn, 136
Zesty Egg Salad Sandwiches, 108
Zesty Potato Salad, 106
Zesty Sausage Sandwiches, 148
Zesty Sausage Skillet Dinner, 172
Zesty Summer Cottage Salad, 88
Zucchini Snack Cake, 234

About Solid Rock

A portion of my books' profits go to help support the noteworthy and honorable efforts of an inner-city children and teens outreach program called Solid Rock in Toledo, Ohio. With hands-on involvement Pastor Keith Stepp and his wonderful wife, Shannon, along with their growing support staff, focus on the needs of the central city, crossing over racial and economic barriers.

Through their children and teens' programs they are establishing a moral foundation for our future generations based on biblical principles. We are in constant need of volunteers to help in many areas, including child sponsors. To be a child sponsor, simply contact Solid Rock and let them know you would like to sponsor a child:

Solid Rock Outreach Program
1630 Broadway
Toledo, Ohio 43609
Or call (419) 244-7020.

On behalf of the children and teens I thank you very much for your support of the Solid Rock Outreach Program through your purchase of my cookbooks.

Dawn

About the Author

Dawn Hall is currently publishing her Busy People's line of cookbooks, including *Busy People's Slow Cooker Cookbook*. She is a successful recovering compulsive overeater and food addict. She was born watching her weight. As an accomplished aerobics instructor and facilitator for W.O.W. (Watching Our Weight), Dawn walks her talk and is living proof that you can have your cake and eat it, too.

She strongly believes her talent for creating extremely low-fat, mouth-watering foods that are made quickly and effortlessly is a gift from God.

As a popular inspirational speaker and veteran talk show guest, Dawn has appeared on *The 700 Club*, CBN, *Woman to Woman*, *Good Morning, A.M.,* along with numerous other TV and radio programs nationwide.

To contact the Dawn or for more information on booking her for your next women's event, conference, or retreat call, write, or fax:

Dawn Hall
5425 S. Fulton-Lucas Road
Swanton, OH 43558
(419) 826-2665 or Fax (419) 826-2700
DawnHallcookbook@aol.com